Please don't
make me go

Please don't make me go

The true story of the little boy who couldn't be beaten

JOHN FENTON

HarperElement
An Imprint of HarperCollins*Publishers*
77–85 Fulham Palace Road,
Hammersmith, London W6 8JB

The website address is: www.thorsonselement.com

and *HarperElement* are trademarks of
HarperCollins*Publishers* Ltd

First published by HarperElement 2008
This edition 2008

2

© John Fenton 2008

John Fenton asserts the moral right to be
identified as the author of this work

A catalogue record of this book is
available from the British Library

ISBN-13 978-0-00-726378-3
ISBN-10 0-00-726378-3

Printed and bound in Great Britain by
Clays Ltd, St. Ives plc

Acknowledgement

I would like to thank Harry Bingham and Helena Drysdale for all their initial assistance, and my agent Euan Thorneycroft for all his help. I would also like to thank Natalie Jerome and the team at HarperCollins for all the help and advice that made the publication of this book possible and Martin Noble, my editor, for all his efforts.

In the recesses of our mind lurk the memories and fears we try to hide.

John Fenton
April 2008

Dedication

For Shelley and Maggie
Your support and faith were inspirational to me

Chapter 1

Mum and I were sitting at the kitchen table, eating bread and jam and talking about what we would do if we won the football pools. The top prize, £75,000, was a fortune to us. We often discussed this and I never got bored of speculating about all the great things we could do together, such as buy a big new house, go on holiday to the seaside, and get a television set of our own. I loved those moments of closeness with my mother when I got home from school in the afternoon. It was just the two of us in our private little world.

I flung my arms out to indicate how big my new bedroom would be and my sleeve accidentally caught the edge of my plate. It toppled off the table then seemed to fall in slow motion to the floor, where it smashed into tiny pieces. My remaining slice of bread fell jam-side down on the wreckage.

'Sorry, Mum,' I said, slipping from my chair to pick up the pieces.

'Not to worry. Accidents happen. Careful you don't cut yourself.'

Suddenly we both froze as the floorboards of the room above creaked. My mother looked up at the ceiling fearfully. The sounds of my father moving around his bedroom always signalled the end of our little tête-à-têtes. She hurried into the scullery and lit the gas under the kettle, holding her finger to her lips to signal that I should be very quiet.

I quickly gathered the broken plate and dropped it in the bin, then hurried to the far side of the table, opened my English homework book and pretended I was engrossed in my studies. I could hear my father's footsteps stamping down the stairs and all of a sudden I wanted to pee. I always got the urge to pee when trouble was imminent.

The scullery door burst open and my father rushed in. He scowled angrily at my mum and strode purposely over to where I was sitting.

'You little bastard.' His right hand shot out and slapped me hard around my ear. 'How many times do I have to tell you to be quiet when you get in from school?'

My Dad worked nights as a bus cleaner, so he slept during the day.

'Leave him alone,' Mum screamed. 'We were just talking quietly.'

'This one doesn't know the meaning of the word "quiet".' He clipped my ear again and Mum rushed over to try and grab his arm.

'Stop it!' she yelled. 'You only pick on him because he's too young to hit you back. You wouldn't dare pick on someone your own size.'

Mum's sharp tongue often got her into trouble with Dad. This time, he drew back his fist and punched her hard in the centre of her face. She stumbled backwards and held up her hands to protect herself as Dad let loose a flurry of punches. One of them hit her high on the head and she slid down and sat dazed on the floor. Her nose and mouth were bleeding and she was totally at his mercy.

I was screaming at him to stop and in desperation I kicked him on the shin. It was the first time I had dared to attack him. I was only nine years old and a skinny, wiry kid – definitely no match for him – but I had to do something to protect my mother. He turned and backhanded me across the room.

'So you think you're big enough to fight me, do you?' He smiled as he picked me up by the scruff of my neck and one of my legs. 'I'll show you how big you are, you little bastard.' He threw me with all his strength across the kitchen. I crashed onto the table and bounced into the chairs. They toppled over backwards and I landed on my back on the chair legs, hurt and winded.

Dad glanced round at Mum, who was slumped on the floor, then back at me, and he seemed satisfied with his handiwork. I'd seen that expression before. He got real pleasure from being violent, as if it released all his pent-up tension. Through the pain I heard the scullery door slam shut and the sound of his footsteps going back up the stairs.

I couldn't cry. I couldn't catch my breath. I just lay gasping. Suddenly my mother was beside me and her hands were desperately trying to disentangle me from the chair legs. She was sobbing bitterly. 'Are you alright, darling? Oh, he's a wicked man.'

She lifted me up by my waist and I saw that her nose and mouth were bleeding, dripping large drops of blood onto the floor.

'Please tell me you're alright.' Once she had got me upright, Mum wrapped me in her arms and we clung to each other for ages, both trembling and crying.

I watched my mother as she rinsed her face under the cold tap in the scullery. I had seen her do this so many times before and it always broke my heart. I loved her so much but there was nothing I could do to stop the endless misery she was suffering at my father's hands.

Later, after Dad had left for work, we listened to our favourite programme 'Journey Into Space' on the radio, and tried to pretend nothing had happened. We were big fans of Jet Morgan and his crew and I always imagined that one day Mum and I would blast off into space on a spaceship like the *Luna*: travelling far, far away, through countless galaxies, never returning and living a life full of happiness and amazing adventures.

There is something comforting in dreams. Anything is possible and you can escape the misery of your day-to-day life. I often wished I could just live in a dream world and never wake up.

My Mum and Dad should never have married. They didn't love each other. They only married because he got her pregnant in a moment of lust and in those days, with the stigma attached to being a single mother and the shame that would be brought on the whole family by her condition, there was only one course of action left open to them. But right from the start it was a marriage made in hell.

My mother was a fun-loving girl of eighteen. She was very bright, but was forced to leave school at fifteen and work in a shop in London to help support her mother. The fifteen shillings a week she brought in was all that kept the family from going under. My father was thirty years old and had recently arrived from Wexford in southern Ireland. He'd come to England looking for work and had got a part-time job as a barman in the West End. It was in this bar that he met my mother.

Elizabeth, my sister, was born in May 1939 just six months into their marriage. Four months later the Second World War broke out and my father enlisted in the army. Because he had flat feet, he was given a home posting in the big army stores in Southampton. This meant that he could get back to London quite regularly and, as a result of one visit, my mother gave birth to my second sister, Jean, in October 1942. Then, on April 22nd, 1944 I exploded into the world. My mother told me that I had rushed my way out – but maybe it was because a V1 rocket had gone off a few streets away at the critical moment.

My father was a small, slightly built Irishman. He was strictly teetotal; both his parents had died from alcohol abuse and, like so many small men, he walked around with a permanent chip on his shoulder. He fancied himself as a ladies' man and went from affair to affair without a shadow of remorse. He had no qualms about hitting women and it was not long before my mother felt the power of his fist in her face. He had a job on London Transport as a night cleaner for the buses. He was not averse to hard work, so earned a decent wage, but never divulged the amount to my mother and only gave her the minimum for food. All of his extra money went on keeping up his appearance and conducting his extramarital affairs.

My earliest memories are blurred snatches of pictures here and there, but violence was always around – from the Carmelite nuns who used to whack our hands with a bamboo cane at my first primary school through to Dad's explosions of temper at home. By the age of seven, just after my kid sister Jennifer was born, I had a pronounced nervous stammer and had to attend a speech therapy clinic in Hanwell. The therapist gave me tongue-twisting exercises to repeat. I still remember one: 'Look at Lily, Lily up the lamppost; come down Lily, you do look silly.'

Because of my stammer I became a prime target for the bullies in my school. Having a stammer was nearly as bad as having to wear glasses, which got you called 'four eyes'. Whenever I had to stand up to read aloud, the entire class would look in my direction and start sniggering. This made me stammer even more and the teacher would tell me angrily to sit down again. It wasn't long before I developed a massive inferiority complex and tried to hide in the background away from the cruel jibes and laughter.

St Gregory's Catholic Primary School was situated in an affluent part of Ealing and most of the children came from quite wealthy backgrounds. Mum had very little money, so while the clothes I wore were clean, they never came close to being like the other children's. She had a nose for finding the best bargains in a jumble sale and she'd carefully scrub them in the large stone copper in the scullery. I was always excited when I tried them on, never noticing the odd frayed collar or sewed-up hole in my trousers. I'd feel proud as I strutted off to school with my nice new clothes but I was soon brought back down to earth when the children laughed and taunted me unmercifully about the way I looked. I stood out like a sore thumb in my shabby, second-hand clothes.

I hated having to get changed into my sports kit to play football. My underwear, vest and pants, were always hand-me-downs from my two older sisters. I complained to mum on several occasions about wearing girl's knickers but she told me not to be stupid as no-one could see what I was wearing under my trousers. She had no idea the taunts I had to endure from the other boys when they saw them. 'He's got a fanny!' was their favourite. I would feign illness to avoid school on days when we had physical education or sports. If I was forced to go I would sneak into one of the toilet cubicles and struggle into my kit in private.

My home life was equally unhappy. My father seemed to hate me and would hit me unmercifully for no apparent reason. On my eighth birthday, I remember I went into the back garden with my mother and sisters to play a game of cricket with a bat and ball my grandmother had given me. I accidentally hit the ball against the kitchen window and cracked a pane of glass. My father rushed out into the garden and pulled one of the cricket stumps out of the ground then proceeded to beat me all over my back and legs with it. The beating went on for two or three minutes, and when at last he stopped, I was left on the ground unable to move. My mother kept me off school for over two weeks until the bruising had gone.

Of course, she fared no better. I lost count of the number of times she came crawling into my bed of a night after yet another violent row. She was always inconsolable. I would cuddle up to her in the hope that it would make her feel better, but it was always to no avail. On these occasions it was the sound of her whimpering that sent me into a troubled sleep. I grew to hate my father and promised myself that when I was grown up there would be a reckoning.

He usually got out of bed around four o'clock in the afternoon. I never knew what to expect when I arrived home from school. Sometimes I would hear the shouting before I entered the house and would sneak up to my room and bury my head under my pillow to shut out the noise. Other times I would arrive home to find my mother already crying and my father scowling angrily. These were the worst times. Invariably, my father would hit me for just coming into the room. One day, I had fled the room screaming out how much I hated him. I went to my bedroom and cried myself to sleep but awoke some time later to the agonising pain of my father hitting me with a piece of timber, which he was wielding with exceptional ferocity. The next day at school I passed a lot of blood in my urine. It was then that I decided that my best option was to arrive home after six o'clock, which was when my father usually left for work.

My favourite place to go after school was Jacob's Ladder railway crossing, where trains from Ealing Broadway and West Ealing passed under a bridge on their way to and from the West Country. I had a little book of train numbers and underlined them every time I saw a new train thundering down the track. It was always exciting when the Flying Scotsman came speeding by. I would run to the part of the bridge where the funnel smoke would engulf me in a thick cloud and breathe in the glorious aroma of smoke and steam. Sometimes I was enjoying myself so much that I would still be there at seven.

But I couldn't stay out of my father's way all the time. There were still weekends to get through and the evenings when he started work at a later hour. By the time I was twelve years old I had become hardened to my father's beatings and nastiness, and I no longer hid with fear in my room. Whenever I witnessed one of his violent outbursts against my mother I would do my best to help her. I would try to kick him or throw something at his head. This meant, of course, that I got another beating but at least it stopped him hitting my mother. I hated him with a passion that was almost as strong as the adoration I felt for my mother. Often I would lie in bed and think about how I would pay him back in kind when I was older.

It seemed to me that things couldn't get worse at home, but on a January day in 1958 I found out that they could. Dad and Gran had joint tenancy of the house we lived in. He hated her living with us, even though she only inhabited the front room and rarely came out of it. She hated him for the way he treated her daughter. They rarely spoke to each other and, when they were forced to, the conversation was always strained with underlying venom.

On that day Gran had come into the scullery to fill her kettle with water and my father was shaving in the mirror over the sink. She reached across to turn on the tap and accidentally jogged his arm, causing him to nick his face with his razor. He screamed out, 'You clumsy old bitch. Get back in your own room.' She retorted, 'It's a pity you didn't cut your throat.' That was it. Sixteen years of pent-up fury was unleashed. He grabbed her by her scrawny throat and started to strangle her, making no allowance for the fact that she was an old woman, nearly deaf and half blind. My mother jumped on his back to pull him away and his anger was then diverted onto her. He started to beat her unmercifully and the sound of her screams brought me running into the room. I found my Gran on the floor, clutching her throat and gasping for air, and my mother getting beaten to a pulp over the cooker. I grabbed the first thing that came to hand – a three-inch, sharp vegetable knife.

'Leave her alone, you bastard!' I screamed.

My father turned to me. I knew it was my turn to face his fury and gripped the knife tightly. His face blanched noticeably when he spotted it and he said quietly, 'What are you going to do with that?'

'If you don't leave them alone, I'll kill you.' My voice was trembling with emotion but my eyes showed that I wasn't bluffing. I knew that this could be my moment of destiny and I welcomed it. I made a move towards him and couldn't believe it when he ran from the room.

'Give me the knife, John.' My mother gently took it out of my hand. 'Help me with Gran.'

We lifted Gran off the floor and sat her down in the kitchen. She was in shock and her whole body was shaking as if she had been out in the cold for days. My mother wrapped her in a coat and made her a cup of hot, sweet tea. It must have been at least two hours before she was fit enough to return to her room and, even then, she was still whimpering. We didn't see my father for the next two days.

Life slowly returned to normal, but in my heart I knew that it was only a matter of time until my father had his revenge on me. What was he going to do? Would he kill me? These thoughts troubled my mind and kept me awake at night worrying.

The bright, early-morning sun shining through my threadbare bedroom curtains woke me from a troubled sleep. Momentarily, I struggled with drowsiness and reached down to adjust the coats that I had piled on top of my blanket to keep me warm. Suddenly, I became alert. Why was the sun shining? It was a school day. It was always dark when I got up for school in winter. I jumped out of bed and shivered as I placed my feet onto the cold, lino-covered floor. The book I had been reading the night before, *The Count of Monte Cristo*, was lying on the floor so I picked it up and put it back on the mantelpiece. I hurried downstairs to see why Mum hadn't called me. I found her sitting in the kitchen weeping silently. My father was sitting on his stool by the coke boiler, tracing patterns in the air with the glowing tip of his cigarette.

'Why didn't you call me, Mum?' I asked.

'You're coming out with me for the day,' my Dad said as he looked up at me. 'Get yourself dressed.' I noticed that he was wearing his Sunday best clothes.

'Where are we going?' I asked. 'Are we going to see Uncle John?' I liked my father's brother. He was nothing like my father and was always full of fun and mischief.

'Maybe we will and maybe we won't. You'll just have to wait and see.'

I hurried back upstairs and quickly got dressed in my own Sunday clothes – basically my school clothes, but with a nice blue jumper that my mother had knitted for me. I looked at myself in the mirror: with my dark hair in the typical short, back and sides of the day, dark eyes and scrawny features, I didn't think I was anything special.

When I came back downstairs there was a steaming bowl of porridge waiting on the table. I sprinkled it liberally with sugar and wolfed it down. I was eager to be on my way – treats in my life were rare and a day at my uncle's was definitely a treat.

My father looked at his watch. 'Right,' he said 'it's time for us to go.' My mother followed us to the front door. I turned to kiss her goodbye and she wrapped me tightly in her arms. She whispered, 'Take care of yourself, John. Remember how much I love you.'

I was puzzled by her remarks and looked deeply into her tear-filled eyes. 'I'll be fine mum, don't worry. I love you too.'

I was surprised when my father led the way towards West Ealing. I thought we would have gone to Ealing Broadway to catch an underground train to Paddington. I walked by his side, not speaking, but curious as to where we were headed.

We went over Jacob's Ladder and I could see the Uxbridge Road in front of us. It suddenly occurred to me that we could get to Paddington by bus. I had never been by bus to my uncle's and I wondered which way Paddington was. Just before the Uxbridge Road, my father led me down a side street and up some wide flagstone steps to a large red-bricked building. Above the door was a printed sign: 'Ealing Juvenile Court.'

I stared at the sign. My heart started to race with fear. I said, 'Why are we here?'

My father took hold of my arm firmly and led me through the door. 'You'll see when you get there. Don't give me any trouble as,' he pointed to a policeman standing in the entrance hall, 'he'll deal with you if you do.'

He pushed me towards the large room the policeman was standing in front of and said, 'It's nearly time for your hearing.'

I looked appealingly up at him. I begged, 'Please don't make me go. I promise to be good.'

He shoved me forward again and I walked into the juvenile court with my head bowed and feeling an overwhelming urge to pee.

Chapter 2

24 January 1958

I was led into a courtroom and made to stand in front of a purple-draped table, above which two fluorescent lights hung from a discoloured yellow ceiling. My foot tapped uncontrollably on the highly polished slats of the floor and my eyes flitted nervously round the room. There were policemen standing under every window and two especially burly ones guarding the entrance. I wondered why they thought such precautions were necessary when faced with a scrawny thirteen-year-old. What did they think I was going to do?

Behind me and slightly to the right sat my father, his cold blue eyes staring unblinkingly through gold-rimmed glasses. He was in deep conversation with a woman sitting next to him. I noticed how often she nodded her head sympathetically then glanced in my direction with a distaste that wrinkled her thin mouth into a crooked line of red lipstick that appeared to be underlining her bulbous nose.

'Everybody rise.'

A man in a black pin-striped suit who had been sitting at a side table now stood up and looked around the room. Everyone stopped talking and rose to their feet.

A small anteroom door swung open and three people came in – one woman and two men. They walked purposefully to the draped table and, with the briefest glance at the assembled onlookers, sat in the three seats behind the table, the woman in the middle.

The men could have been twins they looked so alike. Both were wearing grey, pinstriped suits, white starch-collared shirts, military striped ties and black brogues. They both had slicked-back black hair and black horn-rimmed glasses. The woman was dressed extremely elegantly in a light-coloured tweed skirt and mohair sweater with a string of pearls round her neck. She had lovely twinkly grey eyes, and these calmed me a little. She seemed nice, I thought.

'Case number 247 in respect of John Fenton. The charge is brought by his father, Dennis James Fenton, who states that his son is beyond parental control. You may all be seated.'

'Mr Fenton,' the nice woman said, 'please come forward.'

I heard a movement behind me and then my father was standing beside me. I turned to look at him but he never glanced in my direction. He was looking straight ahead at the nice woman with an expression of self-pity on his face.

'Mr Fenton, we have read the charge that you have brought against your son and would appreciate a little more enlightenment as to why you think he is beyond your control.' The nice woman smiled at my father. 'Take your time – we are in no hurry.'

My father coughed quietly to clear his throat. 'Your Honour. His mother and I are at our wits' end as to the boy's behaviour. We've turned to you as a last resort.' There was desperation in his voice. 'Please help us.'

I turned to see if my father was crying, as this was said with such anguish.

'He kicks and hits his sisters without any reason. He comes in late from school and never lets us know where he has been. He is rude to his mother and grandmother and seems to get a perverse delight in using wicked and vile language. If I try to give him any corporal punishment he turns violent and tries to attack me.' He took out a hand-kerchief and wiped his eyes.

'Are you all right, Mr Fenton?' the woman asked sympathetically. 'Would you like a short recess?'

'I'm sorry, Your Honour. I'll be fine now. It's so distress-ing.' Again, the handkerchief came out and my father blew his nose loudly. 'If only you knew what we've been through. He'll send us to an early grave.'

I couldn't believe my ears. I was supposed to be the violent one in the house? I was amazed at his tirade of lies.

'I am sure we can help you, Mr Fenton. Try not to distress yourself.' The woman sounded even more compas-sionate. 'I have dealt with situations like this before and I have always found a solution.'

'I do hope so.' My father's voice was now under control. 'We want him to be a normal boy – play football, go swimming, work hard at school and be a success when he grows up. Did I tell you he smokes? Well, he does, and I've been called up to his school about it, and worse than that, he steals money and cigarettes from his mother's handbag.'

I turned to look at him, but he wouldn't catch my eye.

The three magistrates were regarding my father with sympathy. He seemed to be having difficulty controlling his emotions and sniffed loudly behind a large white handkerchief. With an exaggerated wiping of his eyes he put the handkerchief away in his jacket pocket.

'Thank you, Mr Fenton. I know how hard it must have been for you and your wife to take this course of action and I will now do my very best to help you both.' She smiled sweetly at my father. 'Please return to your seat.'

'Well, John, what have you got to say for yourself?' The woman's eyes were no longer twinkling; they had turned flinty grey. 'Explain yourself.'

'Explain what?' I thought. I didn't know what to say. My dad had just told her a giant pack of lies. Why wasn't Mum there to tell her that I only attacked him when he was hitting her and making her cry? Why wasn't she there to tell this court woman that I bought my own cigarettes from the wages I got doing a milk boy's job every Saturday and Sunday? Why wasn't she there to tell her that I didn't come home early from school because I knew my dad got out of bed at that time and he was always angry with me? Why wasn't she there to tell her that most nights she climbed into my bed crying after yet another violent row with my father and how I cuddled her to make it better?

'I am waiting for your explanation.' The woman glared at me.

'I don't know what to say,' I tried to mask the trembling in my voice, 'and anyway it's got nothing to do with you.' I was too ashamed to tell her the truth about my home life.

As if one, the three people behind the table were gawping at me with incredulity. 'It has nothing to do with me! I can't believe what I have just heard.' The woman virtually spat out the words. 'I'll show you what it has to do with me.'

They huddled together in a hushed conversation for a few minutes then she addressed me again. 'It is quite clear', she began, 'that you have a total lack of respect for anything and everyone. You seem to be hell-bent on self-destruction and because of this we have to protect you and society from what you, no doubt, are becoming.' She paused for a few seconds. 'Therefore, it is the ruling of this court that you be remanded in a secure young persons' establishment for a period of two weeks while reports are obtained.'

The three people behind the table stood up. Without another glance in my direction, they returned through the small door from which they had appeared.

What was all that about? I didn't have a clue what had just been decided. I turned around to go back to my father but found he was no longer beside me and was, in fact, walking towards the exit. I started to follow him but a strong hand on my arm halted my progress.

'You're with me, sonny Jim.'

I looked up at a burly police officer.

'Don't even think of trying to get away,' he said. 'Just come along with me.'

The officer led me out of the courtroom and down a corridor. His grip on my arm became tighter as he opened a glass-panelled door and led me through.

'Take a seat,' he said firmly, 'and no noise.' These words were spoken so forcibly that they sounded like a threat. I quickly sat down and stared at the floor, utterly terrified. I had never had any dealings with the police before and this man was scaring the shit out of me.

The police officer stationed himself in the corridor opposite the door and stood staring at me through the windows. I looked around the room. It was about twelve foot square with no windows. The walls were green and defaced in places by names scratched on them. The floor was covered in faded green linoleum that was cracking noticeably in one of the corners. The only furniture was an equally defaced wooden table and six black plastic chairs. I checked the chair I was sitting on and found it was black plastic as well.

It seemed an interminably long time before the door was opened again. The officer asked if I needed the toilet but the nervous urge I'd had in the courtroom had passed, so I declined. It was shortly after two o'clock in the afternoon when they came to fetch me. I knew the time as I had heard a clock chime somewhere in the building. The two men that came were not as fearsome-looking as the one outside the door but they were equally as forceful. They led me by my arms out of the building and into a blue van with bars across the side and back windows.

'Where are you taking me?' I asked, at last plucking up the courage to speak.

'St Nicholas House, Enfield,' was the terse reply from the driver. That was all that was said during the thirty-minute journey out of London and into Middlesex. I was overcome with fear and confusion and battling within myself not to cry. Why was this happening? What had I done to deserve this? Who was going to look after Mum? I badly wanted my Mum to come and get me, tell these men it was all a mistake, give me a big hug and take me back home again.

Chapter 3

The van turned off the main highway and through a stone archway onto a long drive, which cut through some dense woods. After about five minutes of twisting and turning, a large Georgian manor house came into view. I was struck by how white it was and how big the windows were. I had never been in the country before and had certainly never seen such a magnificent building. If this was St Nicholas House, it didn't look at all intimidating and I was looking forward to seeing the insides. My fear was dissipating and rapidly being replaced by excitement. I imagined that this must be how people felt when they went on holiday. I had never been on holiday and had always envied the rich children who went away to places like Southend and Margate that to me sounded exotic.

The van pulled up in front of two large wooden doors and I was led in through one. The interior of the building was even more inspiring than the exterior. The huge entrance hall had a floor of grey marble flagstones, which seemed to reflect all of the winter sunlight shining through the large windows. Everywhere I looked there were huge double doors with ornate brass doorknobs, or white walls with beautiful carved cornices. A wide marble staircase with a well-polished banister dominated the hallway.

The van driver knocked softly on one of the doors and opened it in the same motion. I was led into a large room whose grandeur was diminished by lots of modern office furniture. Several people were sitting behind desks and the clicking of typewriters reverberated. A suited man got up from his desk, came over to one of my escorts, and took the sheaf of papers he was holding out. His eyes briefly scanned the papers.

'That's fine,' he said in a Geordie accent that sounded peculiar to me.

'He's all yours. See you later.' My escorts let go of my arms and left without a backward glance. I heard the van engine start up again and the sound fading as it pulled away down the drive.

'What size shoes do you wear?'

I turned to look at the suited man, who was eyeing me questioningly.

'Six, sir,' I said timidly.

The man went to a side cupboard and rummaged around for a few minutes. When he reappeared, his arms were piled high with items of clothing. He dropped them at my feet.

'Pick them up and follow me.'

With great difficulty, I scooped them up from the floor and hurried after the man who was now climbing the staircase.

'Get a move on boy,' he shouted. 'I haven't got all day.'

I staggered under the precariously balanced pile and hurried to catch him up.

'In here.' The man opened a door halfway along the upstairs corridor. 'Take all your own clothes off and put them in that basket.'

He gestured to a large wicker basket leaning against a side wall. The room was obviously meant for washing as there were two large sinks on the far wall and several on the floor. I had never seen washbasins on the floor before. As if the man had been reading my mind, he pointed to one of them.

'Shower yourself and make sure you do your hair well. I will be checking for lice.'

Self-consciously, I stripped off my clothes and stepped into the basin. It took me a few nervous minutes to figure out how this new-fangled contraption worked but at last I did and the lukewarm water felt good as it pelted down on my shivering body. The soap the man handed to me smelled the same as the one my mother used for scrubbing the front doorstep at home. After about five minutes of heavy soaping and scrubbing I was handed a threadbare white towel. I rubbed myself dry and dressed myself in the clothes the man had given me.

The clothes were far from being new but were definitely clean. They had a distinct odour of mothballs and I wrinkled my nose as I put them on. The vest and underpants were a greyish white and the shirt – which was too large – was blue and had a frayed collar. The brown corduroy short trousers were slightly tight but the matching tunic jacket fitted me well. To round everything off, I had grey ankle socks and a pair of well-worn-in brown sandals.

After briefly inspecting my hair and scalp, the man pointed at the wicker basket I'd put my clothes in.

'Bring that and follow me,' he ordered as he walked away. Virtually scampering, I followed him as we retraced our route back to the entrance hall. Pointing at the floor outside the office door he said, 'Leave the basket there and come with me.'

This time the man opened one of the doors to the left of the staircase. I heard the voices of lots of young people coming from within and entered the room with trepidation.

'One for you, Mr Jenkins,' the man shouted across the noise.

A silver-haired man came over. 'What's your name, lad?' he boomed out.

'John Fenton, sir,' I replied quietly.

'Right, Fenton, go and meet the others and try not to make too much noise.'

There were about thirty boys in the room, their ages ranging from nine to sixteen years old. I was self-conscious about my appearance, but relieved to see that everyone was dressed in the same ill-fitting apparel as me. They paid me scant attention and just carried on with their various activities. Some were sitting talking, others were playing board games, and a few were standing by a table-tennis table watching two of the older boys having a game.

'Where are you from?' I turned to see where the voice had come from. A boy of about the same age as me was standing beside me. 'I'm from Barnet.'

'I'm from Ealing,' I replied. 'Where's Barnet? I've never heard of it.'

The boy looked shocked at my ignorance. 'Everyone's heard of Barnet. Are you fucking stupid?'

I shrugged my shoulders. 'If you're so *fucking* clever,' I emphasised the word fucking, 'tell me where Ealing is.'

The boy laughed loudly. 'That's fucked me.' He looked at me with a friendly expression. 'My name's Bernard. What's yours?'

I smiled back. 'John, John Fenton. What's your last name?'

'Connors.' He hesitated for a moment. 'What are you in here for?'

'I don't know. My dad said he was taking me out for the day and I ended up in Juvenile Court. Next minute I was told I had to come here for reports. I haven't a clue what they were talking about or what happened.' I felt tears springing to my eyes and turned away so the boy wouldn't see them and think me soft.

'You're lucky. They're just going to do probation reports. You'll be going home the next time you go to court.' Bernard spoke with such assurance that I immediately felt better. Then he added, 'I've had probation already – this time I'm going down.'

'Going down where?' I was in awe of the way Bernard spoke. 'What have you done?'

'Played truant. Nothing big, just truant.' He laughed again. 'The wankers were always round my house. My old lady would take me into school and I would leg it out the back gate. I hated the fucking place.'

'So what happens to you now?' My admiration for him was growing by the minute.

'I reckon I'll get three years' approved school,' he told me. 'Quite likely I'll go to St Vincent's. I'm a Catholic. Yer, I'll get Vincent's.'

'Let's go and sit down.' Bernard started towards an empty table. 'I'll put you wise as to what goes on here.'

I listened intently as my new friend outlined the daily procedure at St Nicholas's. The routine was simple. Out of bed at 6.30 am. Wash and shower and then tidy the dormitory. Get dressed and go down for breakfast at 7.30 am.

Between 8.30 and 10 am scrub and clean the interior of the house. After the morning house inspection it was off to help the gardener with weeding and cutting the lawns. At 1 pm lunch and at 1.30 until 2 pm recreation. Between 2 and 4 pm it was back to helping the gardener. All boys were required to bathe after work and to be inspected for cleanliness. Tea was at 5.30 pm and there was further recreation between 6 and 7.30 pm. We would then be given a watery cup of cocoa and a slice of bread and jam. Into bed by 8 pm and lights out at 9 pm.

All the boys smoked. It was strictly forbidden, but that made not the slightest difference and boys were always being caught having a crafty smoke in some shaded part of the building. The 'Bosses' – the name given by the boys to all who worked in 'St Nick's' – tried their hardest to stamp it out, but always failed. I was amazed at the hiding places Bernard showed me to secure my cigarettes so they were not found in the frequent searches. They were taped underneath the table tennis table, or in the potting shed in the garden, or inside the chimneys. Visitors usually smuggled cigarettes in on a Sunday. One of the gardeners would also buy them for you if you had the money. The Bosses were fighting a losing battle and this alone made smoking worthwhile.

I followed Bernard around like an obedient lapdog. He made sure that I sat next to him in the dining room and he showed me how to get a steaming mug of tea out of the silver tea urn on the serving counter. He also advised me what were the best sandwiches to put on my plate and how to sneak food out of the dining room so that I could have a feast later in bed. The only thing he couldn't do was arrange an exchange of dormitories so that I slept in the same one as him. He patted me on the back as I headed towards my room and said, 'I'll see you in the morning.'

I walked into my dormitory and looked nervously around me. Bernard had been my support since I arrived, but now I was on my own again. There were eight beds in the room and I didn't have a clue which one was mine. I looked at a boy who was sitting on the bed closest to the door and asked quietly, 'Which is mine?'

He pointed to the other end of the room and said, 'The one under the window.'

Even though all the boys were friendly, I felt ill at ease. I was embarrassed as I slipped out of my clothes and struggled into an ill-fitting pair of striped pyjamas. I had never exposed my body to other boys' scrutiny and did my very best to hide my willy from their view. I dived into bed and pulled the bedclothes up tight under my chin then watched enviously as my room mates larked around and threw pillows and books at each other. I would have loved to join in but I didn't have that sort of confidence, so I watched and laughed at their stupid antics from the confines of my bed. Mr Grey, one of the Bosses, soon appeared in the doorway and ordered everyone into their beds. He looked around the room to make sure everything was in order and turned off the light.

'Goodnight boys and no more noise,' he said as he closed the door behind him.

I think I half expected the riotous fun to continue and I was surprised when, apart from a few snickers, the room fell into silence. I lay quietly staring up at the ceiling and listening to the muffled sounds of the house settling down for the night. My mind was racing and I blessed my good fortune at having been sent to such a fun place. I closed my eyes and said my prayers and asked Jesus to watch over my mum. Momentarily I worried about her, but without warning the day's events overtook me and I fell into an exhausted but happy sleep.

The first five days flew past for me. I had never had such a good time. Bernard taught me how to play table tennis, and although I was well and truly thrashed every time, I loved the game. Boys seemed to come and go and Bernard always knew what had happened at their court appearances. Trevor, a ten-year-old, had come back from court crying and was put into the infirmary for a few days. Bernard told me that he had been given three years in a junior approved school and the Bosses were keeping him in the infirmary so he couldn't try to run away. 'He'll be OK,' he said in his usual matter-of-fact voice. 'He's just got to get his head round it.'

I nodded as if I knew what Trevor was going through. 'It wouldn't bother me if they gave me ten years. I love the place.'

'Then you're fucking nuts,' Bernard said harshly. 'This may be a doddle of a place, but approved school's a completely different ball game.' He noisily cleared his throat and spat a big globule of phlegm between my feet. 'It's full of nasty bastards. They kick the shit out of you for nothing and, if you're not careful, they'll put it up your bum.'

'How do you know that?' I was staring down at the phlegm. 'You've never been in one.'

'Everyone knows what goes on in those places. Where have you been? Don't you know anything about life?' He seemed to be getting annoyed and I was shocked to see tears in his eyes.

'I'm dreading it,' he said, 'and if you were facing it, you would be dreading it too.'

'Then why did you play truant? You knew what might happen.'

'Fuck off, John. You're starting to piss me off.' Bernard's voice sounded menacing. 'Don't talk about something you know fuck all about.'

'Sorry, Bernie. I didn't mean to annoy you.' It was the first time I had shortened Bernard's name and it came out quite naturally. 'Maybe you won't get approved school.'

'I wish,' Bernie said quietly. 'I just know in my heart that I'm going down.'

'Maybe I'll go down with you. I'm a Catholic and would go to the same one as you. That wouldn't be so bad. Would it?' I was trying desperately to reassure my friend.

Another globule of phlegm landed between my feet. 'You're getting probation. That's for certain.' He cleared his throat and sucked more phlegm into his mouth. 'There's no chance of you going down.' This time the phlegm hit the wall by the side of me and slid down leaving a slimy green trail behind it.

'I know you'll think I'm stupid,' I needed to ask the question, 'but what exactly is probation?'

'You really don't know, do you?' Bernie looked at me sympathetically. 'It's nothing really – a load of piss. I bet you everybody in here, apart from you, has had it. All you have to do is report to a probation officer once a week, usually after school, and listen to a load of bullshit. It only lasts for about half an hour. As long as you pretend you'll do as he says, he'll be happy.'

'Is that all?' I was amazed it was that easy. 'You're kidding me? Right?'

'No. That's all there is to it.' Bernie lowered his voice to a whisper. 'When your mum comes to visit, get her to get you an ounce of baccy – Golden Virginia – and a couple of packets of fag papers. It lasts longer than fags.'

'If she's got the money I know she'll get them for me.' I felt embarrassed. 'But, she might not have the money.' I had written to her every day since I'd been there but I wasn't sure I wanted to ask her about the baccy because she might be upset if she couldn't afford it.

'It's no big deal,' Bernie seemed to understand. 'I'll get my dad to get plenty for both of us.' He put his arm around my shoulder. 'We'll be OK.'

I had never felt such an overwhelming feeling of friendship – virtually love – as I felt for Bernie at that moment. I would do anything for him. I would repay his friendship tenfold. I felt ten feet tall as we sauntered over to the table-tennis table.

I awoke early on Sunday, excited because my mother was coming to visit that day. I wondered what time she would arrive and worried that she might not find the place. I was relieved when at last my name was called to report to the visitors' hall. She hadn't got lost, so I had been worrying over nothing.

I was led into the hall and hurried over to where Mum sat beside one of the large windows. I was disappointed to see that she was alone as I had hoped she would bring my sisters along so I could show off my new home.

She stood up and hugged me tightly. 'Oh, my poor little darling. I've missed you so much.' She started crying. 'How are they treating you? Are you all right?'

I returned her hug and guided her back into her chair.

My mother was thirty-six years old but looked fifty. The unhappiness of her life had left indelible grooves scored deeply in her face. Her eyes had heavy bags under them and the thick lines around her mouth could never be mistaken for laughter lines. Her forehead had permanent wrinkles and her once-bright auburn hair was now streaked with grey. She had generously applied a cheap face powder in an unsuccessful attempt to hide a fading bruise on her cheekbone. Her clothes were shabby and her beige raincoat was at least one size too small. She had on a thick pair of stockings with a visible ladder running from her right shin to where it vanished under a scuffed pair of brown shoes.

She reached under the table and picked up a carrier bag which she handed to me. 'I've brought you a few little treats.'

I opened the bag and looked inside. There were three apples and two comic books. She took out her purse and handed me a shilling piece. 'And here's something for you to buy some sweets during the week.'

I took the money reluctantly. 'Are you sure you've got enough to get home?'

Mum smiled. 'Of course I have. I want you to have it. Now tell me how you're getting on.'

The next two hours flew past as I related everything that had gone on since I arrived at St Nicholas's. Mum was very interested in my new friend Bernie and asked lots of questions about him. 'Don't admire him. You should really feel sorry for him,' was the advice she gave me, but I didn't understand why she was saying that. I thought he was the bee's knees.

When I asked about my sisters and home, she was a little vague and only wanted to talk about me. Then when I asked how my dad was, she replied, 'Forget about him. Tell me more about how you're getting along at table tennis.'

All too soon the visit was over. I knew that Mum had very little money so I didn't ask her for any cigarettes or baccy. It would only upset her if she couldn't give me any. I decided that I would lie to Bernie and pretend that I had asked but she had no money. As she walked away and out of the main doors, I found myself crying and ran to the toilet so that no-one saw my weakness.

That night, for the first time since I had arrived, I found it difficult to sleep. My mind wouldn't let me rest. I missed my mother badly. I worried about her. For hour after hour I lay awake thinking about my home and my old life there.

Chapter 4

February 1958

In February the whole country was gripped by icy winds and freezing fog. It was an ordeal to get out of bed in the morning as the coldness seemed to bite into every exposed part of me and left my flesh sporting a blueish tinge. The rest of Europe was experiencing the same cold spell and it was during this weather front that England was plunged into mourning. On 6 February in Munich, Germany, the plane carrying the Manchester United football team crashed on take-off. The news spread around the remand home like wildfire. Seven of the famous 'Busby Babes' were killed and England lost some of its finest players. Duncan Edwards, a shining star and one of England's finest young players, died of his injuries fifteen days later. The tragedy of the air crash affected every boy in St Nicholas's and united the country in grief.

I reluctantly climbed out of bed the day after the plane crash. I could hear the rain lashing against the dormitory windows and the howling winds shaking their sturdy frames. In places that were invisible to the naked eye the wind found apertures and whistled noisily into the already cold room. I shivered as an icy blast of air swept over my feet. As I hurried out of the dorm and down the hallway, my footsteps made a hollow sound on the polished floor-boards and I regretted not putting on my socks because my feet were exceptionally cold. I threw open the washroom door with such ferocity that it crashed noisily against the wall, and hopped across the stone-covered floor to a hand basin on the far wall.

The cold water I splashed on my face stung me with the ferocity of a thousand bee stings and my teeth began to chatter uncontrollably. I spent very little time cleaning my teeth and could taste the peppermint flavour on my lips all the way back to the dorm. I reached under my bed and pulled out the wicker basket that contained my own clothes and, still shaking, hurriedly put them on. My two weeks in St Nicholas's were over and it was the day I was due back in court. I hurried to the dining room because I wanted to have as much time as possible with Bernie before we went our separate ways.

Bernie sat hunched over our usual table. There wasn't the usual cheery greeting; he looked dejected and lost in thought. We had become firm friends over the last two weeks and the other boys affectionately called us Pinky and Perky. Bernie looked up and gave me a weak smile. He reached into his tunic pocket and handed me a slip of crumpled paper.

'It's my address. My mum or dad will let you know where I am.'

I felt despair washing over me. I would be going home today but Bernie was facing an uncertain future. This boy had given me loyalty and friendship at a time when I needed it most and I was profoundly grateful to him.

'Bernie, I wish I was staying with you,' I said. 'I promise I'll come and see you, wherever you are.'

'When you do come, make sure you bring plenty of baccy.' It was obvious that Bernie was holding back tears. 'Can I have your address?' He produced a scrap of paper and a small stump of a pencil.

I scribbled down my address and handed it back to him. 'If you get a chance to write, please make sure you do. I'll write back.' I spoke with such conviction that Bernie at last managed a warm smile.

'I know you will.' A serious look followed. ''Don't forget to say sorry when you speak to the judges today. Tell them that you're ashamed of the way you behaved and that you will never do it again. They love all that shit.'

'Did you say that when you went to court last Tuesday?'

'I didn't get the chance. They gave me three years before I could open my mouth.' I remembered how Bernie had come back from court the previous Tuesday. He had just walked nonchalantly into the recreation room and said, 'I told you I would get three years.' Then, as an afterthought: 'Bastards. I hope they're all dead by Christmas.'

'Do you think I'll get a chance to speak?' I enquired.

'How many times have I got to tell you? You're getting probation. They'll give you some bullshit lecture and send you on your way.' Then with an embarrassed look, 'I'm really going to miss you. You're a bit of a wanker, but a nice one.' He grinned. 'You'd never have survived in an approved school. You're too soft.'

The door to the dining room swung open letting in a cold blast of air from the hallway. Boss Lewis stood in the doorway with two uniformed police officers. 'OK, Fenton. Time to go.'

I stood up slowly and, with a despairing glance at Bernie, walked towards the waiting officers.

As the two large doors were closing behind me I heard Bernie shout 'See you soon.'

I sat quietly in a small room that was an annexe to the much larger courtroom. I was not alone. There were three other children in the room: two girls and a boy. I wondered if I had looked as terrified two weeks ago as they all appeared to be now. One of the girls had been crying, and though she had stopped, every few seconds she sniffed loudly. I would have liked to tell her that she had nothing to worry about but we had been told we had to be completely silent so I didn't dare.

The door opened and a very tall police officer signalled with one finger for me to follow. My heart was beating rapidly as I walked into the courtroom and it was hard to stay calm. I spotted my father immediately. He was sitting in the same seat as when we were here the last time. All of the seats were occupied. I wondered briefly which of the adults were the parents of the sniffing girl. The three judges were already in their seats and were looking at me intently. The policeman walked me over to the table and stood me in front of the same grey-eyed woman as before. She and her companions looked down at some papers and spent several minutes reading. More than once they huddled together whispering. Occasionally they looked in my direction and then resumed their secret discussion. At last they sat up and looked directly at me.

'Well, I think we have all the necessary facts now.' The woman sounded friendlier than the last time she had spoken to me. 'It was for your own good that we sent you on remand and after reading your reports it would appear that it has done you some good.' She smiled. 'You must remember that your parents only brought you here for your welfare. They wouldn't want you to stay in a place like that for an indefinite amount of time.' She paused briefly. 'I am sure you wouldn't want to either.'

'Yes I would. I loved the place.' The words were said with sincerity. 'It doesn't frighten me. It was great.' The respite from the life I led at home and at school had been welcome. I had slept peacefully for two weeks. I had heard and witnessed no violence. No one had teased me about the clothes I wore. I had a friend. A real friend. I felt good about my experience. I felt good about myself.

The woman was astounded. 'What did you say? It was great – you loved the place – is that what you said?' She was looking at me with amazement. 'It would appear that these reports are wrong. You haven't changed. You're still as brazen with defiance as you were before.' The three judges once again went into a huddle then raised their heads and glared at me.

'You've got your wish,' the woman said. 'Three years' approved school.' She looked towards a police officer. 'Take him away.' The woman barked to the police officer. 'We have heard enough.'

I was led away to the holding room. The same green-painted surroundings, the same green linoleum, the same black plastic chairs greeted me.

'I'm going to tell you your future, sonny, whether you want to hear it or not,' the tall policeman said, scowling down at me. 'When you've done your three years in the approved school, you will only be out a short while and then you'll go to Borstal. After Borstal you'll end up in prison and after prison,' he grinned, 'I have no doubt you'll kill someone and then we'll hang you. I wonder how smug you'll be when the judge puts that black cap over his wig.'

I didn't understand what he was saying. 'Thank you, sir,' I murmured quietly and flinched as the policeman lifted his arm as if to hit me.

'You cheeky little bastard. You deserve everything that's coming to you.' The policeman slammed the door and stationed himself on the other side, glaring at me through the windows.

I was relieved when at last they came to collect me and take me back to St Nicholas's.

'You said *what*? I can't believe you're that stupid.' Bernie was staring at me in complete amazement. 'No wonder they gave you three years.'

'I meant it. I do love the place and I did have a good time here.' I grinned. 'It means you and I will be together in Vincent's.'

Bernie gave me an appraising look. 'You're hardly equipped to handle an approved school. You're not exactly Mr Universe.' He shook his head slowly, still finding it hard to believe that I had come back from court with a three-year sentence. 'Have you ever had a fight? Do you know how to look after yourself? If you don't, you'd better learn quickly. We're going to a shithouse of a place.'

'Maybe it won't be as bad as they say.'

'Oh, it'll be as bad as they say and possibly worse. We're both in deep shit now and if we're not careful,' he pretended to cut his throat with his finger, 'we'll be dead meat.'

'If anybody hurts us,' I said nervously, 'why can't we just report them to one of the Bosses?'

'Don't be stupid. Nobody goes to the Bosses. You'd be a grass and, believe me, you wouldn't want to be one of them.' Bernie had a serious look on his face. 'Promise me that you'll never be a grass. I mean it, John. Promise me.'

'OK, I promise.' Bernie looked relieved. 'So how do we look after ourselves?'

'With difficulty I expect. We'll stick together until we know the ropes and then do our best to survive.' He nodded at my feet. 'You'll need to use them when you fight.'

'How do you know so much about these things, Bernie? You've never been in an approved school. How do you know for certain what it's like?'

'My brother Jimmy did three years in St Swithin's on the Isle of Wight. He told me all about it.' He nodded his head approvingly. 'Jimmy's a real hard case. Nobody fucks with him. He's great.'

'Are you a bit of a hard case, Bernie?' I asked hopefully. 'I know I'm not. I've never had a fight.' I remembered how often I had been hit by other boys at school and how I had run away, usually crying. 'I don't like fighting.'

'I'm no hard case. But I've had a few fights.'

'Did you win?' I asked with admiration. 'I bet you did.' I couldn't imagine Bernie not being good at everything he did.

'I did OK. But the boys I fought won't be anything like the ones in Vincent's.' He smiled ruefully. 'They'll be nasty.'

For the first time since my first appearance in court I viewed my future with trepidation. Everything Bernie said filled me with dread. How would I survive in an environment like the one he claimed would exist in Vincent's? My only consolation was that Bernie would be with me. At least I would have a friend.

'How long do you think we'll be here before we get a place in Vincent's?' I asked.

'Maybe a couple of weeks. Who knows?' Bernie reached into his tunic pocket and produced a squashed cigarette. He rolled it expertly between his fingers until it was back to its original shape. 'Let's go for a quick fag before tea.'

I stood up and followed Bernie as he strolled towards the door. I still had an overwhelming feeling of doom but was determined not to show it. I would take a leaf out of Bernie's book and be nonchalant about my situation. I would survive. Bernie would help me. *Fuck them all*, I thought. *I hope they're all dead by Christmas*. I liked that expression and decided I would use it more often. It made me feel better.

Bernie was wrong. It wasn't two weeks before we were taken to Vincent's. It was four days.

Chapter 5

I remember very little about the journey. I know we travelled across London but I didn't recognise any of the towns we went through. Bernie spent the entire journey regaling me with tales of his exploits with truancy officers. Our laughter must have been infectious as our two escorts – the driver and his mate – smiled on more than one occasion. We could see them through the grille that separated us from the front of the van.

'OK, lads. Quiet down.' The driver was putting on his peaked cap. 'We're here now.'

We both peered out to see where we were. The Black Maria van was reaching the top of a steep incline. On the right-hand side of the road was a field that was fenced off with mesh wiring. The fence was about ten feet in height with a string of barbed wire draped above it. Bernie raised his eyebrows.

'Do you think they don't want us to get out?'

I smiled weakly. I was more interested in the gateway the van was turning into. Two large black wrought-iron gates halted our progress. The gates were attached to two red-brick pillars and stretched across the top of the pillars was an arched, black, wrought-iron sign with the words 'St Vincent's' standing out boldly on a fancy beaded surround.

The driver got out and rang an electric bell on the right-hand pillar. It was only a short while before a black-robed figure appeared on the other side of the gates and proceeded to unlock them with an ornate black key.

He seemed to work at a laboriously slow rate. Every movement was precise. When at last the gates were open he stepped slowly backwards, leaving just enough room for the van to enter. As it manoeuvred past, I could just discern a white face peering in at us from beneath the black hood. Bernie had also been looking at the man and I was surprised to notice that fear blanched his face.

St Vincent's came into view. It was monastic in appearance, with a small square bell tower situated in the centre of a grey slated and slanted roof. The walls were of red brick and punctuated with two rows of white, arched windows. In the centre of the bottom row of windows was a large stone arch above two large oak doors. The building was surrounded by a well-maintained garden and some early daffodils gave it an appearance of serenity. There was a big, gnarled oak tree in the centre of the front lawn, with clumps of daffodils around its roots, and large rose bushes were dotted around.

The van pulled up outside the oak doors. We waited patiently until the robed man came walking slowly up the gravelled path. He reached inside his cassock, produced another key and opened the right-hand door. He beckoned us forward with just a slight nod of his hooded head and disappeared inside. My escort held tightly onto my arm as we entered the building, as if he expected me to run at any moment.

The door opened into a large hallway. The floor had black and white ceramic tiles that struck me as looking like a chessboard; they were so highly polished that, looking down, I could see myself clearly. A tall statue of the Sacred Heart stood on a wooden plinth by the right-hand wall and opposite it, also on a wooden plinth, stood a statue of a saintly looking monk.

It has to be St Vincent, I thought. My eyes wandered over to a large framed print of the current Pope that was displayed proudly in the centre of the right-hand wall. Hanging five feet from the floor on the far wall was a large wooden crucifix.

'It's like being in bleeding church,' Bernie whispered. I nodded my head in agreement and smiled at the irreverence of the remark.

We were ushered through a door to the right of the Sacred Heart statue. Hanging from the wood-panelled walls were numerous pictures of saints and one very large one of the Blessed Virgin behind a desk. Seated behind the desk was a monk, about forty years old and with the most penetrating stare I had ever seen. His hair was jet-black and heavily greased with Brylcreem. His nose was long and straight and there was a profusion of black, stubbly hairs sprouting from both nostrils. His lips were thin and cruel-looking and there was a blueish tinge around his chin and under his nose from where he shaved. His eyes were constantly switching from me to Bernie as if he were inwardly appraising us both. He turned his attention to our escorts.

'Did they give you any trouble?'

I hated the way the monk spoke, his voice at least an octave above a normal man's voice. He had a strong Irish accent which seemed to come from down his nose and not out of his mouth.

He whinges, I thought. *He doesn't talk, he whinges. It's not far off sounding like my old man.*

'No trouble at all.' The driver patted me and Bernie lightly on our heads. 'A couple of nice lads.'

The monk's mouth twisted into a cold smile. 'Brother Francis will take you to the kitchen and get you a nice cup of tea before you head back,' he said to the escorts. His eyes switched to the hooded monk standing quietly just inside the door. 'Brother Francis, if you would be so kind.'

Brother Francis and the two escorts left the room, quietly closing the door behind them. Bernie and I stood in front of the desk being reappraised by the monk's penetrating stare. Eventually, he diverted his eyes to the paperwork the driver had handed him. Slowly and methodically he worked his way from sheet to sheet until at last he gathered them all together and placed them in a neat pile. He turned to Bernie and me and seemed to stare at us interminably, though it may only have been a few seconds. I was relieved when at last he started to speak.

'Which one of you is Connors?' he asked. 'Who's the one with the itchy feet?'

'I am, sir.' Bernie was hardly audible.

'Well, Connors, don't try any of your disappearing tricks here. We won't put up with any of your nonsense.'

He was now staring at me. 'Unruly behaviour! We will soon get that out of your system. If you open your mouth out of turn here you'll be in big trouble.' His voice seemed to go up yet another octave. 'Do I make myself clear?'

I nodded. I had lost the power of speech.

'I will now tell you the rules of the school, so listen carefully, I will not repeat myself.' He closed his eyes as if he were meditating. 'I am Brother De Montfort and the head-master of this school.' He opened his eyes. 'We have rules in this school that have to be obeyed. Any breach of the rules and you will be disciplined. I will not hesitate to cane you if you deserve it. You have been sent here because you are not fit to live with ordinary people. You are shit and nothing but shit. Forget about your parents for the next three years. You have no parents – no brothers and sisters – you have nothing but this school. Do you understand that?' De Montfort stood up menacingly, and leant over the desk until his eyes were only inches from our faces. 'Do you understand that?'

We both nodded our heads violently. Our fear was evident and De Montfort eased himself back into his seat.

'You will attend Mass daily at seven o'clock in the morning. On Friday and Sunday you will take Communion. Confessions are heard on Thursday evening and you will attend Benediction every Sunday afternoon. If you are bright enough, which I doubt, you will get the chance to learn to serve Mass with the priest.' He paused and took a deep breath. 'If you had had God in your life before, you wouldn't be here now. A child brought up in a house that loves Jesus is a good child. I hope and pray that by the time you leave my school, Jesus and the Blessed Virgin will be an integral part of your lives.' I noticed how he bowed his head reverently as he said the name Jesus. 'You will address all of the Brothers by their full title and all of the civilian staff as Mister. It is common practice to refer to the Brothers as Bro and I am quite happy for this term to be used as long as it is used with respect.' He stood up and faced the picture of the Blessed Virgin and blessed himself with the Sign of the Cross. He turned to face us again.

'Every boy is awarded 18 points at the start of the week. Each point is worth one penny. This means that every boy will be given one shilling and sixpence every week providing he has had no points deducted. If you are caught smoking it will cost you four points. If you are heard swearing it will cost you four points. If you decide to fight it will cost you 10 points and you will have to come and see me. At the end of the week I will inspect all of the masters' notebooks and deduct points from any boys who have been booked. Do you understand that?'

Once again we nodded.

'If a boy has a total of 18 points left at the end of the week this will be referred to as a very good week. If he has between 12 and 15 points left it will be referred to as a good week. If he has between seven and eleven points left it will be referred to as a satisfactory week. If he has between nought and six points this will be referred to as a blue-poor week. Anything below nought is a red-poor week. Do you understand that?' De Montfort was looking at us and nodding his head. 'Is it perfectly clear?'

'Yes, sir,' we both answered in unison.

'I'll continue then. All the boys that achieve either good or very good in a week will be allowed to go to the cinema on Saturday afternoon. Nobody else goes. If you get a blue-poor week, this will mean the loss of a quarter of a day's holiday off your annual leave. You only get 21 days, 14 days in the summer and seven days at Christmas, so every quarter of a day means a lot. We understand that a boy may slip up occasionally, so we allow a very good week to cancel out a blue-poor week. Nothing can redeem a red-poor week. That quarter of a day's holiday is lost for good.' He slowly adjusted his cassock and looked down at his shoes. 'Is everything I have just told you perfectly clear?' He looked up as Brother Francis returned quietly to the room.

'Yes, sir.'

'Good, so let's go on. After you have been here three months, and providing your points are good enough, you will be allowed to go home on the first Sunday of the following month. You leave the school at nine o'clock in the morning and return by seven o'clock in the evening. If you are late back, you will never have this privilege again.' He reached into a drawer in his desk and took out a book. He flicked through the pages until he found the one he wanted. 'Fenton – you will be in the bricklaying department. Connors – you'll be in carpentry.' He closed the book. 'Have you any questions?'

'What class am I in, sir? You never told us.' I felt my legs quaking under me but managed to sound calm as I asked the question.

De Montfort looked at Brother Francis and smiled. 'I think Fenton believes he's a scholar, Brother. What do you think?'

Brother Francis reached up and pushed back the hood that had masked his face so that it now rested neatly on his shoulders. He had the squashed nose of a boxer and I guessed he was around fifty years old. 'Maybe he thinks he's too good for bricklaying, Brother. Maybe we should change the curriculum so that he can sit in a classroom all day and pretend he can read.' The sarcasm in his Irish brogue was evident to all in the room. 'Maybe he should run the school.'

Both brothers laughed. De Montfort regarded me disapprovingly. 'All of the boys attend class on a Tuesday morning. The rest of the week you will be taught a trade.' He walked around the desk and stood staring down at me imperiously.

'The average IQ of the boys in this school is 95. None of them, including you, has any academic capabilities. The Government has decreed that boys with such low levels of intelligence should be taught a trade. Is that all right with you? Are you going to question the Government as well?'

'No, sir.'

De Montfort was silent for a moment, evidently deciding what to say next. He nodded his head slowly. 'I think that covers everything,' he said, still peering down at me. 'You may take them away now, Brother Francis. I will tell Matron that you'll bring them to her shortly.' He was about to turn away when he decided to have a last few words. 'Don't forget, Fenton. I will not tolerate any insubordination.'

As we were led from the room, I thought to myself: *I hope he's dead before Christmas*.

As he led us through the corridors to the uniform room, Brother Francis told us a little about the history of St Vincent's. The school had been founded by Brother Augustine in 1878. Because of its success the government had awarded the Brothers the running of another five schools. The school was proud of its achievements in rehabilitating wayward boys back into society and teaching them a worthwhile trade that would help them make a living. The school's sporting achievements were second to none. They expected their boys to win any tournaments they were entered into and they especially prided themselves on their boxing and football teams. Failure was not an option. Brother Francis told us that he was the boxing coach and boasted that he had three boys competing in the junior ABA semi-finals in two weeks' time.

'Once you're settled in, I will give you the chance to join the team,' he said. 'You're never too young to learn.'

'How many boys are here?' Bernie asked.

Like the strike of a cobra, Brother Francis slapped him hard on his left cheek. 'How many boys are here, *Brother Francis*?' He stood menacingly in front of Bernie. 'Don't forget the "Brother".'

'Sorry, Brother Francis.' Bernie was close to tears and his left cheek showed the imprint of the slap.

I reached out and touched him lightly on the shoulder in a token gesture of comfort. He was my friend and he was hurting. Brother Francis was staring at me. His satisfied expression was similar to the one my father had after he hit my mother. Something in my look must have upset him because he suddenly attacked me with the ferocity of a rabid dog. The blows were fast and numerous and I cowered against a wall trying to protect myself, utterly stunned at what was happening to me. He was a monk, a religious man. Was he allowed to beat me like this? He was punching me as if in a boxing match, but without the gloves. When at last the beating stopped, Brother Francis was out of breath and noisily gasped in lungful after lungful of precious air.

I leaned against the wall and gingerly felt the growing lump on my forehead caused by his bony knuckle. I kept my eyes focused on the floor.

I hope you're dead by Christmas. You ugly fucker. I hope your entire family die screaming. These thoughts comforted me and when I lifted my head I made sure there wasn't a glimmer of emotion in my eyes.

'You'll get more of the same if you ever dare look at me like that again. Do you understand?' Brother Francis was staring at me, waiting for a reply. He shouted loudly, 'Do you understand?'

I nodded reluctantly. His hand lashed out and slapped me hard on my right cheek. 'Answer me when I speak to you. Do you understand that?'

'Yes, Brother Francis.' My voice was barely audible.

Another slap landed on my cheek. 'Speak up. I want to hear what you say.'

'Yes, Brother Francis,' I said more loudly.

Brother Francis stood staring at me for several seconds. I think he was trying to interpret the tone in my voice. Was it said with defiance? It certainly wasn't submissive. He couldn't be certain, but I knew he didn't like it. I'm sure he would have liked to slap me again but the sight of the bruising he had already inflicted on my cheek probably stopped him.

'No more speaking. No more questions. Just follow me.' He spun on his heel and walked swiftly onwards.

We followed Brother Francis to the uniform room in complete silence. Bernie kept glancing in my direction. It was obvious that he had been surprised at the onslaught on me and amazed at my reaction. I had shown no fear, keeping my expression blank. This was a new side to my character that Bernie had never imagined. I was hardened to beatings, of course, from Dad's violence at home and I'd learned not to fight back and not to show fear – just to take it. Bernie smiled at me quickly. Any worries he'd had about me surviving Vincent's had gone. I knew I had impressed him with what he regarded as toughness. I occasionally touched the lump on my forehead, which seemed to be getting larger every time I touched it.

'Take all your clothes off,' Brother Francis ordered, glaring at us from within a walk-in cupboard. He watched impatiently as we scrabbled out of our clothes and quietly smirked in satisfaction at my discomfort as I pulled my shirt over my bruised forehead. 'Put these on and be quick about it.' He threw a selection of clothes on the floor in front of us.

In a very short time, both of us were kitted out in our new uniform. The clothes were not new but were in good condition and fitted us well. White underclothes, short grey trousers, grey shirt, maroon pullover, long grey socks and black hobnailed boots. We were also given a maroon blazer to be worn whenever we left the school premises.

'You will be given overalls in your workshops. All of your sports equipment will be given to you when you need it.' Brother Francis looked distastefully down at the clothes we had been wearing. 'Those you will keep in your locker. Pick them up and follow me.'

Brother Francis opened a door opposite the uniform cupboard and led us through it. The size of the room we were led into took both of us by surprise. It was rectangular in shape, over 200 feet long and 30 feet wide. The left-hand wall had several doorways leading off it and I wondered where they went. The right-hand wall had windows along its entire length that were covered on the outside with a protective wire mesh. Glancing through the windows I could see what appeared to be a large concrete quadrangle, securely encased on three sides by school buildings and on the far side by some large wooden workshops. Between two of the workshops was an entrance that led onto a large sports field. I knew this as I could see some netted goalposts in the middle distance.

Turning my attention back to the room I saw that long wooden memorial benches lined every wall. The walls were all painted brick – the top half cream and the bottom half pine green. Two evenly spaced rows of pictures adorned all available space on the left-hand wall, showing football teams or boys standing in a classical boxing stance surrounded by trophies. I couldn't make out the writing underneath and promised myself that I would look more closely at them when the opportunity arose. I wondered briefly if I would ever see my picture on the wall. I doubted it but thought how proud I would be if it ever happened.

'In here.' Brother Francis opened the last door on the left-hand wall. We entered a large square room filled with several rows of steel lockers. Each locker was six feet in height and divided in half by two doors. Each door had a number embossed on it and a name tag stuck on beneath. Brother Francis was scanning the names, searching his memory, looking towards the ceiling to seek guidance from above until at last he pulled open a locker door and peered inside. He gave a sigh of satisfaction when he saw it was empty. 'This one is yours, Fenton.'

He checked the number on the door. 'Your number is 71. Don't forget it as that will be your number for everything you do for the next three years. Put your clothes in your locker and then wait outside the door.'

I stood outside the locker room and listened to the commotion coming from within. 'Jesus Christ! Give me patience.' Brother Francis was losing it again. His voice boomed out: 'Jesus Christ! Where the hell is it?'

I heard a noise that sounded like a slap.

'Get out of the way you little bastard.' It sounded as though Bernie had been slapped again and I was tempted to go back in the room to help him but a shouted 'At last!' from Brother Francis meant that the trouble was over. When Bernie reappeared he had blood trickling from his nostril and tears in his eyes. I didn't dare look at the monster in case I got another beating, but kept saying over and over again in my mind: *I hope you're dead by Christmas. I hope you're dead by Christmas.*

The journey to Matron's office was made in complete silence. Bernie occasionally wiped his bloody nose with the back of his hand. My eyes never left the back of Brother Francis. I was engrossed in praying for his early demise.

Matron was a tall, stout woman in her mid forties. Her hair was light brown and permed into tight curls. Her face was plump and not unattractive, though she had on far too much face powder, which gave her a very pallid complexion. Her lips were covered in the deepest red lipstick and there was a smear of red on one of her front teeth. She was dressed in a crisply starched white uniform and her more than ample bosom strained to break free from it.

'I see you've been in the wars already,' she said in a soft Irish voice as she looked at both of us in turn. She handed Bernie a ball of cotton wool. 'Wipe your nose with that.' She briefly inspected the lump on my forehead. 'You'll be OK. The skin's not broken. Maybe you'll both think twice about fighting next time.' She naturally assumed we'd been fighting each other and we didn't contradict her.

She went to an open cupboard and produced two toothbrushes, two bars of soap, two circular tins of Gibbs Dental Powder and two face flannels. She handed one of everything to each of us and smiled at Brother Francis. 'I'll put them down to see the doctor next week.' She looked at a calendar that was hanging on the wall behind her desk. 'He is due to visit next Tuesday.'

'Say thank you to Matron,' Brother Francis demanded.

'Thank you, Matron,' we said politely.

Bernie was straining to look down the front of Matron's dress and catch a glimpse of her breasts. Matron saw what he was doing and immediately straightened up and adjusted the front of her dress.

'That will do, Brother. You can take them into the school now.' She dismissed us by sitting down at her desk and writing on some papers in front of her. I noticed that her cheeks had lost some of their pallor and there was just the slightest hint of pink showing through the powder. I had to stop myself smiling.

Brother Francis led us out of the room and down a small flight of stairs. He stopped in front of a plain wooden door and looked at his wristwatch. 'It's just after five o'clock. The boys will be getting ready for tea soon. You can go and join them.'

He produced a key from somewhere in his cassock and opened the door.

Chapter 6

The door opened into the large rectangular room we'd been in before but now the benches were lined with boys. We couldn't even see the entire length of the room as other boys moving around obstructed the view. Two boys who had been standing close to the door looked at us with interest. When we tried to get past they made no attempt to move out of the way and we were forced to squeeze gingerly around them. I was scared and glanced at Bernie for comfort. The look on his face showed me that he was feeling exactly the same and he nervously gestured with his head for me to follow him. We made our way over to a bench that only had one boy sitting on it.

'Where are you from?' The boy looked at us with mild curiosity. 'What Remand Home?'

'St Nicks,' Bernie replied. 'My name is Bernard,' he pointed in my direction, 'and he's John.'

'What number have you got? I'll tell you what house you're in.'

'I'm 116 and he's 71.'

'You're in St David's,' he said, looking at me, 'the same one as me. You,' he switched his attention to Bernie, 'you're in St George's.'

'How does the house system work?' I asked.

'Simple. All numbers between 1 and 30 are in St Patrick's; between 31 and 60 are in St Andrew's; 61 to 90 are St David's; and 91 to 120 in St George's. When we have to line up we do it in houses and in numbers. You should always be standing behind the same person.' He looked around the room furtively. 'Be careful about who you upset.' He gestured towards a group of boys standing against the opposite wall. 'All of those are nasty. The tall one with the blond hair is called Jimmy Wilkinson and he's the governor. You can't have any smokes unless you buy them from him or his mates. If he sees you smoking and you haven't bought it from him …' He never finished the sentence. He just smiled wanly. 'Put it this way; you'll regret it.'

I looked more closely at the group of boys opposite, especially the blond one. He looked about fifteen years old and was approximately five feet ten inches tall and of medium weight. He had a pronounced Roman nose and watery blue eyes. As I was watching him, he squirted a stream of saliva from between his front teeth, hitting a boy who was walking past him. The whole group laughed uproariously. The boy who had been spat on didn't react and hurried about his business.

'Do you see what I mean?' He stood up. 'Just be careful.' He started to walk away, stopped, and came back to where we were sitting. 'My name is Bill Hedges. I've been here two years and if you want to know anything, just ask.' He gave us a wink and walked away.

'He's a nice lad,' I remarked. 'I wonder what he's in here for?'

'Don't ask. It's none of our business and until we know the ropes, let's keep ourselves to ourselves.' Bernie shook his head slowly from side to side. 'I don't trust any of these scumbags and you had better do the same.'

We sat quietly watching the boys in the room. Their ages ranged from our age, thirteen, to possibly sixteen years old. We were definitely two of the youngest and this thought gave me little comfort. I knew there was going to be a pecking order and we were at the bottom. Bernie was right; we had better keep ourselves to ourselves.

My attention was diverted by raised voices from the middle of the room. As if by magic the crowded floor cleared, except for four boys standing staring at each other. The remainder of the school stood on benches or leant against walls to watch the proceedings. It was quiet, like the lull before a storm.

'Go for it, you mouthy fucker.' One of the boys in the centre started walking belligerently towards another boy. 'Kick it off, you piece of shit.' Suddenly and without warning he shot out his right fist. The fist landed forcibly in the centre of the other boy's face and blood leaked out of his damaged nose and trickled down his mouth and chin. From nowhere the aggressor produced a two-foot dangling toilet chain and it hummed and whirred as he swung it above his head in a circular motion.

The injured boy backed away and smiled through his bloody mouth. He spat a mouthful of blood and spittle straight into the face of his assailant and kicked him hard in the crotch. He ran in fast under the swinging chain and crashed his forehead into the startled boy's face. The momentum of their coming together made both boys lose their footing and they crashed to the floor in an untidy heap.

One of the other boys, who had been standing in the centre, ran forward and kicked the head of the boy with the chain. He was immediately jumped on by the fourth boy and they also fell to the floor.

I was horrified at what I was watching. I had never seen anything remotely like the extremity of this violence. I was so engrossed that I didn't see two of the Brothers in their black robes approaching the writhing bodies on the floor.

'If you want to see the nastiest bastard in the school, look at that young Brother.' Bill had appeared at our side again. 'Brother Arnold. He's one nasty cunt.'

I watched the Brothers as they separated the four boys on the floor. The young one that Bill had pointed out seemed to enjoy the task. He had a smile of satisfaction on his face as he yanked a boy off the floor, grasped his left cheek between his thumb and index finger and twisted so hard that the boy screamed in pain. He then slapped the boy on his other cheek with a sound like a pistol shot. It must have really hurt. He released the boy's cheek and shoved him in the centre of his face with the flat of his hand. The boy staggered backwards for a few strides before falling hard onto his backside. The Brother stood over him, legs slightly apart, swaying gently from side to side.

'Get up, you little bastard.' He challenged the boy. 'I'll teach you not to fight.'

The boy watched him warily.

'Get up, I said, or do I have to kick you up?'

The boy rolled sideways away from the Brother's feet and scrabbled quickly to standing position.

'Now you can come with me to see Brother De Montfort.' He shoved the boy in the direction of one of the doors. 'Get going.'

I was so engrossed in watching the young Brother that I had failed to notice that the other Brother had got the remaining three boys to their feet and was walking them in the direction of the same door. No shouting, no hitting, no kicking – just walking them quietly towards the door. The difference in the two monks' behaviour was startling.

Bill was right. The young Brother was a nasty cunt. I thought I had best try to stay out of his way. I watched the two Brothers and the four boys disappear through the doorway.

'Brother Arnold has been here five or six years,' Bill told us. 'Don't let him catch you smoking. He hates it. You don't just get booked; you get a good smacking as well.'

A shrill blast on a whistle brought our conversation to an end.

'Line up.' A man dressed in blue overalls was standing at the far end of the room. He was tall and heavily built, about fifty years old with wiry ginger hair. His ruddy face was covered in pockmarks. 'Line up and be quick about it.'

The entire school briskly lined up in four rows. I was in the row nearest the wall, Bernie was two rows away. A Brother I had not seen before walked quietly down the length of each row counting the boys. 'I make it 115,' he called out to the ginger-haired man. 'Is that correct?'

The man checked a black marking board attached to the wall. 'We should have 119. Is this board up to date?'

'I'm sorry, Mr Lawson. There are four boys with the headmaster that haven't been put on the board. Everything is correct.'

'Thank you, Brother Michael.' He pointed at the right-hand row, 'File in, and no noise out of any of you.'

There was no talking permitted during mealtimes and any boy who breached this ruling was booked and got the customary slap to go with it. Brother Michael stood on a podium at the front of the room, watching us like an owl seeking its prey. He had a small black notebook in his hand and every so often he would open it and write someone's name in it; then he would signal that person to come to the podium with a shout and a beckoning gesture with his talon-like finger. When the boy arrived at the podium the Brother reached down and pulled him up onto his tiptoes by grabbing his hair. He gave the boy a sharp cuff around his ear and sent him back to his seat. This was repeated at least five times during tea and I wondered how any of the boys would have points left at the end of the week, at the rate of bookings I had seen so far.

After tea I met up with Bernie again and we sat on the same bench as we had before tea. Bernie wasn't his usual self. He seemed unusually quiet and withdrawn, and something was obviously worrying him.

'What's up?' I asked. 'What are you thinking about?'

He had tears in his eyes. 'Look at my ankle.' He rolled his right sock down. The inside of his right ankle had a purple and blue swollen lump on it and the skin had been grazed. Small red specks of blood oozed out of the graze and it looked very painful.

'What happened? How did you do that?'

'I reached for a cake at the table. The boy on the other side of the table wanted it, so he kicked me.' A tear trickled down Bernie's cheek. 'He was too big to fight. He must

have been fourteen or fifteen. He told me that he will
always have my cake from now on and there's nothing I can
do about it.' He angrily wiped away the tear. 'I hope the
bastard is dead before Christmas.'

I put my arm around my friend's shoulder. I was hurting for him. I wished I had been stronger and older and
could have helped him. 'You always said this place would
be rough. Your brother Jimmy was more than likely
bullied before he toughened up. He survived and came
through it. So will we, Bernie.' I squeezed his shoulder.
'Our turn will come. We just have to learn how to fight by
their rules.'

We sat quietly together. I was frightened but too scared
to show it. The Brothers and their attitude towards discipline terrified me. I had expected the boys to be rough and
maybe bully me, but cruelty by the staff had never entered
my mind. I was finding it hard not to cry and my whole
being was awash with self-pity.

I closed my eyes tightly and concentrated on saying a
prayer to the Blessed Virgin. My Catholic schooling had led
me to believe that deities could hear your silent prayers and
I felt sure that the mother of Jesus would help me through
these troubled times.

'Hail Mary, full of grace, the Lord is with you.

*'Blessed art thou amongst women and blessed is the fruit of
thy womb, Jesus.*

*'Holy Mary, mother of God, pray for us sinners, now and at
the hour of our death.*

'Amen. Hail Mary …'

I must have said at least three decades of the Rosary in
my mind before I reopened my eyes and, as for all fervent
believers, it had a soothing effect on my troubled mind. I

looked at Bernie and saw that he too was lost in deep reverie, so rather than disturb him, I returned to my silent prayers for divine help.

'*Hail Mary, full of grace, the Lord is with you.*

'*Blessed art thou ...*'

Chapter 7

I had been awake since the break of dawn. It was the first Sunday in June and I was going home for the whole day. I was anxious to be on my way because I hadn't seen my mother since February. There were no visits from relatives at St Vincent's. I missed her badly and had read each of her letters to me at least fifty times. They made me feel less isolated and comforted me, helping me to endure the bullying I was being subjected to daily. I ran my tongue along the inside of my bottom lip. I could feel the bumps and scars from being punched in my mouth, causing my teeth to penetrate and bruise the inside of my lips.

I knew with certainty that the bullying would go on. It was the way of the school and nothing was going to change it. The only way to stop it was to fight the bully and hurt him sufficiently that he would never, ever, target you again, but I couldn't do that because I was a coward, a boy who was frightened of his own shadow, a boy who would be bullied and abused for the rest of his days. I shook my head hard, trying to shake off the shame and fear that had taken over my life.

Fear is like a cancer. It eats away at your mind and gives you no respite. I'd try to hide from it in shadowy corners, but it always found me. I pulled the bedclothes over my head at night, only to find it lurking in the darkness. I shut my eyes tightly to erase it, but it lay in wait for me and jumped out without warning. I felt weary from the constant battle going on in my mind. I needed the luxury of crying. I wanted to let my emotions out without the fear of someone seeing me. I wanted to sleep without fear.

Sleep without fear. I doubted if I would ever be afforded that luxury again. Jimmy Wilkinson had made sure of that. He was a constant reminder of my weakness, my cowardice, my shame and humiliation. He had destroyed any small amount of belief I had in myself and I could find no way to excuse my lack of action. I had lost my self-respect and felt like shit. He almost destroyed my belief in God and weakened my faith in the power of prayer. That dreadful night would live with me forever.

It was in my second week at Vincent's that I was woken in the middle of the night by Wilkinson. He was kneeling by the side of my bed and had shaken me gently to wake me up.

He held out an unlit roll-up. 'Do you fancy a smoke?'

'I – I suppose so,' I whispered. Bernie and I had often spoken about the dangers of Vincent's. I knew I should refuse, but I couldn't. It seemed that all my senses had been paralysed with fear and that to refuse his offer would be unwise.

'Follow me and no noise.' He waited silently by the dormitory door as I climbed out of bed. When I got near where he was standing, he crouched low and hurried along the corridor that ran parallel to the dormitories. I followed

him in the same crouching manner until we reached the
first-floor showers and toilets. He ushered me in and closed
the door behind us quietly.

A match flared into light and briefly illuminated our
surroundings. The plain white ceramic tiles that covered all
four walls reflected back our gloomy shadows. Wilkinson's
face appeared chalky white as he puffed the roll-up into life
and his watery blue eyes stared at me in a peculiar way. I felt
uneasy. The match went out and we were plunged into
darkness. I could just discern the red glowing tip of the
cigarette as it wove intricate patterns en route to and from
Wilkinson's mouth.

'Here. You have it,' he whispered. I took the offered
cigarette and puffed in a welcome lungful of smoke. My
teeth began to chatter and I clamped them tightly
together. I knew in my heart that I shouldn't be in this
place, that it didn't feel right. I gulped in another mouthful of smoke.

Bernie and I had bought several roll-ups off Wilkinson
by this time so while I already regarded him with fear and
suspicion I was at least on first-name terms with him.

'I think we should go, Jim. We don't want to get caught
by Arnold.' I reached out to hand him back the cigarette. 'I
– I think we should go.'

'In a minute.' Wilkinson's voice sounded husky. 'I've
just got to do something first.'

I jumped like a scalded cat when I felt him starting to
lift my nightshirt. 'What are you doing?'

'Stay still, you little wanker. You knew you'd have to pay
for that roll-up.' He pushed me hard, face first, against the
tiled wall. 'Don't worry; I'm not going to stick it up you. I'm
just going to put it between the tops of your legs.'

My legs felt weak and I'm sure that if it wasn't for the fact that I was pressed up against the wall they would have crumpled under me. *Sweet Jesus. Please help me. Mary, mother of God. Please help me*, my mind screamed out. I could feel his hand on my buttocks and I clamped them tightly shut with straining muscles. His breath was warm against the back of my neck and coming out in short, laboured gasps. *Oh, Jesus. Please help me.* He was fumbling with his own nightshirt and with absolute horror and revulsion I felt his erect penis pushing against me.

Suddenly, without warning, his right forearm smashed into the back of my head.

'Loosen up your legs,' he said through gritted teeth 'or I'll break your fucking neck.'

His arm was pushing my face onto the wall. I felt dizzy and confused; the initial blow on the back of my head had hurt me and I thought I might pass out at any time.

'Loosen your fucking legs,' he repeated.

I think I may have lost touch with reality for a few moments as I suddenly became aware of his penis sliding rhythmically in and out between my upper legs. I clenched my eyes tightly shut and tried to erase from my mind what was happening to me. I'd never felt so completely alone and unloved. There wasn't a person alive who could help me and now I had been deserted by God and the Blessed Virgin.

Wilkinson let out a shuddering gasp of breath and pushed me even harder against the wall. I could feel a warm viscous flow trickling down my legs and I couldn't help but let out an involuntary cry of anguish. I felt defiled. He pushed his mouth up against my left ear.

'If you ever mention this – I'll fucking kill you.' He hit the back of my head with another forearm smash and pulled away from me, opening the door quietly. 'Stay there until I've had time to get back to bed.' The door closed behind him and I stood alone and trembling in the dark.

Time seemed to stand still. I leant against the wall, not moving, alone in the darkness. I haven't a clue how long I stood there – maybe ten minutes, maybe an hour; time meant nothing to me. It was the sound of footsteps coming down the hallway that brought my frozen heart back to life; it hammered against my ribs and forced me to scamper into one of the cubicles and close the door quietly behind me. The footsteps stopped outside and I could hear the handle of the door turning.

Fear took hold. I was unable to move and every nerve in my body was tingling in terrified anticipation. With a resounding crash the door was flung open and the lights switched on.

'Are you in here, Fenton?' It was Brother Ambrose. He had found my bed empty on his two-hourly check. 'Why are you sitting in the dark?' I let my breath out in an audible sigh. Ambrose was alright – a grandfatherly kind of man with horn-rimmed glasses, who seemed very pious.

'I'm sorry, Bro. I have diarrhoea. I didn't have time to put on the light.' There were a few moments of silence then the sound of his footsteps going back down the corridor. As he went away I could hear him softly reciting the Lord's Prayer. *'Our Father, who art in heaven, hallowed be Thy name, Thy kingdom come …'*

I sat without moving until I could no longer hear him, then I stood up and walked, trembling, out to one of the shower basins. I had to wash away all traces of that filthy discharge that was still clinging to my legs like a slug's trail on a garden path. The water from the shower was only lukewarm but that didn't bother me. Even the limited foam from the carbolic soap acted like a healing salve as it washed away that filth. When at last I stepped out of the shower I felt clean again but bitterly ashamed. I stood naked in front of a long mirror and watched the tears streaming down my cheeks and dripping off the end of my chin. My right cheekbone was red and swollen from being smashed against the tiled wall and there was a small graze on my nose. It took me all of me limited willpower not to scream out in torment at my misfortune.

You will pay for this, you bastard. No matter how long it takes; you will pay. I stood looking and talking to myself, imagining the pleasure I would have in seeing Wilkinson dead. I vowed to myself and to God that I would have my revenge on that filthy piece of shit. One day.

I dressed myself and crept along the corridor and back into bed. I buried myself under the bedclothes, trembling and starting at the slightest noise. The thoughts of the revenge I would have helped me cope with my fear and I eventually fell into a deep sleep.

I was wakened in the morning by the boy in the next bed shaking me gently.

I jumped up and snapped at him, 'Don't touch me like that.' I swung my legs out of bed and onto the floor. 'Don't you dare touch me.'

'It's time to get up.' The boy looked surprised at my reaction. 'Next time, I'll leave you in bed, you wanker.'

'I'm sorry.' I whispered. The boy had been doing me a favour. I would have got booked for being in bed after the first call. 'I didn't mean it. I was half asleep.'

'No damage done,' the boy replied. Although he grinned, I knew he wouldn't forget my rebuke. I shrugged my shoulders. I had bigger worries than some boy who'd had his feelings hurt; I had to face Wilkinson again. I had resolved the previous night that there would be no recurrence of that abuse, no matter what the consequences. I didn't know how long the shame and humiliation would stay with me but I did know that I would rather be dead than allow it to happen again. I also knew that I would have my revenge, no matter how long it took.

I likened myself to Edmond Dantes in *The Count of Monte Cristo*, one of my favourite books, who seeks revenge on Raymond de Villefort and Fernand de Mondego for the injustices inflicted on him. Wilkinson was now both of these characters rolled into one and although his crime against me was different from the ones against Dantes, I felt equally as vindictive. Wilkinson didn't know what was coming to him. He didn't know what a bad enemy he had made and how much I now thirsted for evil to befall him. I stood up and grinned ruefully. Vincent's was my Chateau d'If but, unlike Dantes, I didn't want to escape. I had a reason to stay. I had my hatred for Wilkinson to see me through.

I had decided that everything that occurred that night would stay a secret. There was no need for Bernie to know; I was too embarrassed to tell him. When he asked me about the new bruising on my cheek I told him I had been punched in the face by one of the boys in the dormitory. He found nothing unusual in this as it was a normal occurrence. I had no reason to come in contact with Wilkinson so it was easy to avoid him, but I watched his every movement from afar. Everything he did I evaluated. I was getting to know him well. When my time came I would be ready. I had already started to formulate an unpleasant surprise for him and when the time was right I would act.

That June, the soporific chugging of the train wheels rattling along the track was the only noise in the carriage. I sat hunched in a corner seat staring unseeing at the landscape flashing past. Every puff of Golden Virginia tobacco I inhaled caressed my throat and relaxed me deeper into a state of euphoria. I was on my way home – only for a few hours, but I was on my way.

The horrors of Vincent's were already fading from my mind; they seemed far away and distant. It was the first time in months that I had looked around me with a feeling of unbridled interest. I didn't recognise the names of some of the railway stations we stopped at – Bexleyheath … Erith – but I knew that I was getting closer to London and home. When we stopped at London Bridge Station I was fascinated at how dirty the surrounding houses appeared to be. The brickwork was filthy from years of soot being dumped on them by passing trains and the net curtains hanging in windows were discoloured and grey. I closed my eyes and tried to imagine the people who lived in these drab surroundings. Were they happy? Did they have problems? How many children lived there? So many thoughts were going through my mind that it wasn't until the very last minute that I noticed we were pulling into my destination: Charing Cross Station.

It was an underground train ride to Ealing Broadway Station and then a ten-minute bus ride to West Ealing and my home. I let my eyes feast on familiar surroundings and even gave an old mailbox on the corner of my road an affectionate stroke as I walked past. I stopped and leant against one of the elm trees, spaced out symmetrically along my road, and expertly rolled myself a cigarette. I was intent on savouring every moment of my day at home. I puffed luxuriously on the cigarette, inhaling deeply and letting the smoke slowly drift out of my nostrils. I knew I had an uncertain future in front of me, but this was now, the future could wait.

I could just discern my house from where I was standing and wondered what sort of homecoming lay in front of me. I had heard from my mother every week since I'd been away but there had been no mention of my father in any of her letters. It was as though he didn't exist, as if he had disappeared off the face of the earth. Could she possibly have got rid of him? I didn't even dare to hope. It was time to walk the last few steps – time to see Mum and the girls.

As I came through the back gate and into the small garden, my heart sank as my father emerged scowling from the kitchen door. His blue eyes stared at me dispassionately. 'I thought I'd seen the last of you.' He turned his head and shouted over his shoulder, 'Your little bastard is home,' then brushed past me and went to the gate. 'What time are you going back?'

I had only been in Vincent's for four months but already my temperament was starting to change. I looked at him with contempt. He couldn't hurt me with his nasty remarks; those days were gone. I didn't give a rat's arse if he didn't want me home. I had come to see Mum and my sisters and he would just have to put up with it. 'About five o'clock,' I replied, 'and, if you don't like it – tough shit.'

He spun around to face me. I knew that he wanted to hit me, but he was wary of what I might do. He could still remember how menacingly I had held that vegetable knife and threatened to kill him. It was because of his fear of me that I had been put in Vincent's.

'Hit me, if you dare,' I said quietly. 'Your days of hurting me and Mum are gone. I just hope you're dead by Christmas and I'm given the chance to piss on your grave.'

His face reddened and beads of sweat glistened on his forehead. I felt sure he would have an apoplectic fit at any moment. He seemed to struggle as he lifted his arm and poked a bony finger in my direction and his whole body was shaking with rage.

'You – you hope I'm dead by Christmas. Well, let me tell you something,' he paused to draw breath. 'I've wished you dead since you've been born. You're not even my son. Your slut of a mother got pregnant by another man when I was in the army.' He spat a large lump of mucous on the garden. 'So how does that news make you feel? You're a bastard,' he sneered, 'and your precious mother is a lousy slut.'

I looked at him in stunned silence. Thoughts raced through my mind as I slowly digested this. Was it true? The thought of not being his son didn't bother me at all, but I didn't like the way he delighted in calling my mother a slut. To me she was the most wonderful person in the world. No matter what he said, he could never bring her down from the pedestal I had her on in my mind.

'I'm glad you're not my father. I hate you and I hate the fucking Irish,' I yelled at him. I remembered a term of abuse used by one of the boys at Vincent's. 'St Patrick was a cocksucking queer who shagged sheep.' I paused and laughed at the shocked expression on his face. 'Just like you are.'

This insult stretched him beyond any form of self-control. His right fist shot out and, although I jumped back, it still made contact with my lip, which immediately swelled and oozed blood from the corner of my mouth. The sight of blood seemed to spur him on. His whole body crashed into me and we fell in an untidy heap onto the grass. He straddled me, pinning my arms underneath his knees, and viciously backhanded me across the face.

The pain brought tears to my eyes but I still managed to spit a mouthful of saliva and blood into his face, where it dripped off the side of his chin. He grinned and back-handed me again across the face. 'Cocksucking queer, is it?' he panted. 'I'll show you cocksucking queer.' He swung back with his other hand, knocking my face sideways. 'By the time I finish with you, you'll never want to come home again.'

The blows came in quick succession. Right to the head. Left to the head. My head was flipping from right to left in rhythm with his blows. I was rapidly losing consciousness but there was no let-up in the amount of hits. I heard a voice that seemed a long way away, screaming, pleading, 'Stop it. You're killing him,' and then there was blackness.

I awoke to the sensation of hot water being dabbed gently on my cheek. I kept my eyes shut and tried to push my battered face even deeper into my mother's lap. I loved the smell and the warmth of her body as it always gave me a feeling of peace and safety. Nothing bad could happen to me when surrounded by such a beautiful aroma. I wanted to cry. I slowly opened my eyes and the tightness around my eyelids told me that they must be swollen. I reached up to touch them but her hand restrained me. I heard her say quietly, 'Lie still, John.' I was trying to focus on her face but everything seemed blurry.

I shut my eyes again to get rid of the weird images. I must have passed out again as I remember nothing until I felt Mum trying to lift me off the floor. I reopened my eyes and slowly her face appeared. I could see she was crying. I struggled to break free from her and with an enormous effort managed to sit up.

'I wanted this day to be so nice,' she said. 'I'm so sorry, son. When you're older I'll explain it all to you. It isn't like he said. He's lying. You *are* his son.'

'You don't have to explain anything to me. I don't care what he said. He's just a nasty bastard.' I strained my neck to look around. 'Where's he gone?'

'I don't know and I don't care.' She smiled through her tears. 'I do know that he said he wouldn't be back until after you've gone. So that means we can have a nice peaceful day and you can tell me all the things you couldn't put in your letters.'

'Come,' she took my hand and pulled me gently to my feet. 'I think it's about time I made you a nice cup of tea. I've also got something special for dinner.' She squeezed my shoulders affectionately. 'We've got an apple crumble.'

I still felt light-headed as I sipped the sweet tea. My head felt sore from the beating I had taken and I occasionally touched the swelling around my mouth and cheekbones, trying to force back the tears. Feeling sorry for myself would do me no good and would upset Mum even more. I had become a master at hiding my emotions so it was easy to switch my attention away from my injuries and into the task of rolling a cigarette. Tobacco had become a tranquilliser for me. I sucked deeply on the cigarette, inhaling as much smoke as my lungs would allow, and watched the diluted smoke drift out of my mouth and disappear into the atmosphere. Eventually, after smoking three I was feeling more like myself.

Mum had been watching me intently since I came into the house. 'Well,' she asked, 'are you going to tell me about your new school?'

'There's not much to tell. It's just a school.'

'Don't lie to me. I know you too well,' she gently rebuked. 'I can always tell when you're bottling something up. It's what you haven't said that makes me believe something isn't right. If you were happy, you'd be chatting away nineteen to the dozen. Tell me all about it, I really want to know.'

I shook my head. 'What's the sense in worrying you with my problems? You can't do anything about them.'

She smiled. 'A problem shared is a problem halved. Even if I can't do anything, I can give you some adult advice. It might help.'

'How do you advise someone into being something that they're not? I'm frightened of the other boys and I'm being bullied. I'm not a fighter and I'm scared of getting hurt.' I angrily wiped the tears away. My voice was breaking up uncontrollably. 'So, tell me what I should do.'

'You're not a fighter! You're scared of getting hurt!' My mother sounded astonished. 'You're the bravest boy alive. What do you think just went on in the garden? The only coward out there was your father. I've seen you take beating after beating and I've never seen you afraid. I know this sounds silly, but you're my hero. Nobody on earth could ever accuse you of being anything but a hero.'

I hated to see her like this and wished I hadn't said anything. I reached out and took her hand. 'That's why I never told you, Mum. I knew you would get upset.'

'Of course I'm upset. It's my fault you're in that place. If only – if only I had been braver, none of this would be happening to you.' Her anger was evident and her maternal instincts were aroused. 'I want you to tell me what's happening to you in that place. Who is hurting you?'

I told her of all the beatings I had seen and how they frightened me. I told her of the cruelty being dished out daily by some of the Brothers, and about the numerous times I had been bullied by older boys and how they had hurt me. I didn't tell her about Wilkinson. That was my secret and I was still trying to come to terms with the shame of what had occurred.

'So now you know everything, Mum,' I said quietly, averting my eyes so she wouldn't detect the lie. 'How do I deal with it?'

I watched as she brought her emotions under control. Her hand was visibly shaking as she opened a packet of cigarettes and put one in her mouth. I lit a match for her and watched as she puffed the cigarette into life. She relaxed back into her chair and blew out a long stream of blue smoke.

'I hardly know what to say,' she said quietly. 'If I could take your problems onto myself, I would do it willingly. But I can't.' She took a long puff on her cigarette. 'You know that, don't you?' She stared at me fixedly until I nodded in agreement. 'You have to believe in yourself. Get rid of all that nonsense in your head that you're a coward. You're not a coward. You're just a young boy being forced to grow up too quickly in a dreadful environment. Did you know that the biggest coward of all is a bully? Well, he is. You never see a bully hit someone he knows will hit him back. Why? Because he's a coward. The only real way of dealing with a bully is to bully him. I suggest that the next time one of these boys decides to hit you, you pick up a big piece of wood and hit them hard across the head with it.'

'You don't really mean that, do you?' I asked, incredulous.

'Yes I do, and don't you forget it. I hate the thought of those little bastards hitting you. I will feel a lot better if I know that you are going to deal with it.' She stubbed the cigarette out angrily in an ashtray. 'As for the Brothers, those evil, sanctimonious bastards, you'll just have to try and keep out of their way. I've always hated the Catholic clergy and the way they behave.' She hesitated, deep in thought. 'I should never have converted when I married your father. I knew what they were like. Every time the parish priest comes around he stinks of drink, and how many of them have appeared in the Sunday papers for abusing young boys?' She took out another cigarette. 'And as for the Brothers, they are notorious for their cruelty. Nothing you've told me about them surprises me. They are all destined to burn in hell.'

I was shocked by what Mum had said. She was advocating that I use weapons to defend myself but I knew in my heart I wasn't capable of that. Weapons frightened me. I needed to speak to Bernie and ask his advice. At the same time, Mum convinced me that I had to somehow bring the bullying to an end and I was determined not to let her down. Maybe Bernie would have the answers.

The rest of the day was filled with a lot of false joviality. We didn't mention anything more to do with Vincent's or my father. Occasionally Mum would get a bowl of cold water and dab my swollen face with a wet rag. I ventured a look in the bathroom mirror and saw that both my eyes were swollen and bruised. My lips were puffy and there was a small cut in the corner of my mouth. My father had done a real job on me and I promised myself that I would pay him back in kind when I was older.

Mum clung on to me tightly as I was about to leave. It was as if she knew that it would be some time before she saw me again and she wanted to give me as much love as was humanly possible. I hugged her back and kissed her damp cheek. 'Don't forget what I told you,' she said. 'And don't forget that you're not a coward. You're my hero. Don't let any of those little bastards bully you.'

'I won't, Mum, I promise you.' I kissed her again on her cheek and prised myself loose from her hug. 'I have to go. If I'm late back I won't be allowed out again.'

It was with great difficulty that I walked away. I didn't want to leave her. I dragged myself to the bus stop and began the journey back to Vincent's. My mind was racing, my whole body tingling with anticipation at what Mum had advised me to do. But lurking in the back of my mind was fear. Would I be able to do what she had said I should? Would I get hurt attempting it? What sort of weapon should I use and could I stand being hit with a weapon?

I was only a month past my fourteenth birthday and I would have to fight boys up to three years older than myself. I felt sick to the pit of my stomach, but I was determined to follow her advice. I had to become nasty and put aside feelings of being a coward and a wimp and replace them with a belief in my invincibility and superiority. I decided that every boy in that school was going to be my teacher. I would watch them all closely and learn from them. Every move, every trick, every bit of nastiness that worked for them I would practise until they all became a natural part of my self-defence. I smiled at my bravado. With Bernie's help and a willingness to learn I no longer had anything to worry about.

'You're fucked, Wilkinson.' I spat the words out and got a startled look from the bus conductor who happened to be passing my seat. I looked out of the window and smiled knowingly. 'Really fucked.'

Chapter 8

I grabbed Bernie by the arm and hurried him to the chapel gateway. 'Kennedy and Robinson are going "around the back". It should be a good one.'

Bernie pulled his arm away angrily. 'Fuck off, John. I'm fed up watching fight after fight. I must have seen twenty fights over the past three months and nothing has changed. We're still getting thumped by the others. If you want to watch it, go ahead – but count me out. I'm going for a smoke.'

I watched Bernie walk away until he disappeared into one of the brick porches that led into the recreation room. I felt slightly disappointed that he no longer had the same enthusiasm for watching and learning about fighting. I was as keen as ever and spent a great deal of my time in the locker room, practising moves I had witnessed in some of the fights. Bernie sometimes came with me and I enjoyed testing which of us could head-butt a steel locker door the quickest. I usually won and prided myself that I could head-butt the door and follow it up with a low kick while still keeping perfect balance. I was now trying to master a third move: after the low kick I would jump slightly backwards and grab a weighted money belt out of the back of my trousers and swing it ferociously downwards. I had nearly mastered this but I was far from happy with my present speed. I needed a lot more practice.

Going 'around the back' for a fight was the *crème de la crème* of violence. It meant that the two protagonists were taking their disagreement out of sight of the Brothers and masters to a place where they wouldn't be stopped. There would be a winner. Somebody could really get hurt. I had been in Vincent's for six months and this was the first time two people had opted for 'around the back'. I would have to be very careful when sneaking out of the yard as I would be taking as much risk as the combatants. If I was seen by any of the staff I would be accused of trying to abscond and duly punished. I would also be in deep trouble if Kennedy or Robinson saw me spying on them. These fights were private, no audience allowed. I knew the risks but my obsession to learn about fighting spurred me onwards.

I crept unobserved into the chapel, quickly making my way into the vestry. My heart was thumping as I tried the vestry door that led into the small graveyard at the rear of the chapel. It slid open easily and I squeezed myself into the small porch, closing the door quietly behind me. I stood quietly, listening for any sounds, until I was certain nobody was following me. Satisfied I was alone, I sprinted to the three-foot-high cemetery wall and dived over it, landing in a crumpled heap on the grass of the playing field. I skinned my elbow on a hidden stone in the grass and cursed silently under my breath. After a brief inspection of the damage done by the stone, I belly-crawled my way along the base of the wall in the direction of the small yard at the rear of the carpenter's shop. This was where the fight was due to take place. I hoped I was in time to witness it.

As I drew near to the yard I could hear sounds of a struggle coming from its confines. I crept forward, closer, closer, until I thought I was near enough to look for an aperture to spy on the proceedings. Luck was on my side. Right next to the place where I was kneeling was a tiny gap in the brickwork that gave a complete, unobstructed view of the entire yard. As soon as I looked through the gap I knew that I was witnessing something nasty. I instinctively drew away to shut out the vision, but like a magnet my eyes were drawn back.

Kennedy was sixteen years old, a tall, good-looking lad, with blond hair and dark blue eyes. He had been in Vincent's for two years and was rated quite highly. He could definitely look after himself. Robinson was also sixteen years old. He was short and stocky with a swarthy complexion. It was whispered that he was a gyppo, but nobody really knew and nobody fancied asking.

Kennedy was hurt, his face a mask of blood. He had been slashed twice across his left cheek with a razor blade that Robinson was brandishing in his right hand. Both cuts would need stitching and the blood was still streaming off his chin and down the front of his clothes. I watched with awe and admiration as he ripped off his bloody shirt and wrapped it around his left forearm. He was going to use his arm as a shield and the shirt would stop the blade penetrating his skin. He showed no fear – even though he must have been in a lot of pain.

He reached into his waistband and pulled out a grey sock. I didn't know what he had in the sock but I guessed it was a large stone or a chunk of lead from the metalwork shop. He walked slowly towards Robinson, swaying slowly from left to right, his left arm out in front of him, ready to protect him from any further slashes from the blade.

Robinson backed away slowly. His movements appeared exaggerated as he feinted left and then right, seeking out a weakness in Kennedy's guard, hoping to find an unprotected spot to slash at. Kennedy kept coming slowly forward. His eyes were riveted to the movement of the hand with the blade in it. He was manoeuvring himself in close enough to use the weighted sock.

Suddenly, with blinding speed, Kennedy jumped forward and swung the sock in a vicious downward arc. Robinson tried to snatch his arm backwards, out of danger, but it was too late; the weighted sock hit his hand with a sickening thud. I clearly heard the sound of the wrist bone snapping. The second swing of the sock caught Robinson on the side of his face. He was unconscious before he hit the floor. Kennedy walked over to where Robinson was lying motionless and kicked him twice in his unprotected face. He then ran to the far end of the yard, climbed over the wall and disappeared from my sight. Robinson was still motionless on the ground when I left the scene and scampered back to the vestry.

Bernie was looking at me with interest. 'Did you see the whole of the fight?'

I nodded. It was the talk of the school. Kennedy had needed thirteen stitches to repair the cuts on his cheek. Robinson had a broken wrist and a fractured cheekbone. He had been admitted to Dartford Hospital and was not expected to be released for at least a week. The police had been informed by the hospital administration that the injuries to both boys were consistent with being assaulted with a weapon.

The only snag was the boys. They both insisted that they had been involved in accidents. The police had interviewed every boy in the school and had found nothing that could shake Kennedy and Robinson's statements. De Montfort was furious. He hated anything that brought the school into disrepute as this could reflect on his ability to control the boys under his charge. The police made it clear to him that they felt sure there was a conspiracy of silence and that they knew both injured parties had been involved in a fight with weapons. However, they were powerless to charge either of the boys with an offence as they had no witnesses and no evidence.

De Montfort gave the officer in charge permission to address an assembly of the entire school before supper that night. I was looking forward to hearing what he could possibly say about the incident. Apart from Kennedy and Robinson, I was the only person who could relate with authority what had taken place, and I hadn't told a soul, except Bernie.

I described the loaded sock and added, admiringly, 'It was a good move. Kennedy's one hard bastard. He deserved to win.'

Bernie looked at me with disbelief. 'You've changed, John. You're starting to admire violence. It wasn't a good move; it was a nasty move. Both Kennedy and Robinson deserved what they got. They're fucking animals.'

I walked away from Bernie feeling annoyed. I knew I was changing but I felt I had no choice. This school was completely run by violence. The masters were violent, the boys were violent, and I thought only violence would get me through my time there. I was dreading my first fight but I was determined that, when that time came, I wouldn't disgrace myself. Why Bernie didn't understand that completely bewildered me.

It had been three months since I had been home. No matter how hard I tried, the blue- and red-poor weeks just kept on coming. In the twelve weeks since I'd been back I'd had two weeks of satisfactory, six weeks of blue-poor and four weeks of red-poor. That meant I had lost two and a half days of my annual holiday. All my bookings were from being caught smoking. Sometimes I got caught four times a day and one day, much to Bernie's amusement, I had been caught six times. I had long since resigned myself to having only a short holiday, as I had no intention of giving up smoking.

Bernie had been craftier than me. He had not lost anything off his holiday and had been home on all of the first Sundays of the month. I was glad that he'd got to go home as it was the only way we had of acquiring tobacco. Wilkinson often tried to bully us into telling him where we hid our stash of tobacco but we never told him the secret. Much to De Montfort's amazement, I had mastered the Latin Mass and Father Delaney, the school priest, had begun using me as a server for all of the services. I kept our tobacco hidden in one of the numerous boxes of hosts that were stored in the vestry. There was no chance of it being found as it was part of my job as the server to ensure that the main chalice was topped up with hosts. It was the safest stash of tobacco in the school. None of the staff would dream of searching the chapel and I felt sure that Father Delaney would never allow it if they ever tried. He was a decent man in his mid fifties, with big bushy sideboards, and we'd got on with each other from the start.

I had an unexpected bonus land at my feet because of the work I did in the chapel: I found Jimmy Wilkinson's hiding place for all the money he extorted by selling cigarettes. I saw him, from the vestry window, sneaking around the small cemetery. He lifted one of the flagstones that made up the pathway and placed a bulging handkerchief into a hole that had been hidden by the stone. After he had gone I went out into the cemetery and lifted this stone. Stuffed into the hole were at least nine or ten handkerchiefs, all bulging with sixpenny pieces, and a small leather purse with four one-pound notes inside it. I estimated that there had to be at least thirty pounds in his cache.

I had never seen so much money. I made up my mind that it would disappear before he had a chance to take it home with him on leave. The thought of his anger and upset when he found his fortune gone gave me an almost orgasmic feeling in my body. Anything that upset Wilkinson pleased me and I knew that losing all his money would drive him berserk. I didn't tell Bernie about what I had found as I didn't want any awkward questions about my hatred for Wilkinson. This was my secret – part of my payback. This was personal.

'I don't think you boys have a clue what an accessory before and after the fact means.' The police inspector had been in full flow for ten minutes. I looked around me and noted that nearly all the boys had a look of bored resignation on their faces as they were forced to endure his lecture. 'It is a very serious crime. Men have been hanged for committing the offence.' He paused and looked around the room. It was obvious he was hoping the last statement would shock somebody into coming forward and telling him all about the Kennedy and Robinson fight.

Bernie nudged me and whispered. 'He's got two hopes – Bob Hope and no hope.' I laughed quietly at the remark and got a disapproving look from Brother Michael.

'There are times when you have to stand tall and speak out. This is one of those times. Two boys have been seriously injured – one of them could have been killed – and none of you know anything about it.' He let out a hollow laugh through almost clenched teeth. 'Do you think we're stupid? Do you think I believe that in a closed environment like this nobody knows what went on? Of course you know what went on. I dare say that most of you admire the boys and the level of violence they used against each other.'

He looked at us accusingly and slowly shook his head. 'You're as guilty as the two boys who were fighting. You may believe that your code of silence is protecting Kennedy and Robinson. Let me assure you that it does no such thing. Your silence is leading them to believe that the using of weapons is all right, acceptable in society. Well, it's not all right and decent society will not tolerate that sort of behaviour.'

Brother De Montfort came forward to stand next to the inspector. His face was a mask of anger. He shouted loudly, 'And I most certainly won't. How dare you refuse to co-operate with the inspector. All first Sundays are cancelled next month. Instead, you will spend the day in the chapel, reflecting on your unacceptable code of conduct.'

De Montfort's punishment got an immediate response. There were whispers of discontent from nearly everyone – 'fucking wanker', 'cunt', 'arsehole' were just a few of the discernible words being muttered. The Brothers and masters tried desperately to catch someone making one of these remarks but were thwarted by the fact that nobody's lips seemed to move and most people were looking down at the floor.

The inspector stared at us open-mouthed, not believing what he had just heard. I had to turn my head away as I knew I would end up smiling. Did he think Vincent's was an ordinary school? Did he think that being locked away and abused would make a boy better behaved? This clown was living in cloud cuckoo land.

Brother De Montfort took a silver whistle from a secret pocket in his cassock and blew out a shrill blast. 'One more remark will mean the loss of another first Sunday. Is that what you want?' His voice was trembling with rage. 'Every boy has lost nineteen points.'

All of the boys went silent. De Montfort had just taken a quarter of a day off our annual leave. He looked at us with imperious satisfaction. He had stopped any form of rebellious behaviour. He knew that our annual leave was the thing we looked forward to the most.

The inspector saw the futility in speaking to us and took De Montfort's interruption as an excuse to leave the room. De Montfort hurried after him. He whispered an instruction to Brother Francis as he was leaving. Brother Francis now took up a position in front of us. 'Strip out of your clothes. Put them in a neat pile on the floor at your feet. I mean all your clothes – that includes your underclothes. I want you standing naked.'

Strip searches were not unusual. They usually produced a few items of contraband. Tobacco, matches, cigarette papers and occasionally a few weapons. Each boy in turn had to walk to the front of the recreation room carrying their clothes. We had to place our belongings on a table and wait while two of the masters searched them. I was always amazed at the amount of black and blue bruising on some of the boys. It would cover the whole of their backsides and sometimes encroach onto the tops of their legs. In a lot of cases they would also have cuts, which had scabbed over, standing out above the bruises. I had been told that these were the marks left after you were caned by Brother Ambrose. I hoped and prayed that I would never have to carry those marks.

De Montfort reappeared before the searches were finished and took a perverse delight in walking up and down the ranks telling every boy that he had lost nineteen points. He never realised that because every boy was now on a red-poor week anyway, they could brazenly smoke for the rest of the week without fear of the consequences. I went to bed thinking about how little the police understood boys who were put into approved schools. I was also proud to have been part of a successful conspiracy of silence. It gave me a feeling of getting my own back on a system that stank.

Chapter 9

St Vincent's was a relic of a bygone age. Time seemed to stand still as boys from all walks of life had to suffer sadistic customs that had been in place since the end of the last century. I was amazed at the dates by some of the initials that had been carved into the wooden pews in the chapel. There was one scratched into the stone step at the foot of the altar where altar boys had knelt since the chapel had been opened in 1889 – '*AL.1897*'. I often knelt on the step and wondered who those initials belonged to. What kind of boy was he? Was he still alive in 1958? I knew for certain that if he ever came back to visit the school he would find familiar surroundings. The only improvements he would find would be electricity instead of gas, hot water for ablutions, showering facilities and mowers for cutting the grass. The rest of the amenities were the same.

All the tools in the workshops were old but very well-maintained. At the end of all working days the tools that had been used were checked for cleanliness. The shovels in the bricklaying department were at least twenty years old and had been used to mix thousands of mixes of mortar and concrete but at the end of the day they were left shining like new. The same applied to the trowels, hammers, plumb lines, bolsters, buckets, mortarboards and any other tool we may have used. The minutest trace of dirt found on a tool would result in being booked and getting a hard slap around the ear. Peter Cornell, who was in charge of our department, was a master bricklayer and a fairly nice sort of man. He would turn a blind eye if any of his boys had a crafty smoke and he would just point a finger if a boy cursed. But show him a dirty tool and one of his big hands would hit your ear like a jack hammer. It was safer to take extra time cleaning your tools.

It was September 1958 and the football season was about to begin. I had wanted to go for football training ever since I arrived at Vincent's, but up until now I had been too timid to put my name forward. I think my self-confidence started to improve as soon as I started to practise fighting. Bernie had already put his name forward and now I decided to have a go as well.

Tom Banks was in charge of the football teams. He was the most popular master in the school. In the seven months I'd been in Vincent's I had never seen him hit a boy around the head or book a boy for smoking. He was a fanatical Charlton Athletic fan and rarely missed any of their home matches. He spent hours speaking to the boys about matches he had seen. He gave a pass-by-pass analysis and tried to bring similar moves into the training matches. I don't think it was possible to find a fault in him. He really was a great guy.

'So what makes you think you're good enough for the team, Fenton?' Tom was staring at me. 'Do you think you've got what it takes?'

'I don't know, sir. I just want to learn how to play properly and maybe get in the team next year.'

'Have you ever played in a team before?'

'No, sir. But I'm a quick learner and don't mind how much I have to practise. I won't let you down.'

Tom smiled at my enthusiasm. 'You wouldn't be letting me down. You'd be letting yourself down and your team down. Last year neither of our teams lost a match. They achieved this by hard work and a well-founded belief in their ability. If I let you join our squad of players I will expect the same sort of attitude from you. Do you understand that?'

'Yes, sir.'

'Do you support a football team?' He looked at me with interest. 'Most of the players support the best team in the country.'

'Why would they support Manchester United, sir? They nearly all come from London.' I was trying to stop myself smiling. 'I thought they'd support Chelsea.'

'Manchester United? Chelsea?' Tom laughter boomed out across the yard. 'You're a cheeky sod.' He patted me on my shoulder. 'You're in. Join the lads for training every lunchtime and evening. And Fenton, let that be the last time you ever mention those two teams. The only team I allow to be talked about is Charlton.'

Bernie smiled at me. 'I take it from Tom's reaction that you're in the squad. What did you say that made him laugh so loudly?'

I told him and he chortled. 'What position do you want to play in?' Bernie asked. 'I want to play on the right wing.'

'I don't mind. I'd just like to get into the team.'

'If you put as much practice into football as you do into learning how to fight you'll have no problem getting in the team.'

'I will, Bernie. I'll put the practice in.' I nodded my head and added, 'But I'll also continue to practise fighting. That's for certain.'

'Jesus, John, what do you think you're going to achieve by it? We've been here seven months and nothing has changed. Both of us are getting thumped by every arsehole in the place and it's going to continue as far as I can see.' He shook his head. 'You're just wasting your time.'

'Maybe I am and maybe I'm not. I don't know, but I intend to keep it up. It makes me feel better about myself.'

A shrill blast on a whistle brought our conversation to an end. Brother Ambrose was indicating that we were to line up in our houses before filing into the washroom before lunch. The washroom was a large, one-storey building recently renovated by the various building departments in the school. We had done a good job and the new tiles and washbasins gave the interior a clean and sterile effect. Above each of the washbasins were two wooden shelves at head height. Each of the shelves had two numbers printed on them. The four numbers on the two shelves above my washbasin were 11, 41, 71 and 101. On the shelf by each number was a tin of Gibbs tooth powder and bar of Palmolive soap. Hanging on two brass hooks by each number was a toothbrush and a face flannel. Behind the washbasins, in the centre of the washroom there was a large, aluminium frame made up of circular pipes with lots of numbered hooks welded on to them and from each of the hooks hung a white towel.

I had just finished washing my face and started to turn around to reach for my towel when suddenly I was pushed violently towards my washbasin. I had no time to put my hands up for protection and my forehead slammed into one of the brass hooks on my shelf. I screamed out in pain and immediately vomited into the sink.

'Don't get in my way again, you fucking wanker.'

I turned around to see who was speaking and had caused me so much pain; it was a boy called David Love. He was nearly fifteen years old and a member of the school's boxing team. He had often hit me and Bernie and we both hated him. He came from Bermondsey in south-east London and loved bullying all the smaller and younger boys. He smirked when he saw the trickle of blood running from the cut in my forehead. It was one smirk too many.

A blinding rage took over me. I jumped at him and we both fell through the towel frame, landing in a heap on the floor. Brother Ambrose pulled us both off the floor and hit us each around the ear. He shoved us roughly away and reached for his notebook. I went back to my washbasin and tried my best to stem the flow of blood from my forehead. I couldn't do it and was forced to go and ask Brother Ambrose if I could see matron. He looked at the small cut and nodded his head.

'It serves you right. That's what you get from fighting,' he said, staring at me angrily.

'Thank you, Bro.' As I hurried out of the door, the blood was starting to drip off my chin and down the front of my clothes.

When I came out into the yard I was immediately jumped on by David Love, who had been waiting for me to emerge from the washroom. He grabbed me in a headlock and tried to smack me in the face with his other hand. Bernie and I had practised getting out of a headlock a hundred times. I threw myself backwards and we both fell back onto the floor. This manoeuvre put Love underneath me and all I had to do was turn over. I rolled over quickly and pulled my head out of his arm grip. As soon as my head was clear I smashed it downwards into the centre of his face. It was the first time I had ever used my head as a weapon and I was relieved to see that it had done damage. His nose and mouth were both bleeding and his eyes were watering so much he couldn't see. I was just preparing to smash my face downwards again when I was yanked to my feet by Brother Michael, who was on yard duty. He smacked me hard around the left side of my face.

'You're both booked and you'll be seeing Brother De Montfort later.' He pointed to the far corner of the yard. 'Get over there and don't come over this side.' He pulled Love off the floor and hit him hard around the cheek. 'I saw the whole thing and you started it. I've sent Fenton over to the other side of the yard, away from you. You stay on this side. You'll both see Brother De Montfort later.'

I went over to the chapel wall and sat on the floor at its base. My forehead was still bleeding but somehow it didn't seem to matter any more. Bernie ran over and stood in front of me, grinning. 'That was great, John. You really hurt the bastard. I couldn't believe it when I saw it was you fighting Love.'

'I told you that it pays to practise.' I was feeling elated. I had had my first fight and I hadn't lost it. 'Did you see how easy it was to get on top of him? It worked just like we had practised.'

'What was it about?'

'He shoved me in the washroom and made me bang my head. I jumped on him and then it was broken up. When I came into the yard, he jumped on me.' I looked over to where Love was standing on the other side of the yard. He pointed his finger in my direction. 'I don't think it's over yet. Look at the way he's pointing his finger at me. I think there's more to come.' I stood up and beckoned him over, taunting him with my arrogance, laughing him into anger. The whole school was watching so he had to come.

'Jesus Christ, John. What the fuck are you doing?' Bernie was horrified. 'He's going to kick the fuck out of you for taking the piss.'

'He's coming, Bernie, so get out of the way.'

Bernie spun around and saw Love sprinting across the yard in my direction. He stepped a few paces away. 'Watch yourself,' he shouted as Love swung a looping right hand punch at my face.

It was easy for me to move out of the way of the punch because Love was angry and wild in his swing. I kicked him hard in his shin, just above his right foot and saw his mouth grimace in pain when it connected. He hopped a few paces on his good leg.

'You fucking wanker,' he shouted. 'I'm going to kill you.'

'Don't talk about it. Do it.' I had heard a boy called Peter Larch say that in a fight once and had decided there and then that if I ever got a chance, I would use it.

Love's left hand shot out and hit me just above my left eye. It really hurt and I could feel the swelling straight away. From the corner of my eye I could see Brother Michael running across the yard in our direction. Love saw him coming also and in that moment, while he was distracted, I managed a good kick to his left knee.

'Fuck,' he yelled and reached down to hold it.

I kicked him again. This time it was his right knee and he shouted out angrily, 'You little bastard.'

Brother Michael grabbed me by the scruff of my neck and hauled me towards the classroom porchway. Brother Arnold had come into the yard and was beating and pushing Love in the same direction. Brother Michael unlocked the classroom door, opened it and shoved me through the doorway and in the direction of De Montfort's office. I could hear Brother Arnold and Love coming in the same direction. Before we reached the office, Brother Francis came hurrying towards us. He looked at the damage done to Love's legs, shook his head at the sight of his two swollen knees and signalled to Brother Michael.

'Come with me, Brother, and you can tell us what happened.' They both disappeared into De Montfort's office.

Five minutes later I was standing in front of De Montfort. He peered at me as if he had a bad smell under his nose.

'So you've decided to take up fighting. You've decided that school rules no longer have to be obeyed.' He smiled with his mouth only. 'I'm sure that after you've visited the small dormitory with me and Brother Ambrose your views will change for the better. I told you when you first arrived that I would not hesitate to discipline you. Now you are going to find out that I did not lie.'

I stepped apprehensively through the doorway that led into the small dormitory. A long row of beds, each with a chair beside it, lined both sides of the room. At the far end was another door, which led into the toilets and wash room. I didn't know what to expect and every noise or sound made me jump with fear. Brother De Montfort followed me into the room and threw a pair of silk boxing shorts onto the nearest bed.

'Get out of your clothes – including your underpants – and put on the shorts.' His whinging voice echoed around the closed room. 'Brother Ambrose will be along shortly.'

I self-consciously undressed and pulled on the shorts. They fitted me snugly and the silk seemed to cling to my genitals. I pulled them slightly downwards to loosen their grip. Brother De Montfort never took his eyes off me and seemed to be enjoying my discomfort. A cruel smile crossed his face when I jumped at the noise of Brother Ambrose coming into the room. He was carrying a bundle of bamboo canes, held together by two pieces of string, and it was then I knew for sure I was about to be caned. My heart began to race and I was sweating with fear. I remembered the fierce, hot pain when Sister Mary struck my palms with a bamboo cane back at primary school and the time when fear made me urinate on the floor in front of the class. *Please, God, don't let me humiliate myself this time*, I thought.

Brother Ambrose was a trained teacher but only taught one morning a week. He had two other jobs: one to supervise the cleaning of the school, the other to discipline the boys. I had heard that after he caned a boy he would have tears running down his face but I didn't believe it. Why would a person do something that made him cry?

He selected a three-foot-long cane from the pile and pulled it loose from the string. Slowly and methodically he placed the rest of the canes on a bed and began to do some practice swings with the cane in his right hand. It swished through the air, making a humming noise like an angry bee. After about a dozen practice swings he nodded at Brother De Montfort.

'Right, Fenton, I think we're ready for you.' De Montfort's eyes closed as if he were meditating. 'You are here because you cannot obey simple rules that allow this school to run efficiently.' He opened his eyes and pointed to a spot in the centre aisle. 'Bend over and touch your toes.'

I had hardly reached my toes when, with a large swishing sound, the three foot cane slashed against my scarcely protected backside. The blinding pain I felt is impossible to describe but I know I screamed in agony. I ran like a scalded cat to the far end of the room and jumped up and down on the spot. I don't know what made me do this but it seemed to help me until the pain subsided. I'm sure that it was not an uncommon sight to either of the brothers as neither of them reacted to my sudden demonic dash. Brother De Montfort waited a short while before he signalled me back to his end of the room with a bony finger.

'You have to understand that the sort of behaviour you've shown today will never be tolerated. I will not have fighting in my school. Do you understand that?' His face was expressionless as he spoke. 'Do you understand that?'

I nodded, unable to speak. Never in my worst nightmare had I seen or imagined such fear and pain.

'Touch your toes.'

Again the deadly swishing sound and the excruciating pain. My scream sounded even louder this time and I actually crashed into the toilet door at the far end of the room. Tears were streaming down my face and I was finding it hard to catch my breath. Both brothers were staring at me impassively. When De Montfort signalled to me I limped back to where he was standing.

'Don't think we get any pleasure out of caning you boys. We do it for your own good. It is only through this sort of punishment that you truly learn what is right and what is wrong.' He pointed at the floor. 'Touch your toes.'

I didn't scream this time. I couldn't. It took all the breath out of my body. I did manage to run to the far end of the room and beat the door with my clenched hands. The whole of my lower body seemed to be on fire. My breathing eventually returned to normal and I found myself emitting loud guttural sobs. De Montfort's bony finger signalled me again.

I limped back to where he was standing and looked up into his cruel face. 'I've learned my lesson, Bro. I'll never fight again,' I sobbed.

'I don't believe you. All you boys are liars.' He definitely seemed to be enjoying himself. 'Touch your toes.'

This was no longer punishment; it was torture. Every slash with that bamboo cane challenged my sanity. My legs felt weak and hardly able to support my body. My tears flowed but no sound came out of my mouth. The dash to the far end of the room no longer helped me. I feared looking in De Montfort's direction and seeing his bony finger signalling me back for another slash of bamboo. The fourth, fifth and sixth slash with the cane took my pain to a new level. My chest was heaving as I fought for breath. My hands were shaking with shock or maybe fear. My whole being was exhausted from the brutality it was enduring and the muscles in my legs were twitching uncontrollably. When, after the sixth bamboo slash, De Montfort told me to get dressed again, I fell to my knees in relief. I looked up at Brother Ambrose and through my tears I could see tears rolling down his cheek. It was true – he cried when he caned you. But I felt no pity for him. Just hatred.

I must have stayed kneeling for two or three minutes before I was able to stand up and get dressed. I slowly pulled down the shorts. I thought at first I must have urinated in them as they were wet and sloppy but then I saw that my hands were bloody from touching them. I strained my head around trying to get a glimpse of my backside. I couldn't see that far but I noticed that there was a lot of blood on the backs of my legs. I knew then that the bamboo cane must have cut me with one of its slashes. De Montfort saw what I was looking at.

'Go to the washroom and shower yourself down.' He smiled coldly. 'It's all over now and you'll soon feel as good as new.'

I walked slowly and deliberately towards the washroom. I was no longer self-conscious about my nakedness; in fact, I was devoid of any feelings. I stepped into a shower and turned on the water. I adjusted the temperature so it was just above cold and let the water beat down on my shoulders and run in soothing streams over my lower regions. It felt wonderful and I stood in that position for several minutes. When at last I stepped out of the shower I felt almost human again and the memory of the caning and the pain I had endured was receding from my mind. I walked back along the dormitory to where both of the brothers were still standing and put on my clothes.

'I hope you have learned your lesson,' De Montfort whined. 'I never want to have to bring you up here again. Do you understand that, Fenton?'

I nodded my head. 'Yes, Bro,' I said quietly, but inside my brain I was screaming, *I hope you're dead by Christmas, you ugly cunt. I hope all your family dies by Christmas.*

'Good. I knew that you would see sense. You're an intelligent boy and Father Delaney thinks highly of you. Your parents would be proud of the way you have mastered all the Latin responses at Mass.'

Fuck off, you cunt. Die, you ugly cunt. Die, die, die.

De Montfort was appraising me with his lifeless eyes. I wondered briefly if he could read my mind. I decided he couldn't because if he could he would be beating me into a pulp by now.

'I've decided that you will miss lunch today. You can go instead to the chapel and polish the floor of the vestry. And, while you're on your knees polishing the floor, maybe you can ask Jesus for his forgiveness.'

'I will, Bro,' I said submissively.

Fuck you, you cunt.

We walked at a sedate pace down the stairs and back to De Montfort's office. Love was standing outside the office with Brother Arnold and looked at me with hatred. I was glad he was about to suffer the same caning as I had and I forced a smirk onto my face to annoy him. It didn't go unnoticed and De Montfort shoved me angrily towards the yard door.

He looked at Brother Arnold. 'Take him to the chapel. I've given him work to do and he's to get no lunch.'

Brother Arnold grabbed me by the scruff of my neck. 'Do you want me to stay with him?'

De Montfort shook his head. 'That won't be necessary. He knows what he has to do and can be trusted to get on with it. He's worked alone in the chapel for the last two months.'

I was shoved unceremoniously out into the yard and all the way to the chapel door by Brother Arnold. He couldn't resist giving me a hard cuff around the back of my head as he let me go. 'I'll be checking your work later. Make sure you do a good job or you'll be back upstairs.'

I didn't even turn around to acknowledge what he had just told me. I just opened the chapel door and went inside.

As I shut the door behind me I whispered, 'I hope you're dead by the end of the day, you sadistic cunt.'

The vestry floor needed nothing doing to it. I took out the polish and cloths and positioned them around the floor to give the impression I was doing something. I rolled myself a cigarette from the tobacco hidden in the hosts then I lit the charcoal in the thurible and sprinkled a small amount of incense over it. I waved the thurible around until the smell of burning incense permeated the entire room and then I lit my cigarette. I sat down carefully on the floor in the corner of the room, wincing at the tight hot feeling of my backside from the caning, and blew the inhaled smoke from my cigarette over the smoking incense. Safe in the knowledge that the smell of cigarette smoke would go undetected, I allowed myself the luxury of smoking two cigarettes in quick succession.

I heard the chapel door open. As quick as a flash I opened the thurible and threw the remains of my cigarette inside. I blew on the charcoal, which immediately glowed red and started to consume the tobacco and paper. I closed the lid of the thurible and knelt on the floor with a duster in my hand. I listened carefully and could hear someone approaching stealthily towards the vestry door. I began rubbing the cloth along the floor. The door flew open and Brother Arnold rushed in. He seemed surprised to find me on my knees working. He looked around the room like a hawk seeking out its prey until his eyes came to rest on the smoking thurible.

'Why are you burning incense?'

'I had to make up some more charcoal as the thurible was running out. Father Delaney asked me to do it,' I lied, knowing that he wouldn't ask Father Delaney to verify my story. 'I'll put it out if you want, Bro.'

He was sniffing loudly, trying to identify the aroma of cigarette smoke. 'Stand up. Put your hands above your head and spread your legs.'

His search of me was thorough. He felt and looked everywhere. When, at last, he was satisfied I was hiding nothing he stepped away from me and stared in my face. He was trying to detect a flicker in my expression that might betray where I was hiding any contraband. As Bernie had said, he stood two hopes – Bob Hope and no hope. I stared back at him without any emotion in my face. For at least a minute it was like a contest of who could outstare whom.

Brother Arnold broke the staring by looking critically at the floor. 'Get on with your work.' He pointed to the far side of the room where there were no dusters on the floor. 'I want it all as clean as that.'

'Yes, Bro,' I said. I watched him walk away and followed him with my eyes until I saw him leave the chapel and close the door behind him. I immediately went back to my hidden cache of tobacco and rolled myself another cigarette. I lit it, blew the smoke contemptuously in the direction Arnold had just taken and whispered, 'Fuck you.'

I felt the need to be alone. I didn't feel up to going back to the bricklaying that afternoon so I decided to polish the pews. I could take my time doing it and smoke as much as I liked. I could also have a heart-to-heart talk with God. I enjoyed talking to God in chapel and I often used him as my confidante. He never answered me but, at the end of my conversation with him, I always felt as if I had unburdened my troubles onto someone else. When Brother Arnold returned to the chapel and found me polishing the pews I told him that Father Delaney had asked me to do it and asked if he could tell Mr Cornell where I was. Arnold never even queried when I had seen Father Delaney; he just nodded his head and went back out into the yard.

I knelt down on the step of the pew I was polishing and looked up at the large wooden crucifix that was hung above the altar, suspended by two white ropes attached to a rafter. The figure of Jesus had been beautifully carved and the pain and suffering he had endured showed clearly on the face. I always felt like crying when I thought of how he was tortured and ridiculed before being nailed to that terrible cross. He knew what it was like to feel totally alone, to be frightened and to need help. Those words from the Bible, 'My God, why hast thou forsaken me?' – they could have been written for me.

I brushed a tear angrily from my face. I had read somewhere that God only helped those who helped themselves. Crying wasn't helping my cause; it was hindering it.

With my eyes riveted to the effigy of Jesus, I spoke softly to him. 'Well, Jesus, I am here again. I'm sorry about all the swearing but it's just a way of letting out my anger. You know I'm telling the truth as you can read my mind. You saw how Love hurt me in the washroom. He deserved what he got. I'm not sorry I hit him and to tell the truth I was quite proud of myself. I think that you must have been helping me as I couldn't have done it on my own. Thank you, Jesus.'

I paused and polished the seat in front of me, then looked up again. 'I got really hurt when I was caned and if you can make sure I don't get caned again I promise to say five decades of the rosary to your mother. Are you still looking after my mum? I've got another favour to ask you, Jesus. I'm not sleeping well at night and I'm always tired when it's time to get up. I know I've got a guardian angel, but in this place I think I could do with your help as well. I'm having terrible nightmares about what Wilkinson did to me and I'm terrified it could happen again. If you could make him ill and die then I know I would be all right. Please help me, Jesus. I'm frightened and need your help.'

The chapel door opening brought my little chat to an abrupt end. It was Father Delaney and he looked pleased to see me kneeling and polishing the pews.

'Are you trying to clean yourself into Heaven, John?' Father Delaney smiled at his own remark. He was a tall, robust man with a voice that could penetrate the noisiest of assemblies. He noticed the lump and cut on my forehead. 'What have you been up to? I hope you haven't been fighting.'

'I'm sorry, Father. I had a fight this morning and I've been caned.'

Father Delaney's face went white. He looked at me sympathetically. 'Are you all right, John? I've seen the damage done by caning and I want to assure you that I do not agree with it. I can do nothing about it as it is part of the rules of the school.' He reached out and put his hand on my shoulder. It was as if he had turned on a tap. Tears streamed down my face and I began sobbing uncontrollably. He patted my shoulder affectionately. 'Go into the vestry and have a cigarette.' He smiled at my expression of surprise. 'Don't worry, I've known about it since the first time you lit up and used the thurible to mask the smell of your smoke.'

I looked up at him through my tears. His face was filled with compassion. 'Go on, John. Go and have yourself a smoke. I won't be coming into the vestry for at least half an hour. Make sure that you burn enough incense to fool me.' He turned on his heel and disappeared into a small side chapel that was often used by visiting monks and priests on an ecclesiastical retreat.

I followed him into the side chapel and found him kneeling in front of the small altar. He had his rosary beads in his hand and was deep in prayer. I said quietly, 'Thank you, Father.' He never looked in my direction. He just nodded his head. I crept quietly away and went into the vestry and closed the door behind me.

'It's about time we had payback on the lot next door,' Pete Boyle grinned. 'It's been three weeks since they did us. They'll have forgotten it by now and won't be expecting anything.'

Boyle was an inspiration to everyone in our dormitory. He disregarded all the rules of the school and had a zest for fun. All the boys liked him and I was not surprised to see them all nodding in agreement and smiling in anticipation of what was to come.

Three weeks earlier the boys from the next dorm had taken us unawares and attacked us at eleven o'clock at night. The whole assault lasted less than a minute and none of us had even made it out of bed. It had been a triumphant success and they took great delight in rubbing our noses in it for days afterwards. Tonight it was going to be our turn.

Dormitory fights were not common but were enjoyed by everyone. The art of it was to catch the other boys sleeping and inflict as much damage as possible in the shortest amount of time. Because of the noise when the assault took place it was imperative to get back to your bed and pretend to be asleep before the Brothers arrived on the scene. I couldn't help smiling as I saw all our lads preparing for war. Pillows were discarded and pillow cases filled with books and boots. I put my work boots into mine and had a practice swing of it above my head. I was ready.

'We'll use our blankets so they don't hear us coming,' Boyle whispered.

We all put our top blankets on the shiny linoleum floor and placed our pillow case weapons in the middle of them. We then sat on our blankets and pushed them silently along the floor using our hands. Although there were thirty of us sliding along the floor you couldn't hear the slightest sound. We slid along the corridor and into our opponents' dormitory, taking up positions so that every bed was covered. Doyle suddenly screamed out, 'Payback, you arseholes.'

I jumped to my feet and smashed my pillowcase down into the stomach of my sleeping enemy. His eyes flew open in alarm and he just managed to get his head out of the way of my second swing. The pillowcase crashed into his shoulder and he let out a gasp of pain. I grabbed my blanket back off the floor and ran like hell for my own dormitory. I dived into bed and slung the blanket untidily over my head and body. Every one of our lads made it back to their beds before we heard the rushing footsteps of Brother Arnold and Brother Ambrose.

We listened to the commotion coming from our enemy's encampment. Brother Arnold was having a field day.

'Who's been fighting?' he screamed and I heard the sound of someone being slapped. 'Why is your nose bleeding? Who have you been fighting with?' Eventually things quietened down and the brothers returned to their quarters.

Pete Boyle climbed out of his bed and crept quietly back along the corridor. We all listened as he called, 'Who's laughing now?' There was the sound of crashing objects as he was pelted with everything the boys could lay their hands on. He ran back into the dorm laughing and jumped into his bed. 'Well done, lads,' he said quietly. 'We stuffed them.'

Chapter 10

'I want you to slide in on your left knee and side with your right leg out in front of you. Imagine that you are tackling a fast winger. Your right leg has to connect with the ball.' Tom Banks had the entire squad lined up on the sidelines of the pitch. 'Sprint forward across the pitch and when I blow my whistle you slide in with your imaginary tackle.'

We had been practising the sliding tackle for two solid weeks at training. Tom demanded that everyone in his football squad should be able to tackle hard and fair. I had developed an image in my mind of Jimmy Wilkinson running with the ball and I was more than a little enthusiastic in diving in with my tackle. In my mind I never got the ball. My right foot always crashed into his ankle and he was left on the side of the pitch, crippled and writhing on the ground in agony. Tom liked my enthusiasm and after training called me over to speak to him.

'You've really mastered the sliding tackle. Well done. I'm going to give you a game on Saturday in the second team.'

I couldn't believe what I was hearing. Never in my wildest dreams did I think I stood a chance of breaking into one of the teams. I was lost for words and stood looking at him with an inane grin plastered all over my face.

'I'm going to play you at right back. You'll be the last line of defence on that side of the pitch and as long as you tackle like I've seen you practise, nobody will be going past you.' He patted me warmly on my shoulder. 'You deserve your place.'

I was in a daze when I walked away. I jogged over to Bernie and grabbed him by both his arms. I shook him wildly and screamed. 'I'm in the team. I'm in the team.'

Bernie didn't look happy. 'How come you got in the team? My ball control is better than yours.'

I shrugged. 'I don't know. I think Tom likes the way I do the sliding tackle. He's put me at right back.'

Bernie shook his head. 'You're not big enough for right back.'

'Well, that's where he's put me and I'll make sure I don't let him down.' I noticed how peeved he seemed at my news. 'I thought you'd be pleased for me, not jealous.'

'I am pleased for you.' Bernie looked contrite. 'I just wish he had given me a chance as well.'

I put my arm around his shoulder and said, 'He's bound to pick you soon, Bernie. You're too good to be left out.'

We walked back to the schoolyard in silence. I was thinking about St Gregory's and the taunts of the children. I wish they could see me play on Saturday in a team that hadn't been beaten for eighteen months. I idly wondered if the team would win any trophies this year and if we would have our photograph taken and see it hung on the recreation room wall.

I fell asleep that night with wonderful thoughts going through my mind. I had lulled myself into a false sense of security, which was shattered and smashed to pieces in the early hours of the morning.

I woke up and wondered why I was awake. I lay quietly with my eyes shut and listened for noises in the dormitory. Slowly I became aware of a cold draught on my right leg. I presumed that the bedclothes had shifted and my leg was exposed to the elements. Without opening my eyes I reached down to adjust the covers. My eyes flew open when my hand encountered an arm. I looked straight into the face of Jimmy Wilkinson, who had his hand underneath my bedclothes. I threw them back and was horrified to see that my penis was hard and Wilkinson was masturbating me. I screamed at the top of my voice in fear and shock. 'Get the fuck away from me.'

Wilkinson immediately let go and scrabbled to his feet. He looked across the dormitory and signalled to someone. I spun my head to see who he was signalling to.

To my horror I saw another fifteen-year-old boy called Tony Birch kneeling by another bed. He was obviously doing the same to that boy as Jimmy Wilkinson had been doing to me. 'Keep your mouth shut,' Wilkinson hissed down at me.

'Get the fuck away,' I screamed even louder. Wilkinson and Birch ran out of the dormitory and disappeared along the corridor. By this time nearly all the boys were awake. My screaming had been loud enough to wake the dead. The door from the Brothers' quarters was flung open and Brother Francis and Brother Arnold rushed in. They switched on the lights and looked angrily around the room.

'Who was shouting?' asked Brother Francis.

I held my arm up and both Brothers came over to my bed and peered down at me. 'So why were you shouting,

Fenton? You had better be dying, seeing that you've decided to wake up the entire school.' Brother Francis was not pleased.

'I didn't mean to wake up the school, Bro. I had a bad dream and screamed in my sleep.'

'What were you dreaming about?'

'I can't remember, Bro. I just found myself sitting up in bed screaming.'

Brother Arnold slapped me hard across my right cheek. 'Maybe that will knock the bad dream out of your mind.' He glared at me. 'If you have any more bad dreams we'll make you sleep in the middle of the sports field.'

Brother Francis looked around at the dormitory. 'Go back to sleep. The fun's all over.'

The room was plunged into darkness again and the two brothers went back through the door and presumably back to bed.

I lay quietly looking up at the ceiling, trying to come to terms with what had just happened. How could someone have been masturbating me without me knowing about it? Had it ever happened before and I hadn't woken up? How the fuck was I ever going to shut my eyes again? I was terrified. Jimmy Wilkinson was my worst nightmare and now I had to worry about Tony Birch as well. How many more queer and perverted bastards were there?

I toyed with the idea of going to De Montfort and telling him what was going on, but quickly dismissed that idea. To grass on someone was the worst possible offence and could be very dangerous for the boy who did it. I wondered if it would be possible to poison Wilkinson. This thought appealed to me but I knew nothing about poisons and didn't have a clue what I should use. That didn't stop me thinking about it and planning how I could put it in his drink. I enjoyed the thought of him dying in agony.

I was still awake when the school bell chimed six o'clock. I climbed out of bed and went slowly towards the washroom. To my horror Jimmy Wilkinson came out of his dormitory and followed me. He must have been waiting for me to go past his door.

'What the fuck did you think you were doing last night? You could have got me and Birchy in deep trouble.'

'I will never let you come near me again.' My voice was trembling with fear. 'If you ever come into my dormitory after lights out I will scream the place down.'

I didn't see the blow coming. Suddenly my head hit the tiled wall with a dull thud and Wilkinson was smirking. He had got me hard in the mouth with a right-hand punch. I had the distinctive taste of salty blood in my mouth and I ran my tongue over the inside of my lip. I could feel a swelling and a cut on the inside of my bottom lip which was caused by the punch knocking my teeth into my lip. The second punch hit me high on my cheekbone.

'Don't ever tell me what I can do. I'll go where I like and you'll keep your mouth shut.' He tried to punch me again but I managed to block it with my arm.

He was frightening me but I knew that I couldn't let him think I was an easy target. 'You can beat me up as much as you like but it won't stop me screaming if you ever come near my dormitory again.' For some unknown reason my teeth were chattering. 'I mean it. I will scream the place down.'

I only half blocked his next punch and I felt another swelling on my lips. The taste of blood was horrible and I spat a large mixture of spittle and blood onto the floor.

Wilkinson grabbed the top of my nightshirt and shoved me against the wall. 'You'd better stay out of my way, you little wanker. And don't come near me if you ever want to buy a roll-up. You can go and fuck yourself.' He shoved me angrily away and went back out of the washroom.

Though I had been hurt, I was elated with the outcome. Wilkinson wouldn't dare risk coming into my dormitory. I could go to sleep without the fear of him sneaking in to molest me. I went over and looked in a mirror at my mouth. My teeth were all bloody and nasty looking and I sucked in a mouthful of cold water from the tap and swished it around before spitting it into the sink. I heard footsteps coming towards the washroom door. The door opened and Brother Michael came in.

'Get yourself dressed, Fenton, and get over to the chapel. Father Delaney is over there already and you're needed to serve a special Mass.' He stood holding the washroom door open as I rinsed my face. He was impatient. 'Hurry up,' he said, 'they're waiting for you.'

He followed me from the washroom and stood at the foot of my bed while I got dressed. 'We'll go through the school to the chapel; it's quicker.' He held open the door that led through the Brothers' quarters then led the way via a maze of passages and down a flight of stairs until at last he took out a key and unlocked a door. I was surprised to find myself walking out of a door at the front of the school and only a few yards from the side of the chapel.

When we entered the chapel I saw nearly every Brother and master kneeling in prayer. They were equally divided on both sides of the chapel and were saying decades of the rosary. Father Delaney was standing by the vestry door and nodded his head approvingly when he saw me. I hurried over and he led me by the arm into the vestry. I looked up at him questioningly.

'Brother Ephraim was taken seriously ill during the night and we are going to say a Mass for his recovery. We will have to use the side aisle when we go to the altar as Brother Ephraim will be lying in his bed at the front of the middle aisle. Now that you have arrived they will have gone to fetch him, so hurry up and put on your serving robes.'

I found it difficult to walk sedately behind Father Delaney and not look over to where Brother Ephraim was lying. I was curious about what was wrong with him and, as I knelt down on the bottom step at the foot of the altar, I had an overwhelming urge to turn around and look at the bed that was behind me. I was so engrossed in fighting it that I nearly missed my first response.

Father Delaney's Mass voice brought me out of my curiosity. '*Introibo ad altare Dei.*' (I will go to the altar of God.)

I quickly bent my head and said quietly, '*Ad Deum qui laetificat juventutem meam.*' (To God, the joy of my youth.)

Father Delaney said, '*Judica me, Deus, et discerne causam meam de gente non sancta: ab homine iniquo et doloso erue me.*' (Do me justice, O God, and fight my fight against an unholy people, rescue me from the wicked and deceitful man.)

I replied with a response that could have been written for me. '*Quia tu es, Deus, fortitude mea: quare me repulisti, et quare tristis incedo, dum affligit me inimicus?*' (For Thou, O

God, art my strength, why hast Thou forsaken me? And why do I go about in sadness, while the enemy harasses me?')

The Mass took just under an hour before Father Delaney was genuflecting in front of the altar and saying, '*ET VERBUM CARO FACTUM EST et habitavit in nobis; et vidimus gloriameius gloriam quasi Unigeniti a Patre, plenum gratiae et veritatis.*' (AND THE WORD WAS MADE FLESH, and dwelt among us, and we saw His glory, the glory as of the only begotten of the Father, full of grace and truth.)

I replied, '*Deo gratias*' (Thanks be to God) and stood up.

Father Delaney came slowly down the altar steps and went directly to the foot of Brother Ephraim's bed. I followed him and took up a position on his right. Father Delaney lifted his right arm and elaborately made the sign of the cross over Brother Ephraim saying, '*Pax, Domini sit, semper vobis, cum*' (May the peace of the Lord be always with you).

I replied, '*Et cum spiritu tuo*' (And with thy spirit).

As Father Delaney turned to walk back to the vestry I took a lingering look at Brother Ephraim. He was definitely very ill. His face was as white as the pillow he was resting on. I tried to detect a movement in his chest to show he was breathing but it didn't seem to move at all. His eyes were shut and there was not a flicker of movement on his face. I noticed that his nose looked strange; marble in appearance and pinched. I quickly followed Father Delaney into the vestry.

'Father, may I ask you a question?' He nodded and closed his eyes briefly. 'Was Brother Ephraim dead? I've never seen a dead person, but he looked dead.'

'No, he isn't dead. But he is very ill.'

'Why isn't he in hospital, Father?'

'His illness was not unexpected. He has been ill for a very long time.'

'I'd have thought they would have still kept him in hospital.'

Father Delaney took me by the arm and led me to a chair in the corner of the room. 'Enough of the questions, John. Take my word for it; Brother Ephraim has been very ill for a long time. He was a very brave man and wanted no fuss over his condition.' He took out a packet of Senior Service cigarettes from his trouser pocket and lit one. He puffed on it hungrily and blew the smoke out in long blue streams. 'You did very well this morning. I was surprised at your response when I blessed Brother Ephraim. How did you know the response *Et cum spiritu tuo?*'

'It's the same response as when you bless the congregation at Mass. You said the same words so I did the same response. Was it wrong, Father?'

'So you remembered the words without looking at your response sheet.' He took another cigarette from the packet and dropped it at my feet. 'The Brothers are keeping a prayer vigil in and outside Brother Ephraim's room. I must go and join them. Can I rely on you to put everything in order and shut up the front door?'

'You've dropped a cigarette, Father.' I bent forward and picked it up from the floor and held it out for him.

'It's been on the floor. I'll trust you to put it in the bin when I've gone.' He looked thoughtful. 'Fancy you remembering the response. Well done, John. Well done indeed.' He left the vestry and I felt sure he was smiling as he walked away.

I waited a short time before lighting the cigarette.

Brother Ephraim died at midday.

Jimmy Wilkinson lost all his secreted cigarette money at 2 pm.

Chapter 11

I was called out of the bricklaying department just before lunch and ten minutes after Brother Ephraim's spirit had left his body. Father Delaney sent for me and I was taken by Mr Lawson across the yard to the chapel. The chapel was nearly full, with most of the Brothers kneeling in silent prayer. Father Delaney was removing the stole that was hanging over his shoulders and down his front. He nodded sombrely at me.

'Brother Ephraim has died. I have just come down from giving him the Last Rites.' He folded the stole up neatly and kissed its hem before putting it away tidily in a cloth pouch. 'He is being laid out at the moment and we will be accepting his body into the chapel at six o'clock.' He blessed himself. 'There will be a lot of coming and going in the next few days and quite a few dignitaries visiting the chapel. I have spoken to Brother De Montfort and he has released you from school duties so that you can be on call in the chapel. You may find yourself serving several masses a day with different priests; Brother Ephraim was a very well-loved brother.' He peered down at me thoughtfully. 'You might find yourself alone in the chapel for some periods of time. Just you and the body of Brother Ephraim. Will you be able to cope with that, or will you be frightened?'

'I'll be fine, Father. The dead can't hurt me; only the living.' I didn't know how I would react but I didn't want anything to get in the way of me having chapel duties.

Father Delaney smiled. 'A very wise saying, John. Where did you hear it?'

'I've never heard it. I read it in some book.' I tried to remember what book I had read it in. My mind was blank. 'It made a lot of sense to me, Father.'

'You really are an enigma, John. Most boys in this school haven't got past looking at pictures in comics and yet you are quoting sayings out of books and giving Latin responses out of your head.' He shook his head. 'It is such a pity to see a clever boy throw his life away. You could have done so much better.'

'What's an enigma, Father? I've never been called one of them before.'

Father Delaney gave a throaty chuckle. 'It means you're a mystery. Hard to fathom.'

'So, what do you want me to do before this evening, Father?' I asked.

'I'd like you to tidy up the small chapel cemetery. It's been recently weeded but the path needs sweeping and the leaves picked up. Take the flowers from the chapel and share them out between the graves. They are bringing fresh flowers from the gardens for the chapel.' He heaved a sigh and asked, 'Do you think you can manage all that?'

I nodded my head. 'What shall I do after that? It won't take me all afternoon to sort out a few leaves and twigs.'

Father Delaney shrugged. 'When that is done, just hang around the chapel. I'll be in and out all afternoon.' He took me to the door that led into the cemetery. 'There should be a rake and a hard broom in the small shed.' He pushed me gently out and closed the door behind me.

I stood perfectly still, looking at the task in front of me. There were about forty headstones spread randomly around the small cemetery. They were all celtic crosses made out of a sort of grey gnarled stone and some of the inscriptions were hard to read as they were faded by wind, rain and age. The majority of the graves were those of boys who had died in the school from various illnesses in pre-war years. The last boy who died in Vincent's was in 1937. The path that led from the door I had just emerged from curved in a gentle arc until it reached a small gate, which led onto the front lawn of the school. In a niche in the chapel wall was a small wooden shed that had been recently treated and varnished in a dark oak colour. I walked over to the shed and took out a long-handled garden rake and a rather well-worn broom.

It took me very little time to rake the leaves and twigs off the graves and grass and onto the flagstone path. I swept the path slowly and carefully until there was a nice neat heap of waste in the middle and next to a small dustbin I had placed there. I used my hands to put all the leaves and twigs in the bin until only a small amount of dust and dirt was left and then swept that down a small grated drain by the gate. I leant on the broom, looking down the drain, and suddenly I thought about Wilkinson's stash of money. I let my tongue run over the damaged inside of my lip and an idea came into my mind.

I casually walked over to the dustbin and lifted it over to where it obstructed any view of the flagstone I wanted to lift up. I then went to the vestry window and checked that the room was empty and no one was looking out. Satisfied it was safe, I hurried to the stone and prised it up. There in all its glory was Wilkinson's money. Quickly, I lifted out one handkerchief and ran to the drain by the gate. The sixpenny pieces made a lovely sploshing sound as they hit the water at the bottom. I ran backwards and forwards thirteen times before I had disposed of all his silver. There was over twenty-five pounds' worth and it would have been too cumbersome to carry around with me. All that remained in the hole now was a small black leather purse. I opened it up and took out its contents. Four one-pound notes and a ten shilling note went into the bottom of my sock beneath my foot. I replaced the empty purse and handkerchiefs and put the stone securely in its place then smiled to myself and said quietly, 'Not me. It's you that can go and fuck yourself, Wilkinson.'

I quietly went about my work for the rest of the afternoon. I would have liked a cigarette but the chapel always had one or two Brothers praying in it and it wasn't worth the risk. I managed to make a roll-up and hid it in my trousers so that if a chance arose for me to have a smoke I would be ready. Father Delaney came into the cemetery and complimented me on how nicely I had done the flowers and told me he had arranged an early tea for me so I could be back at the chapel in plenty of time for the acceptance ceremony.

I arrived back at the chapel at half past five and was amazed to see that there wasn't an empty seat. There were loads of people present that I had never seen before. I counted at least six priests. There were a lot of brothers and monks and our local bishop had been given pride of place on a large seat at the side of the altar. I quickly got changed. Father Delaney had already lit the thurible and the incense smoke was so thick it made my eyes sting. The coffin stand had been placed in front of the altar and the only thing missing now was Brother Ephraim.

It was exactly six o'clock when Brother Ephraim, in an open pine coffin, was brought into the chapel on the shoulders of four brothers. They gently lowered the coffin onto its stand and moved quietly to their seats. I remembered very little about the ceremony as I was staring at the lifeless face of Brother Ephraim. I made all the right responses and handed Father Delaney the holy water but my eyes kept going back to Brother Ephraim. He had changed colour from this morning. I remembered clearly how white he had looked in his bed as Father Delaney blessed him. He was now an off-colour sort of cream. His face looked as though it was carved out of wax. It didn't frighten me; it fascinated me. All of a sudden the ceremony was over and I was walking behind Father Delaney and back into the vestry.

'You can go out through the cemetery gate back to the school. I am sure the Brothers are going to take turns in doing a vigil until Brother Ephraim has been buried and you might disturb them if you keep walking through the chapel.' The sounds of a Gregorian chant filtered into the room from the chapel. Father Delaney lifted his eyes up to the roof and listened, enjoying every note. 'Be back at six in the morning. One of the brothers will call you.'

I closed the vestry door quietly behind me and stepped into the cemetery. I noticed that I hadn't put the rake away so I took it over to the shed and put it inside. I looked at the interior of the shed and decided it was big enough for me to stand in and have a crafty smoke without being seen. I squeezed into the cramped surroundings and lit the roll-up that I had hidden in my trousers. The smoke seemed to caress my throat and I leaned against the wall of the shed with a blissful sigh. It had been an interesting day. I had seen a dead body. I thought about what I had done with Wilkinson's money and grinned. It had been a great day. I took a last puff on my cigarette and stepped out of the shed and walked away in the direction of the yard.

As I entered the recreation room I very nearly collided with Jimmy Wilkinson, who was walking past the door. He shoved me hard and snarled, 'Keep out of my fucking way.'

I turned my head, not daring to look at him in case I gave myself away. I would have loved to have been big enough to tell him how I'd just fucked him from a dizzy height. Instead I hurried away and went over to where Bernie was sitting looking glum. 'How's it going, Bernie?' I greeted him cheerily. 'I've had a great day.'

Bernie sighed. 'I got a letter from home today. Jimmy, my brother, is back inside.'

'What's he done?' I asked.

Bernie shrugged his shoulders. 'My mum didn't say. All she said was that he's been put in the Scrubs.'

Wormwood Scrubs was a big prison situated in West London, next to Hammersmith Hospital. One of the prison's wings was used entirely for young men awaiting Borstal. I could see he was upset. He doted on Jimmy. I put my arm affectionately around his shoulder. 'Don't worry about him, Bernie. You said he's a hard case so he'll be well able to look after himself.'

Bernie grunted. 'I know, but it doesn't make me feel any better.'

I grabbed his arm and squeezed it. 'You can't worry about Jimmy, Bernie. De Montfort was right when he said we've got no families for the next three years. We can only worry about ourselves and our survival.'

There was a long pause and then in a subdued voice Bernie said, 'I know you're right but I can't just forget about my family.'

'I'm not saying you should. Just try and put them to the back of your mind and concentrate on how we're going to get through the next couple of years.'

Bernie stared at me, then shifted his gaze to the floor. He said quietly, 'You've changed so much since St Nicks. You're not the same boy. I think you're better suited to this place than me.'

'I hate this place,' I said. 'I hate the boys, the masters, the Brothers and most of all I hate myself. Believe me, Bernie, when I say that the only time I'm not unhappy is when I'm in chapel.'

'Don't tell me you're turning into a Holy Joe.' Bernie's eyes searched my face to see if I had been joking. 'Nothing surprises me about you any more. Just don't expect me to start learning to say Mass.'

'Speaking about Mass,' I said, 'you won't be seeing much of me for the next two or three days as Father Delaney needs me for services. He said I might have to serve six or seven masses a day.'

Bernie spat on the floor. 'Fuck me, John, you must be nuts.'

I smiled a little. 'I get a chance for a quiet smoke. I don't get booked and I'm sure Father Delaney will see me all right after Brother Ephraim is buried.' I shook my head. 'I'm not nuts. I'm doing myself a favour.'

'You're still going to have to come back into the school when it's all over. Nothing will have changed. You'll still be in this shitty place.' Bernie spat a large globule of phlegm on the floor. 'So don't get too happy with your lot.'

I brooded for a few moments, thinking about Bernie's comments. He was right in what he said. No matter how good a day was, the next day I would still be in this place. But worrying about it wasn't going to make it disappear. I was determined to enjoy the feeling of fucking up Jimmy Wilkinson.

The whistle sounded for supper. As Bernie and I walked towards our lines, I said, 'I'm sorry about your brother, Bernie. Try not to worry about it.'

'Cheers, John,' he replied. 'I'll see you tomorrow.'

As I made my way to my place in line a sticky stream of spittle hit me in my face. I looked to see where it had come from and Jimmy Wilkinson and Tony Birch stood laughing and pointing at me. I lowered my head and hurried to my place. I wiped away the spittle with my sleeve.

I stood in line with my eyes shut, trying to block out all sounds. I was imagining Wilkinson's face when he lifted the stone. I thought, *I wonder who'll be laughing then, you queer cunt.*

I welcomed lights out when it came. I lay in the darkness listening to the rhythmic breathing of the other boys in the dormitory and revelling in the ecstatic feeling of having at last hit back at the perverted cunt Wilkinson. When sleep came it was peaceful and tranquil.

Chapter 12

I stood in the small cemetery looking down at the fresh mound of earth that hid the recently buried body of Brother Ephraim. I wondered idly what it was like being dead. Could your spirit see its old body? Did your spirit feel sadness? Where did your spirit go after death? There were so many questions I didn't have the answers for and so many questions I wanted to ask.

Over the three days before Brother Ephraim's funeral I had served sixteen masses and two benedictions. Father Delaney seemed to be always in the background and I lost count of the number of cigarettes he dropped on the floor. After the graveside service he had given me a leather-bound book by Charles Dickens called *A Christmas Carol*. He said he felt certain that I would enjoy the story and I was looking forward to starting to read it tonight in bed.

I knew that I had come to the end of spending all day in the chapel and I dreaded going back to my old routine. I had been spoilt by being left alone and out of the reach of the Brothers and the boys. I had seen Bernie briefly every day and his mood seemed to be getting better. Jimmy, his brother, was no longer the main topic of his conversation and he kept me informed about what was going on in the school. He told me that he'd seen David Love's arse in the shower and it looked awful. Black and blue all over and cut in two places. That news pleased me as my own backside was still in equally bad shape.

I walked back to the vestry and into the chapel. There was nobody around and I thought I would take this last opportunity to have a quiet smoke before I headed back to the school. I rolled myself a cigarette and went out into the cemetery to the small shed. I was enjoying the freedom of peaceful smoking and felt sure that my little shed was safe. I never heard the small gate open or the sounds of Brother De Montfort's shoes on the path. He suddenly appeared at the door of the shed and grabbed my hand as I was about to take another puff on the roll-up. His face was a mask of fury.

His whinging voice screamed, 'How dare you defile sacred ground. Brother Ephraim has only just been covered over and you are smoking. Have you no respect for anything or anyone?' He pulled me out of the shed and scraped the sole of his shoe on the roll-up that had dropped out of my hand. His left hand hit me hard across my mouth. He said menacingly, 'Get up to the small dormitory.' He shoved me angrily towards the schoolyard.

I had begun to tremble and shake with fear. Every time he shoved me closer to the stairs I seemed to tremble more. I kept saying to him in a quivering voice, 'I'm sorry, Bro. I'm sorry.' My apologies fell on deaf ears and he shouted loudly for Brother Ambrose as he shoved me through the school. Ambrose hurried into the small dormitory shortly after we got there, carrying the big bundle of bamboo canes.

De Montfort slung the silk shorts into my face. He snarled, 'Put them on.'

I had difficulty getting undressed as I was in a state of pure terror. I struggled out of my shirt and shorts and stood in front of De Montfort in my underpants, shaking. He said, 'Take off your pants and put on the shorts.'

'Please, Bro. I'm sorry. Please don't cane me,' I pleaded with him.

'Get your pants off and the shorts on.' His voice was filled with menace. 'And be quick about it.'

I pulled down my pants and heard a gasp from Brother Ambrose. He pointed at my backside with the cane he was holding and shook his head. De Montfort said, 'Don't worry about that, Brother. I caught him desecrating Brother Ephraim's grave. He deserves no consideration.'

He pointed to the shorts. 'Put them on.'

I pulled them on slowly and looked at Brother Ambrose for help.

Brother Ambrose no longer felt sympathy for me. His eyes were angry. He had been a Brother for a considerable amount of time and had no doubt been good friends with Brother Ephraim. His practice swings with the bamboo cane made a swishing and humming sound as they cut their way through the air. He nodded his head at De Montfort to signal he was ready.

'In all my years dealing with you boys I have never seen a worse case of disrespect. Brother Ephraim was a wonderful man who loved everybody and everything and yet you decided to desecrate his grave with smoke.' He pointed to the centre of the floor and said through clenched teeth, 'Bend over and touch your toes.'

The pain of the bamboo cane hitting my damaged backside was so severe that I fell hard onto my knees. My mouth opened to scream but no sound came out. I rolled over and over until my body collided with the legs of one of the beds. Slowly, sound returned to my throat and I gasped out the remaining air in my lungs. This was quickly followed by me retching and vomiting all over the floor. Hands took hold of me and lifted me. Brother Ambrose's face came into focus as he manoeuvred me onto one of the beds. De Montfort had hurried out of the dormitory and I could hear his footsteps scurrying along the corridor. At last I managed to get my lungs working and I screamed out the agony I was feeling. I writhed on top of the bed. My entire lower body was in spasm. Brother Ambrose caught hold of my arms and tried in vain to stop me moving around. Slowly my movements subsided and my screams became quiet sobs. He put his face close to mine and I saw tears rolling down his cheeks. He whispered, 'Please forgive me.'

Matron and De Montfort came hurrying into the room. She said briskly, 'Lay him on his stomach.' I felt the silk shorts being pulled down. Matron gasped and stepped back from the bed, her bottom lip trembling. She looked at De Montfort. 'What were you thinking? His skin was bound to split if you caned him again.'

'We didn't see the bruising. Did we, Brother? If we had we would never have done it,' De Montfort lied. 'As soon as he had the first stroke we knew something was wrong and stopped.'

I turned my head and looked at De Montfort. Tears were streaming down my face but the hatred I felt for him and Ambrose was evident in my eyes. He turned his head away and looked sheepishly at Matron. 'Can you treat it, Matron? There's no need for him to go to hospital, is there?'

Matron sighed. 'I suppose so. You'll have to carry him up to the infirmary. I can't keep going to his dormitory to treat that cut and he'll be in bed for at least a week.' She turned her attention to me, stroked my hair and said, 'You're coming to the infirmary for a few days. You're going to have to stay on your stomach or you'll damage the healing process. Is there anything you want to bring with you?'

I gave her a weak smile. 'Father Delaney gave me a book as a present and I've left it in the vestry. Could you have it sent up to me?'

Matron looked at De Montfort. 'Is this the boy who's been serving all the masses?'

De Montfort nodded.

'And you've done this to him?' She stared unblinkingly at him. 'The infirmary has been filled with visiting clergy over the last few days and they all commented on the clarity of his responses. They were impressed about how St Vincent's taught Latin to its boys. I wonder what they would say if they could see how you rewarded him for all his good work?' She turned away angrily. 'Have him carried up to the infirmary straight away so that I can get to work repairing the damage you've caused.' She stomped out of the room without even a backward glance.

Ten minutes later, Brother Francis and Brother Arnold came to the dormitory and carried me through the Brothers' quarters and along to the infirmary. Matron had already retrieved my book from the vestry and it was placed on the pillow of the bed I was allocated. I had to lie on top of the bedclothes with only my socks on and I felt embarrassed when Matron came into the room and checked my backside. She asked why I always laughed nervously as she gently put the healing balm over the open cut, and I couldn't answer her.

She must have guessed how I felt as she told me, 'Don't ever feel embarrassed when a member of the medical profession is treating your body. We are just doing our job. We're not looking critically at your body; we are treating it. You're just a young lad and I am putting ointment on a cut on your bottom.' She ruffled my hair. 'Try to stay on your front and don't stay up all night reading.'

I loved *A Christmas Carol*, the book Father Delaney had given me. Dickens made the characters seem so real that I had vivid pictures of them in my mind. I fell in love with Scrooge's sister and cried at her kindness to her brother. I cried for Tiny Tim and rejoiced at his recovery. I could see clearly the magnificent feast the Cratchit family enjoyed when Scrooge sent his anonymous gift and could feel the fear in Bob Cratchit when he arrived a few minutes' late for work the next day. The wonderful outcome of the story I must have read a dozen times. When, after three days, I finished the book it left me with a warm glow all over. I immediately started from the beginning again.

After eight days of Matron's care I was released back into the school. Bernie greeted me with a huge smile and asked cheerily, 'How's your arse?'

'I'm fine. Matron said it's safe for me to have a shower now; the cut is nearly healed.' I looked up just as Brother Ambrose walked through the recreation room. I felt my anger rising. 'That sick bastard knew what he was doing when he hit me. Then the cunt says he's sorry.' I spat on the floor. I was filled with cold hatred towards De Montfort and Ambrose. I prayed to God to grant me the pleasure of one day getting my vengeance on them.

I said quietly, 'One day, you sick cunt. One day.' I could feel Bernie's eyes on me and turned to look at him. 'I mean it, Bernie. One day, I'll have that cunt.'

Bernie nodded. 'I believe you. After what he did to you he deserves everything he gets. I couldn't believe it when I was told you'd been caned again and were in the infirmary. It must have been awful.'

'Don't worry about me. I'll be fine. My arse is just a little sore.' I watched as Bernie produced a roll-up from the side of his sock. He was careful not to be seen lighting it and handed it to me after he had inhaled two or three lungfuls. Because I hadn't had a smoke for the last eight days the first couple of puffs made me light-headed. I closed my eyes and savoured the beautiful feeling of smoke hitting the back of my throat. Bernie reached over and took the roll-up out of my hand and extinguished it by squeezing the burning end between two of his fingers. I watched him secrete the remainder in his sock. 'That was great, Bernie. Cheers. What's been going on since I've been gone?'

'Nothing much,' Bernie said. 'A couple of silly fights. Oh, and Terry Smith broke his arm at football practice. He jumped for a high ball and fell awkwardly on his arm when he landed.'

'Anything else?'

'Wilkinson's been a right pain,' Bernie said, 'For the last three days he's been thumping anybody who crosses his path. He's searched everybody's locker and everybody's bed. I was glad when he had a fight with John Black and ended up getting caned.'

'How did Black do in the fight?' I asked. I wasn't really interested but I felt I had to enquire in order to mask my jubilation at Wilkinson's bad humour. Bernie didn't have a clue why Wilkinson was behaving so badly, but I did. My eyes searched the recreation room looking for him. I found him sitting with his best mate, Jack Devine, and looking as miserable as sin. Every time someone walked past, Wilkinson looked at them spitefully and spat in their direction. He was definitely in a bad mood. I smiled and pressed my foot on the floor. I could feel his small wad of notes in the bottom of my sock. I'd guarded it carefully the whole time I was in the infirmary and never took it out of my sock, even at night.

Thank you, Jesus, I thought.

'Black was losing,' Bernie said, 'and it was broken up quite quickly by Arnold.'

'Did Wilkinson use the high boot?' I asked. I felt sure that he would have, as every fight I'd seen him in, he always followed up his first punch with a high kick to his opponent's face. This move usually won the fight and also did quite a bit of damage.

Bernie nodded. 'Black still has a swollen chin and a nasty-looking graze.'

'Who's been serving Mass?' I asked. I had been the sole server for the last four months.

'No one. A different brother did it every day.' He took the part roll-up from his sock and relit it. He had a puff and handed it to me. 'I hope they haven't found our tobacco in the vestry.'

'They'd have had to remove all the boxes of hosts. It's hidden right at the back.' I took in a large lungful of smoke and handed the small burning butt back to Bernie. He managed somehow to get another two puffs before he burnt his fingers on the glowing end.

He cursed loudly. 'Fuck it. I'm always doing that.' He ground the butt into the floor until nothing of it remained. He looked furtively around the room to make sure he hadn't been seen smoking. He groaned when he saw Brother Ambrose pointing at him and writing in his small notebook. 'That's three times this week,' he said. 'At this rate I'll be getting a red-poor.'

I laughed. I couldn't remember a time when I didn't have a red-poor week. I always seemed to be getting booked for some infringement of the rules and had long given up trying not to get booked. The quarter of a day's holiday mattered nothing to me because in most respects I was better off here than when I was at home. I sometimes envied Bernie when he spoke about his home and the fun he had there. His father sounded like a great guy and was always sending Bernie money to go in his school account. All the tobacco Bernie smuggled into the school after going home was bought for him by his father, and Bernie said that he was always met at Barnet Station when he went home. They had a good father and son relationship and I wished from the bottom of my heart that I had the same with mine – but then, if I had, I wouldn't be in Vincent's.

Brother Francis came into the recreation room and walked purposely over to where we were sitting. He had disliked me from the very first day I arrived at Vincent's when he saw the insubordination in my expression and gave me a beating with his fists and his views hadn't changed over the last seven months. I had done nothing to improve his opinion of me and quite often smoked on his duty so that he would see I didn't give a shit about him or the stupid rules. He scowled at me and said, 'Brother De

Montfort wants to see you. Get over to his office straight away.'

I stood up and followed him out of the recreation room and across the yard. As we entered the main building Brother Francis turned around to face me. He said, 'As far as I'm concerned you've deserved everything that has happened to you. You don't fool me. I know you're a conniving little bastard and that you have no respect for anyone. The only reason you serve Mass is to further your own ends. If I had my way you'd never serve again.' He slapped me hard across my left cheek. 'Wipe that look off your face. I can see what you're thinking.'

I lowered my eyes to the floor. I must have a very expressive face as I hadn't intended to show the contempt I felt for him. I suddenly realised that I hadn't flinched when he hit me. I wondered if I was becoming immune to ill treatment or if I was getting harder? Bernie was right: I was changing. I was no longer the same frightened child as the one who had come into the school all those months before.

Brother Francis was staring at me. I could feel his eyes boring into me and I had to fight the urge to stare back. That would have been stupid and would only have brought on another assault. I created in my mind a picture of Brother Francis in the nude and his withered willy dropping off onto the floor. I increased the size of the picture so that all of the Brothers were standing naked and all of their willies were dropping off. My mind was soon filled with grotesque images of blood pouring from damaged crotches and I had to blink several times to erase them from my mind. Brother Francis spun on his heel and we carried on our way to De Montfort's office.

Brother De Montfort was sitting at his desk and Father Delaney was talking quietly to him as I was brought in. They both looked up in my direction and Father Delaney smiled. 'How are you now, John?'

'I'm fine, Father.'

Brother De Montfort's face was impassive. 'Father Delaney and I have been wondering how we can reward you for all the services and chapel duties you performed during the time of Brother Ephraim's death. We thought that a suitable reward would be to allow you to go to the cinema on a Saturday afternoon for the next six weeks. Also, to allow you to go home on the next first Sunday of the month.' He smiled coldly. 'So, no matter what your points are, you get to go to the pictures and get to go home.'

'Thank you,' I said politely. 'What do I use for money to go to the pictures? I never seem to get any points, so I never get any money.'

'You'll be paid for eighteen points no matter what you get.' He looked at Father Delaney. 'Is that satisfactory, Father?'

Father Delaney nodded his approval. 'You deserve it, John. You worked really hard and I was told by the Bishop to pass on his compliments to you on how well you pronounced the responses. I do believe that he thought Latin was taught in the classroom here.'

Brother De Montfort looked pleased. 'I told you when you came here that I would allow you to serve Mass if you were bright enough. Well, you proved to us that you were and now you're being complimented by the Bishop. I agree with Father Delaney; you deserve these privileges.'

I didn't want any compliments from De Montfort and I wasn't going to acknowledge any. I looked at Father

Delaney and smiled. 'Thank you, Father. I couldn't have done it without your help.'

'Well, that's settled.' De Montfort stood up. 'You can go back to the school now.'

I was in no doubt that my good fortune was due to the intervention of Father Delaney. He was the most decent man I'd ever come across in my life.

Chapter 13

24 December 1958

Three months later, at mid-afternoon on Christmas Eve, I was in Dartford Station waiting for the Charing Cross train. Most of the boys had gone home on the morning of 22nd December and were returning on the evening of the 28th. Because I had lost three and three-quarter days off my holiday I had to stay in school until 2.30 in the afternoon on the 24th and return a day early on the 27th.

I shivered as an icy blast of air swept along the platform. As I looked along the track I saw a cloud of smoke approaching, then the train pulled up at the station with a noisy screeching of brakes and a loud gush of escaping steam. I climbed into an empty third-class carriage and settled myself comfortably in the window seat. I rolled a cigarette and scratched a red match into life on the carriage door. The smoke burned its way down into my lungs and I savoured the aromatic stream I blew out of my mouth, which quickly permeated the air.

I looked idly out of the window and up at the billowing clouds that were moving across the sky. They had a faded yellowy tint to them and belched out an occasional flurry of fine snow, which swirled around the pavements and roads in powdery whirlpools. An elderly woman hobbled along the platform and glanced into my carriage. Her face was white and pinched with the cold and her watery blue eyes showed her disappointment when she saw it was already occupied. She disappeared from sight and I heard the sound of the next carriage door opening and closing.

The train jerked and emitted three or four loud blasts of steam before slowly and laboriously pulling out of the station. The smoke from the engine was being blown along the side of the carriages and gave an appearance of drifting fog. Although I was quite warm now, I shivered at the sight. I only had a thin jacket and it hardly gave me any protection. I said a silent prayer to keep the weather fine until I reached home, but it was in vain; large snowflakes began falling from the sky and soon hid the countryside outside from view. I looked out at the swirling snow and silently cursed my bad luck. Already a layer of snow was forming on the edges of the windows and the inside of the glass was misting up. I rubbed my window with the sleeve of my jacket and made a porthole in the mist but all I could see was a blanket of snow gusting past. 'Fuck it. Fuck it. Fuck it.' I swore loudly three times.

Over the last three months I had grown to hate cold weather. I stared down at my hands, remembering how I dreaded the sound of Brother Francis's footsteps coming down the dormitory corridor. The man had become a living nightmare. He kept telling me that I needed to be taught humility. What the fuck was humility? I had to look the word up before I understood what he was going on about. It wouldn't have made any difference to him if I had humbled myself to everybody and everyone, he would have still punished me. He just never liked me from that very first day when he saw my expression after he had hit Bernie.

It was in the middle of October when he first came to my dormitory at night and ordered me out of bed. He walked over to one of the large sash windows and lifted the bottom half, then signalled me across to where he was standing.

'I am determined to teach you humility,' he said. 'Since you've been here your attitude has not improved. You may have fooled Father Delaney but you certainly haven't fooled me.' He pointed out into the darkness. 'Stand out there.'

I looked fearfully out at where he was pointing. Two foot below the window sill was the flat bitumen roof of the recreation room. It ran the entire length of the dormitories and stretched out thirty feet in front of the windows. The bitumen was still wet from some earlier rain and small puddles rippled on it as the night breeze gusted over them. I found it hard to believe that he meant me to climb out and stand on it in just my nightshirt. I said incredulously, 'You want me to stand out there?'

'Don't question me. Just do as you're told.' He pushed me towards the open window. I could hear the sniggering of the other boys in the dormitory.

I climbed gingerly out of the window and lowered my feet onto the roof. It was wet and cold. The wind blew my nightshirt tight against my body and a freezing draught gusted up my legs and onto my crotch. I folded my arms against my chest and warmed my hands by tucking them under my armpits. I squeezed the tops of my legs together and rested one foot on top of the other. Brother Francis had closed the window and stood peering out at me with his ugly boxer's face. My teeth began to chatter and my feet throbbed as the freezing water chilled them to the bone. I tried to stop my teeth chattering by gripping my jaws firmly shut but this only resulted in my whole head shaking. It seemed to me that the heavens themselves were laughing at me as the force of the wind increased and my nightshirt billowed up.

I don't know how long I was out there – it seemed like an eternity – but I know it was over fifteen minutes. When, at last, Brother Francis reopened the window and called me in, I ran shaking to my bed and dived under the bedclothes. I honestly think that I would have preferred the cane.

I had been forced to endure this punishment at least three times a week over the last two months but as the weather got colder my resilience seemed to get stronger. I still felt the cold and I dreaded going out onto the roof but I was determined not to let that piece of shit Francis get the better of me. I no longer rushed to my bed and dived under the covers. I walked back to my bed and picked up my book to continue reading. My hands still shook and I found it difficult to turn the page but, whilst he was in the room, I showed no weakness. *Fuck you*, I would think.

Meanwhile, I had secured my position in the school football team. I hadn't yet had a game for the first eleven but I was always playing at right back for the second eleven, and we were doing well in the Kent League. I soon learned that there was as much bullying done on the pitch as there was in the school. Mostly it was against players on the opposite team but occasionally, if someone's performance wasn't up to scratch, against the guilty team member. Losing a game was unheard of and I sometimes felt sorry for the opposition as our lads crunched into them in very hard, but fair, tackles. I hadn't come across one boy on an opposing team who could do a sliding tackle and their sports masters would shake their heads and complain if one of their team hit the floor. The tackles were fair but too advanced for most of our competitors.

Occasionally, the odd boy would retaliate against us and that always brought a swift punch in the mouth and a sending off for one of our team. Tom Banks never disciplined any of us for fighting on the pitch as he said it was a contact sport and occasionally tempers were bound to be lost. I had only been in one little scuffle with an opposing player, when he tried to kick me after I had tackled him. I jumped on him and we both fell to the floor but, before I could hit him with my head, the fight was broken up and we both got sent to the dressing room. Tom Banks complained about my being sent off as he said the other player had tried to maim me with a kick, but his complaint got nowhere. We were both found guilty of fighting.

Jimmy Wilkinson still took a perverse delight in bullying me. There were very few days when I was not spat at or pushed. Occasionally I'd get the odd bang in the mouth as I walked past but he avoided my dormitory and that was the most important thing to me. Every day my hatred for him increased. I still hadn't forgiven myself for allowing him to assault me in the toilet and I was determined that one day there would be a reckoning. I had now mastered another fighting tactic. Practising with Bernie, I could confidently catch his foot every time he tried to kick me in the head.

I peered out of the window again. It was still snowing but now darkness was beginning to obscure the countryside as well. I took out my tobacco and rolled myself another cigarette. I seemed to be smoking more than ever and I idly checked to make sure I had enough to last me the next few days. I had close to an ounce of Golden Virginia and two packets of cigarette papers. I decided that I would buy more when I arrived in Ealing. The money I had stolen from Wilkinson would be put to good use during the next few days. I intended to buy my mother some chocolates for Christmas and some of her favourite cigarettes as well. The train was beginning to slow down and I strained my eyes to make out the name of the station we were pulling in to. I could just read 'Bexleyheath' on the station board and the shapes of a few people standing on the platform. I lit my roll-up and flicked the spent match onto the floor by the opposite door.

I hastily moved my feet backwards as my carriage door was flung open. A man and a woman climbed in and the man reached backwards and slammed the carriage door shut with a resounding bang. He glanced in my direction before stamping his feet on the floor to dislodge the snow stuck to his shoes. The woman looked at me and smiled. She asked, 'Are you looking forward to Christmas?' I nodded my head and turned to look back out of the window. I would have much preferred it if they had got in someone else's carriage and left me alone in mine.

By the time we reached Charing Cross Station the carriage had filled up with people and I was looking forward to getting out. Most of them were carrying festive packages and talking loudly. A man sitting next to me kept drinking out of a bottle in a brown paper bag and blowing foul-smelling cigar smoke over me. He was irritating me and I wished I was older so that I could have thrown him out of the carriage and on to the track. I was apprehensive about going home and my nerves were on edge.

As we pulled into the station everyone stood up and said 'Happy Christmas' to all and sundry. I opened the carriage door and jumped out without a word or a backward glance.

They might well have a happy Christmas but I didn't have a clue what lay in store for me. If past Christmases were anything to go by it would be far from a happy time. I hurried out of the station and down the escalator to the tube train.

By the time I arrived at Ealing Broadway Station the snow had nearly stopped. An odd flake still fell from the sky and gusted around before settling on the ground. I went into the station shop and bought a large box of Black Magic chocolates, five packets of Players Weights cigarettes and a two-ounce tin of Golden Virginia tobacco. I handed the shopkeeper a one-pound note and the ten shilling note and he handed me back four two-shilling pieces and two pennies. I put the change into my pocket and made sure that the other three pound notes were still tucked safely under my handkerchief.

The shopkeeper said cheerily, 'Have a very happy Christmas.' I nodded my head, picked up my purchases and hurried out to catch the 211 bus that would take me close to home.

I was pleased to see a bus waiting at the stop. I climbed on and handed the conductor the two pennies the shopkeeper had given me. He gave me my ticket and a cheerful smile, saying, 'Happy Christmas, sonny.'

I nodded back at him and went and sat on the back seat of the bus. I rolled and lit a cigarette and stared sightlessly out of the window. I wanted to get home and away from all these people who seemed to have a permanent smile fixed on their faces.

I walked slowly along the road towards my home. Fairy lights lit up the windows of several of the houses and I could see beautifully decorated Christmas trees in most front rooms. Somewhere close, but not in my road, I could hear a Salvation Army band playing Christmas carols and I started to hum along. I intended to go to Midnight Mass at St Benedict's Church as I had promised Jesus in one of our chats that I'd speak to him again on Christmas Eve. I didn't want to let him down as most of the time in Vincent's he was the only one I could rely on a hundred per cent. Father Delaney had overheard one of my little chats to Jesus and ever since then he had insisted that after every Mass I had some time alone in the chapel. He said he felt very envious that I had such a close and personal relationship with the Son of God and that I must never stop speaking to him as he was always listening out for me. When I went to clean the vestry that evening I found two cigarettes on the floor.

I gave the front doorbell two quick pushes. The hall light came on and I could see Mum through the frosted glass hurrying along the hallway. She opened the door and flung her arms around my neck.

'It's so wonderful to have you home,' she said. 'What time did you leave to get here?' She planted a big kiss on my cheek and pulled me inside.

She had made an effort to look nice and the flowered print dress she was wearing was immaculately clean and crease-free. She had applied some dark red lipstick and I could smell the cheap perfume she had liberally sprinkled over herself. Her hair was done in tight curls and I knew that she must have had curlers in her hair for hours and hours to get it to look so nice. I hugged her tightly.

'You look beautiful,' I said and saw the look of delight spread across her face. 'I left at 2.30 this afternoon.'

The front room door opened and my grandmother came out, smiling at me. I kissed her on the cheek. She was nearly deaf and only partially sighted and she squinted through her glasses to see me more clearly. Her voice seemed to crackle as she spoke.

'You've grown. Look at him, Joan. Look how tall he's got.' Her feeble, gnarled hands squeezed the tops of my arms. 'Feel how big he's got, Joan. He's nearly a man. Feel him, Joan. Feel him.'

I self-consciously broke free from her and smiled at Mum. She was shaking her head in disbelief. 'She's right, darling, you have grown. You must have sprung up at least two inches since the last time I saw you. You're quite the young man.'

'I'm not even fifteen, Mum. I'm just a kid.' I handed her the paper bag with the chocolates and cigarettes inside. 'I'm sorry they're not wrapped but I've only just bought them.'

She looked inside the bag and started to cry. I couldn't understand why she would start crying at receiving some chocolates and cigarettes for Christmas and I silently wished I'd never bought them. She reached out and hugged me tightly and I could feel the dampness of her tears on the side of my neck.

'You're such a good boy,' she sobbed. 'I don't deserve your presents.'

'You're my mum,' I said. 'You deserve everything in the whole wide world.' I gently pushed her away from me. 'Where is everybody?'

Mum pulled a handkerchief from her sleeve and wiped her eyes. 'Liz is living in Kensington with a very nice young man.'

Elizabeth, my oldest sister, was five and a half years my senior. We had barely spoken when I lived at home as there was too big an age gap.

'Jean has gone to see her boyfriend and should be back later tonight.'

Jean was eighteen months older than me. We were much closer and got on well. I smiled at the thought of her having a boyfriend. 'Jennifer is in the kitchen watching television with your father.' Jennifer was six and a half years younger than me.

'Television. Did you say television?' My eyes opened wide in astonishment. Only rich people had a television. 'When did you get it? You never mentioned it in any of your letters.'

'Don't get excited, John. I didn't get it.' She looked embarrassed. 'Your father got it a couple of days ago. He has put it in the kitchen so he can watch it in there. He said there's no reason for you to go into the kitchen as you're not allowed to watch it and he doesn't want to see you.'

I nodded, unconcerned. I didn't care if I never saw him again for the rest of my life; I hated him and wished he was dead. It would have been nice to watch some of the shows on television, but nowhere near as nice as not having to put up with that nasty bastard. I smiled at my mother. 'So where do we get to spend our time this Christmas? In with Gran or in the back living room?'

'I've lit a nice big fire in the back room and Jennifer has hung up some decorations.' She guided me down there. 'I've also moved the radio into the room so that we can listen to all our favourite programmes. It will be really nice and cosy.' She squeezed me tightly around the shoulders. 'I know how you love reading. You can read to your heart's content in there and no one will disturb you.'

'I'm going to Midnight Mass tonight, Mum. Would you like to come with me?' I asked hopefully. 'I'd really like you to.'

She lowered her head and shook it slowly. 'You're asking the impossible. I will never set foot in a Catholic church again. Did you know that Father Gregory from St Benedict's had the cheek to come around to this house and tell me that your father had done the right thing putting you in that school? He believed everything your father told him. He said I was failing as a wife and a mother in not supporting what he had done.' She looked up at me and the hatred she was feeling, thinking of the incident, blazed out of her eyes. 'I told him exactly what I thought of him, his church, his pious hypocrisy and the entire Irish race. I couldn't go to church now, not even for you. I just couldn't.'

My heart was bursting with pride. It was the first I had heard about the parish priest coming to the house and the thought of my mother giving him a piece of her mind because of me made me immensely proud of her. I gave her a huge hug. I had tears in my eyes and held her close to me until they had disappeared. I asked quietly, 'Do you mind if I go?'

'Of course I don't.' She stepped back. 'I would never stop you going to church. Every person must worship God in the way they are happy with. I don't feel I need a church to speak to God. He knows what is in my heart and what sins I have committed. I don't need a priest as a middle man. Especially an Irish one. You go to church and I'll wait up for you.'

When I arrived home from church at ten minutes past one in the morning she was waiting in the back room with a freshly made pot of tea and a plate of mince pies.

* * *

Mum woke me on Christmas morning by gently tapping me on the shoulder and kissing me on my forehead. I had slept on the couch in the back room, covered with a thin blanket and two large coats and with my head resting on a large feather pillow that Gran had lent me. Much to my surprise the fire was already blazing and the room neat and tidy. I hadn't heard a thing as I was unaccustomed to late nights and had been extremely tired. I heaved my legs over the side of the couch and sat staring into the burning coals.

Mum sat down on the edge of one of the easy chairs and puffed slowly on a cigarette. The smoke drifted past my nostrils and I held out my hand, looking hopefully in my mother's direction. She took another cigarette from her packet, lit it and handed it to me. I slowly sucked in a mouthful of smoke and savoured the great feeling of inhaling it into my smoke-hungry lungs. We sat in complete silence, both of us lost in our own personal reverie and neither wanting to break the spell.

The moment was shattered by Jennifer bursting in. She handed me a small packet wrapped neatly in Christmas paper.

'Happy Christmas, John,' she said and looked at Mum to see if she had done and said everything as they had rehearsed. Mum smiled and nodded her approval.

'Happy Christmas to you, Jennifer.' I pulled off the wrapping paper to reveal a packet of twenty Senior Service cigarettes.

'I really wanted some cigarettes and these are my favourites.' I had said the right thing. Jennifer looked really pleased.

From down the side of her chair, Mum produced a larger, bulkier package wrapped in the same coloured paper that Jennifer had used. She reached across and handed it to me. 'Happy Christmas, darling.'

I opened it carefully, removing the paper and folding it neatly on the side of the couch. I looked down at the two books resting on my lap: *Kidnapped* by Robert Louis Stevenson and *Jamaica Inn* by Daphne Du Maurier. I knew nothing about either book but I trusted my mother's judgement and was feeling a little choked up.

'Thank you, Mum,' I said. 'How do you always know what I want?'

During the remainder of my Christmas holiday I lost myself in *Kidnapped,* totally excluding everything else and virtually living the experiences I was reading about. Alan Breck Stewart and David Balfour became real people to me, just like the shipwreck off the island of Mull and their escape across the wild landscape of the Highlands. With the help of Gran's encyclopaedias, I found out about Culloden and the Jacobites and even read a brief account of James III of England and the Hanoverian King George II. Mum laughed when I had difficulty understanding some of the Scottish dialect, telling me she doubted that any person apart from a Scot would understand it.

All too soon David Balfour retrieved his inheritance, the House of Shaws, from Ebenezer Balfour and the story reached its conclusion. So had my holiday. It was time for me to return to Vincent's. It was the best Christmas I had ever had. I had had no contact with my father.

Chapter 14

1959

The Kent landscape was frozen whiteness and the grass crunched under our feet as we trotted out of the dressing room and onto the playing field for a practice match. The match only lasted for about four minutes as the ground was too hard and pitted to run on. The dressing room was freezing cold as we struggled out of our kit and back into our school clothes. Bernie scratched a match along the wall and puffed a roll-up into life. Other squad members watched us enviously as we smoked the cigarette down until only the smallest butt remained. The temptation was too much for several team members and, throwing caution to the wind, they lit a couple of roll-ups and shared them in two of the cubicles. Nobody had the sense to keep an eye out for any of the masters or Brothers until disaster appeared at the door in the form of Brother Arnold.

He walked slowly into the dressing room, his mouth twisted into a sneer, and sniffed loudly as he tried to locate the source of the cigarette smoke. Stephen Wright, the First Eleven centre forward, started walking towards the cubicles and Arnold pulled him savagely back by his hair and hit him hard with the flat of his hand across his cheek and mouth. The sound of the hit must have alerted the smokers as we heard a toilet flushing. Arnold ran around the corner to the cubicles and was just in time to catch three boys coming out of one.

'You little bastards,' he screamed, 'do you take me for an idiot?'

He grabbed the nearest boy and used him as a battering ram against the other two as he pushed and hit them into a corner. He then turned his attention to the only cubicle with a closed door. He broke the lock with one kick and the door flew open with a crash. Two boys were crouching against the far wall. He dragged them both out by their hair and shoved them into the corner with the other three boys then set about them with a brutal frontal assault, slapping and pummelling them until they lay sprawled in an untidy heap. One of the boys had a bad nose bleed and his blood was spattered over the wall and floor. Arnold stood over them, gasping for breath, his face twitching with anger, watching for any reason to resume the attack. Satisfied that he was an unopposed victor, he turned on his heel and strutted arrogantly out of the room.

One of the boys staggered to a basin and rinsed his face. He patted it dry with a towel and peered out of the window at Arnold, who was walking round the perimeter of the pitch. He rummaged in his kit, produced another roll-up and lit it. It was like a signal for the entire team. In less than a minute there were eight roll-ups burning and we all puffed on them in an unrehearsed act of hidden defiance. We waited until Arnold was about twenty yards from returning to the dressing room to escort us back to school before we all jogged out. As Arnold entered the dressing room we cheered and ran as fast as we could into the yard and out of his sight. I wished I could have seen his face as he found the eight roll-ups still burning on the windowsill. Every member of the squad lost ten points for smoking that day but we all felt it was worth it.

January disappeared with the memory of freezing fog and abandoned football matches. Tom Banks kept the squad fit by making us do circuit training in the recreation room for an hour every evening. We enjoyed the training with Tom as he always left us alone in the showers at the end of each session. This, of course, meant that we got a peaceful cigarette before we went to bed.

Shortly after my fifteenth birthday, in April 1959, Jimmy Wilkinson was released on licence. I was absolutely devastated. Wilkinson had done two years and one month of his three-year sentence and had somehow fooled the licensing committee into releasing him early. It was quite common for boys to be released on licence and I was always a bit jealous when they came into the yard on their last morning and said goodbye to their friends. But Wilkinson's release was a travesty of justice and ruined all my plans for getting revenge on him.

Stealing his cash had just been a bonus: it had been pure luck that I had discovered his hiding place. My intention had always been to do physical damage to him; I had dreamed of that day and knew that once I had mastered catching the high boot, I stood a good chance of exacting revenge. Now that dream was shattered.

He swaggered into the yard on his last morning and revelled in the attention shown to him by mates. I watched him leave the yard with a terrible feeling of being cheated. Bernie just said, 'Thank fuck he's gone. Maybe we'll get a little peace now.'

I said moodily, 'My only wish is that he dies screaming.'

Bernie said, 'So do I, but I think it goes deeper with you. You've been obsessed with him for over a year. I know you were practising catching the high boot with Wilkinson in mind. I never said anything to change your mind but, if you'd ever fought him, he'd have fucked you up good.'

'Well, he's gone now and we'll never know, will we? But I was looking forward to finding out one day.'

Bernie stared at me. 'You did a good job on Love but he wasn't in the same class as Wilkinson and his mates. And don't forget the caning you got for fighting.' He spat on the floor. 'It's really not worth it.'

'It is to me,' I said. 'Every time somebody hits me it makes me more determined to become a better fighter. I'm fed up of being bullied and having to sip my tea carefully because my lips are cut and sore. Believe me, my days of being bullied are coming to an end.' I heard my Mum's words ringing in my ears: 'The only real way of dealing with a bully is by bullying him.' I was convinced she was right and that's what I had to do. Bernie never agreed with me, though.

'You'll end up being caned again,' he said. 'I saw your arse. It was black and blue and had a couple of nasty cuts on it as well. Don't be stupid and have it happen all over again.'

'How many times has Love had a go at us since that fight? How many fucking times?'

Bernie shrugged his shoulders. 'I haven't a clue.'

'The answer is none. Not even once.' I smiled with pride. 'Which proves my point that you have to fight back to win. If Love ever tries to hit either of us again I'll beat the shit out of him. He knows that and that is why he hasn't come near us.'

'There are a lot of better fighters than Love in this school,' Bernie laughed. 'Or have you turned into Superman and can now beat anything and everyone?'

'I never said I thought I could beat everyone. I said it pays to fight back.' I pulled a partially smoked roll-up from out of my sock and handed it to him. 'I know I could get hurt in a fight and I know that the cane hurts but—' I took the lit roll-up from Bernie and sucked on it hungrily before handing it back '—I think it's better than having every arsehole in the school carrying on smacking us in the mouth just for fun. Did I tell you that last night Riley, the prick, had me standing by the side of my bed for over an hour?' He was a big lad in our dorm, and just did it to wield his power – no other reason. 'I stood there because I wasn't prepared to fight back and tell him to fuck off. Well, tonight I'm going to tell him to fuck off and stay in bed, and when he gets out of his bed to thump me, we're going to end up fighting.'

'You're not the only one being pushed around. Look at Peterson, the new kid. 'He's already got a fat lip and a black eye. All he did was sit down on the same bench as Cuddy.' Bernie pulled down his right sock and pointed at a large scab and a purple swelling on his shin. 'I've still got a bruise on my leg from being kicked by that cunt and I'd love to kick the shit out of him, but I know that I can't. You have to be sensible and just try to stay out of the way of the arseholes.'

I looked at Bernie's bruised leg and then scanned the yard for a glimpse of Sean Cuddy. I saw him clumsily kicking a ball against the chapel wall with a few of his friends. He was a stocky sixteen-year-old Irish boy with an unruly mop of curly hair and an acne-scarred face with a few wispy hairs protruding from his chin. I had seen him fight before and I wasn't too impressed. He was definitely very strong and afraid of nothing but he was also cumbersome and clumsy. *He'll do*, I thought. *I have to start somewhere, so why not him?* I reached out for the roll-up and puffed in another mouthful of smoke and handed the butt back to Bernie. I said, 'He'll do nicely. Just wait and see.'

'What the fuck are you talking about?' Bernie said. 'Who'll do nicely?'

Brother Michael blew his whistle loudly and we slowly made our way to our places of work. My mind was racing. I had made a big decision and I knew that it would take all my courage and then some to follow it through. I needed to stay focused and keep reminding myself why I was doing it. My courage came from an unlikely source. I thought of Alan Breck Stewart and all of the Clansmen who fought at Culloden. They must have known fear but it didn't stop them fighting and dying for what they believed in. I was better off than them as I wasn't facing death.

That evening, I filed into the dining room for tea. I had planned how I would fight Cuddy and my nerves were jangling. I sought out his table with my eyes and saw that he was facing forwards, three tables in front of mine. All of the tables seated four people. In the centre of each table was a large metal teapot, which one of the boys would carry to the front of the hall to fill up from a tea urn situated on the dining-room counter.

I picked up the pot on my table and walked towards the front of the room. As I was about to walk past Cuddy's table I swung the teapot hard into his face. 'That's for Bernie's leg, you ugly cunt,' I yelled loudly.

Cuddy surprised me by jumping out of his chair and grabbing me in a bear hug that virtually squeezed all the breath out of my body. I could see a large lump on his forehead where the teapot had hit and knew that I had done him some damage. His face was close to mine and I could smell his stale breath as he strained to squeeze me even tighter. I didn't know what to do to get out of his grip so I got his nose between my teeth and bit down hard. A loud yell of 'You bastard!' burst from his mouth before he let go of me and shoved me backwards and straight into the arms of the approaching Brother Arnold.

Brother Arnold put his knee in my back and pulled me backwards onto the floor. His right foot crashed into my ribs and made me double up in pain. He kicked me again in the centre of my back. It felt as though I'd been hit by lightning as a quivering shock ran through my body. He then lifted me up by my hair and crashed the flat of his hand into my unprotected face. I could taste the blood from my nose as it streamed down over my lips. He shoved me towards the dining-room door.

'It's Brother De Montfort for you. I saw you hit Cuddy with the teapot and heard you call him an cunt. I'm sure Brother De Montfort will be delighted to hear about this.'

Brother De Montfort sat at his desk with his eyes shut as he listened to Brother Arnold relate what had happened in the dining room. When Arnold had finished he opened his eyes and looked at me impassively.

'You have been here nearly fifteen months, Fenton, and still you haven't learnt that fighting will not be tolerated under any circumstances. I had hoped that your previous visit to me for fighting would have taught you not to do it again.' He stood up slowly and turned to look at the picture of the Blessed Virgin. He blessed himself and then turned back to face me.

'I hope sincerely that this visit to the small dormitory will be your last and that you will have learnt your lesson.' He looked at Brother Arnold. 'Could you fetch Brother Ambrose for me, Brother, and tell him to come directly to the small dormitory.'

I suppose I had known this was inevitable but I'd been hoping that Cuddy would get caned as well. It was unfortunate that Brother Arnold had seen me initiating the attack. My heart started racing and my mouth was dry in anticipation of the pain I knew was coming my way shortly.

Brother De Montfort ushered me out of his office and up the wooden staircase to the small dormitory. He took out a pair of boxing shorts from a cupboard, placed them on a bed and said quietly, 'Get undressed and put on the shorts. You know the procedure, you've been here before.'

Brother Ambrose arrived just as I finished putting on the shorts. He carried the same bundle of canes as last time. I watched as he selected a long thin cane from the bundle and tested its flexibility by bending it in half and letting it spring back. He swished it noisily in imaginary swipes and flexed his shoulders in preparation. I closed my eyes tightly and concentrated on an image of Jesus being scourged by the Romans. I was determined to make no noise and not to move this time. I kept repeating in my mind, *Remember Jesus. Remember Culloden. Remember Jesus. Remember Culloden*.

I heard De Montfort say, 'Touch the floor' and I bent forward, keeping my eyes shut.

The first slash of the cane brought an explosion of lights to my brain and excruciating pain to the whole of my body.

I took an involuntary step forward with my left foot then stepped back into place with gritty determination. Every instinct wanted to let out a scream of anguish but I wouldn't allow myself. *Remember Jesus. Remember Culloden. Remember Jesus. Remember Culloden.*

De Montfort's voice penetrated my private thoughts. 'Stand up, Fenton.'

I stood up slowly and opened my eyes.

De Montfort was staring at me. 'Why do I get the impression that this is some sort of test for you? You will not win. I will break this defiance.' He pointed. 'Touch the floor.'

Remember Jesus. Remember Culloden. Remember Jesus. Remember Culloden. I shut my eyes tightly again. I was concentrating so hard I never heard the swishing of the cane. Once again the excruciating pain and the desire to scream overwhelmed me and I knew if I opened my eyes, tears would pour out. I forced myself to stand up. Slowly, reluctantly, I opened my eyes and looked at the face of evil. De Montfort stared back at me. I shut out everything he was saying to me. Brother Arnold was standing by the open dormitory door, looking at me in triumph. The bastard was enjoying my pain and humiliation. I no longer felt the pain after that. I could only feel the deep hatred I had in my heart for the sadistic arsehole standing by the door.

Four more times I touched my toes and four more times I stood up and stared at Arnold. He didn't realise he was helping me through my punishment. While he was there I felt nothing but hatred. The caning meant nothing to me. Showing no pain to Arnold was all that mattered. I was surprised when it was all over to find that I had urinated on the floor. I hadn't even felt it.

When I returned to the recreation room Bernie was waiting for me. He shook his head. 'I didn't believe my eyes when I saw you hit Cuddy. Jesus, John, have you gone nuts? Cuddy told me he's going to smash you to bits.'

'That's what he thinks,' I said. 'They can't cane me again for fighting but they can cane that prick.' I looked around the recreation room until I spotted him. He was sitting on one of the benches, staring at me.

I walked purposely over to where he was sitting and the idiot didn't even stand up so I kicked him hard. Cuddy let out a roar and jumped off the bench to try and land on me. I moved easily out of his way. He ran at me and I grabbed his neck with my left arm and pulled his head under my arm. Both of his arms were flailing wildly as tried to hit me with his huge hands but he soon gave this up and put both his arms around my waist and started to squeeze. I thrust my right hand into his face and tried to poke him in the eye. He struggled like crazy and I was being tossed around like a rag doll but I still had a firm grip on his head.

Arms were pulling us apart and I was forced to let go of Cuddy's head. Tom Banks had hold of me and Brother Michael had hold of Cuddy. We were both marched to De Montfort's office. I knew what was coming so I wasn't worried. They couldn't cane me again as it would do too much damage, so they would deduct a quarter of a day off my holiday. Cuddy would get caned and that suited me down to the ground.

I returned from De Montfort's office with a smile on my face. It had gone exactly as I thought it would. De Montfort had screamed a lot of abuse at me and I had shut it out by thinking of Cuddy getting caned. I had made my decision to bring the bullying to an end and nothing was going to stop me now. I knew there was a long way to go before it would end completely but I was prepared for that. If I had to fight Cuddy ten times it wouldn't matter. He would get fed up before me. I had a temper and I couldn't just walk away from arguments the way Bernie did. Besides, I was doing what Mum had told me to.

Bernie laughed so much when he saw me I thought his sides would split. Tears were streaming down his face and he clutched his sides as if he had a severe pain. 'I have never seen anything as funny as Cuddy trying to get you to stop poking his eye out.' He nearly choked with his laughter. 'And why did he stay sitting and let you kick him? He really is a stupid arsehole.'

I found myself laughing along with Bernie. We were still laughing when Liam Donovan came across the room and smacked me in the mouth. Liam Donovan was a good friend of Sean Cuddy and had decided to exact revenge on me. He was sixteen years old and about two inches taller than I was. A groove on his upper lip and nose gave the impression that he had a hare lip but it was just a large scar caused by a cricket ball hitting him in the face. He was no mug and a far more dangerous proposition than Cuddy.

Just for a few seconds after he hit me, I was unsure what I should do about it. Bernie made my mind up for me by throwing me our weighted money belt. I caught it in my right hand and in the same movement crashed it into Donovan's face. I knew I had hurt him as soon as it connected. One of the zips on the belt had taken a layer of skin off part of his cheekbone and a lump had already begun to form. I swung the belt to hit him again but he blocked it with his arm. He hit me twice in the face with his right hand and I found myself on the floor. He swung his right foot at my face and I just managed to roll out of its way.

I was saved from any further punishment by the intervention of Mr Lawson, one of the masters. He pulled Donovan away from me and frogmarched him towards the door. Brother Michael pulled me off the floor and took the money belt out of my hand. He pushed me back towards the door and once again in the direction of De Montfort's office.

Brother De Montfort looked down at the pile of nails that came out of the pockets of the money belt. He guessed their approximate weight by holding a pile of them in his hand and then placed them back on the table. He looked up and I could see he was furious. His voice was almost a whisper.

'How is this going to end?' he asked. 'Are you intent on killing someone? Do you think that I'm not going to punish you for hitting someone with this weapon?' He held the money belt up and pushed it angrily towards my face. 'I'm putting you in isolation until tomorrow. I'll think of how I am going to deal with you overnight.' He looked at Brother Michael. 'Take him up to the isolation room in the surgery and lock him in. I'll inform Matron why he is there.'

I spent the night in isolation worrying about what would happen to me in the morning. I would like to have told De Montfort about the bullying that went on in Vincent's and how often Bernie and I were on the receiving end of some sort of abuse, but I couldn't. That would have been considered grassing and, in the eyes of the boys, the worst possible offence you could commit. I came to the only decision that was left open to me and that was to keep my mouth shut and take the punishment. But what might it be? I was extremely nervous as I walked into Brother De Montfort's office in the morning.

Brother De Montfort wasn't alone. Standing just behind his chair was Brother Francis and, in the far corner of the room, Father Delaney. My heart began to beat rapidly. I was in deep trouble if Father Delaney was attending. Brother Francis looked at me as if I had just crawled out from under a stone. His nose wrinkled with distaste and his mouth curled into a half sneer. I forced myself to stare at him defiantly. His face reddened under my stare and I knew that he would have enjoyed coming across the room and backhanding me into submission.

Brother De Montfort opened a drawer in his desk and produced the money belt and nails. He sat silently staring at them for several seconds before scooping them into a metal waste paper bin. They made a hollow clunk as they landed. He placed the bin back into its position by the side of his desk and then gave me his full attention. His face appeared whiter then normal and his blue shaving tinge more pronounced. The Brylcreem plastered thickly on his head gave his hair a resemblance to sleek cat's fur. He drummed his fingers on his desk, thinking, and then turned to Father Delaney.

'Well, Father,' he said, 'would you like to start off the proceedings?'

Father Delaney took up a position directly in front of me. His dark blue eyes stared into mine and I was forced to look away. 'I want you to tell me, John, exactly what went on yesterday and why you ended up hitting one of the boys with a weapon?'

I couldn't look him in the eyes so I looked at the floor instead. I said quietly, 'It was just an argument, Father.'

'It must have been some argument for you to go and fetch a weapon and hit a boy across the face with it. You had already had two fights and had been caned by Brother Ambrose, so why did you hit a different boy with a weapon as soon as you returned to the recreation room?'

I shrugged. 'It was just an argument, Father. Really. It was just an argument.'

Brother Francis stepped forward. 'He's got an evil streak in him. I've said that ever since he arrived in the school. This only proves me right.'

Father Delaney shook his head vigorously and boomed loudly. 'No. No. No. I will not accept that. There is more to this story than we're being told.'

Brother Francis looked shocked at Father Delaney's outburst. 'I have had to discipline this boy on more than one occasion. He hates discipline and is completely anti-authoritarian. He is arrogant and proud and thinks he is a cut above all the rest. Believe me, Father, he is a bad lot.'

'Brother Francis, he is just a young boy.' Father Delaney's voice was gentle now. 'What makes you think he's arrogant and proud?'

'It's his whole demeanour.' Brother Francis stared at me with open dislike. 'His eyes don't lie and they show his disrespect for all and sundry. He hides his face in books so that his true feelings are not seen. I'm telling you, Father. He is a bad lot.'

'Can you not see that he is intelligent and in lots of ways he is different from the majority of the boys we get in this school?' Father Delaney sighed in exasperation. 'Look at the way he picked up the Latin Mass. In the twelve years I've been here we have never had a better or a brighter altar boy. I have spoken to him on many occasions and I know he loves reading. He has read many of what I would call good books. *The Count of Monte Cristo, Kidnapped, A Tale of Two Cities, Jamaica Inn* – and that's just a few. No, Brother, he is not a bad lot, he is just an intelligent boy who's in the wrong kind of school. He should be in a grammar school studying English Literature, not in our school studying bricklaying.'

Brother De Montfort coughed quietly and brought the discussion to an end. He said, 'That may be so, but he's here and we have to deal with the problem. He hit a boy with a weapon and this will not be tolerated. In normal circumstances he would be caned and that would be the end of the matter, but he's already been caned and I can't cane him again.'

'Maybe a loss of some holiday,' Father Delaney suggested. 'It seems the obvious solution to the problem.'

'I think that's the only way left open,' said Brother De Montfort. 'I think maybe a three-day loss would be about right.'

Father Delaney nodded in agreement.

Brother Francis looked at me in disgust. 'I think he's getting off too lightly. He'll think he's won.'

I tried to keep my expression blank so that they couldn't see that I did, in fact, feel as though I had won.

Father Delaney said, 'This is not a competition, Brother. There are no winners or losers. I think compassion is the word that springs to mind.'

'Right, Fenton.' Brother De Montfort turned his attention to me. 'I am deducting three days off your holidays. You will also polish the whole of the chapel floor and the pews. Is that clear?'

'Yes, Bro,' I said.

He stood up. 'You can go and tell Mr Cornell that you have work to do in the chapel for the next few days.'

I walked towards the bricklaying hut with a grin on my face. What a result. I would lose three days of my holiday, which I didn't care about, and I'd get to work in the chapel, which I loved to do. Peter Cornell, the bricklaying tutor, nodded his head when I told him of Brother De Montfort's punishment and then told me it served me right. I agreed with him and pretended I was unhappy at having to go to the chapel. I made a great pretence of trudging off reluctantly and as soon as I was out of sight I ran as fast as I could to the chapel.

Chapter 15

July 1959 was a month of blisteringly hot weather. The brightness of the sun made me squint as I stood in line with the rest of the school. Brother Michael came striding out of the school block and looked critically all around.

'When I blow my whistle,' he said, 'I want the entire school to congregate by the chapel wall.' He blew a long shrill blast on the whistle and watched us as we jostled for position by the wall. He blew the whistle again to attract our attention. 'The next time I blow the whistle I want everyone to run around the perimeter of the yard until I tell you to stop.'

He took up a position in the centre of the yard and blew another loud blast on his whistle. We all started to jog around the yard.

After about ten minutes of jogging Brother Michael blew his whistle again. He shouted, 'Speed it up. I want you all to run around the yard. No jogging.'

We set off at a fair sprint. I got into my stride, running at the same pace as the football squad did in training. Lap after lap went past and I felt relaxed and comfortable at my steady pace. Boys were stopping and bending down with a stitch and some were just giving up. Very soon there were only six of us left running around the perimeter and the rest of the school sat down to watch.

Ten minutes later the whistle blew again. Brother Michael said, 'That's enough. You can carry on with what you were doing.' He walked back into the school block and out of our sight.

'What was all that about?' asked Bernie.

I shook my head. 'I haven't a clue but I quite enjoyed it. There were only six of us left at the end and I was hoping that it was going to go on to see who was the last one running.'

'It would have been me,' Bernie said. 'I'm the best.'

'It would only have been you if I'd fallen over and broken a leg.' I playfully pushed Bernie away from me. 'I was tracking you with no problem. I could have overtaken you any time I wanted to.'

'In your dreams, John. In your dreams.' Bernie pointed to the chapel wall. 'Let's start again and I'll show you what a wanker you are.'

We started running around the perimeter again. The pace wasn't dynamic but it was steady. We'd been running for the best part of fifteen minutes when Brother Michael came back into the yard. He blew his whistle again and ordered us to line up in our houses. When we were all lined up he took out a piece of paper from beneath his cassock and announced: 'I have selected the runners to represent us at the Home Office Schools Championship Finals. It is going to be held at Erith Stadium on the 15th of this month. There will be teams from all of the approved schools and the competition will be fierce. All the boys I have selected will be excused from their trades and will train hard for the next two weeks.'

He consulted the piece of paper. 'The 100 yards: Peter Tingle.' There were loud groans of disappointment from some of the boys who fancied themselves as sprinters. 'The 220 yards: David Tate.' More groans. 'The 440 yards: Bernard Connors.'

'Well done, Bernie,' I shouted.

Brother Michael dropped his piece of paper and hastily stamped his foot on it to stop it blowing away. He picked it up and uncrumpled it. 'The 880 yards: Andrew Devine.'

All the boys made a loud hissing noise. Andrew Devine had to walk the walk of shame every morning with his sheets. He had a weak bladder and wet his bed nearly every night of the week and had to bring the wet sheets down to assembly in the morning. When the master called out the words 'Wet beds' the hissing would start. His face was always beetroot red as he walked to the front and dropped his soiled sheets in a large laundry basket.

Brother Michael held up his hand for silence. 'That's enough of that.' The school went silent again. 'The one mile: John Fenton and Liam Donovan.'

I was in a daze. I had been selected to represent the school and I was bursting with pride. I was no longer a nonentity, no longer an also-ran; I was a representative for the school in the mile race. They might even take a photograph of me, providing I won, and put it on the recreation room wall.

Bernie grabbed me in a bear hug. 'We're in the team, John.'

'I know, Bernie. I can't believe it.' We went over to the washroom door and sat down on the top step. 'I'm going flat out to win that race, Bernie. I want to be a winner.'

David Tate came sauntering up. He was a skinny, fifteen-year-old boy with exceptionally crooked teeth and a nervous twitch that screwed up his face three or four times a minute. He grinned, revealing his twisted ivory, and said, 'There will be girls at Erith as well. There will be loads of tits and fanny on show and maybe we'll get some.'

'How the fuck do you know who'll be at Erith?' Bernie asked. 'Have you been there before?'

Neither of us liked Tate much. He had been caned twice for masturbating in the toilets.

'You just want something to wank over,' Bernie sneered.

'It's the Home Office Schools Championship. Not the Home Office Schools for Boys Championship.' His face screwed up in a nervous twitch. 'There are girls' approved schools as well. I'll bet you a roll-up I'm right.'

'Fuck off, Tate,' Bernie said. 'Go and tell someone else about your dreams. We're not interested in your bullshit.'

Tate's face screwed up again. He turned around and wandered away in the direction of Peter Tingle, who was sitting against the far wall with a few of his mates.

'He's one weird cunt,' said Bernie, 'but wouldn't it be great if he was right?'

I nodded my head as I didn't know what to say. Mum had instilled in me from a very early age that girls were to be treated with respect. 'They are not as strong as boys and should always be treated with gentleness and reverence,' she had told me on numerous occasions. 'Never take advantage of them and never lift a hand to them. Only the worst sort of man hits a woman. Treat them the same as you would treat a fragile toy.' I knew in my heart I would honour her wishes but how could I do it without making myself look an idiot in front of the other boys? I looked at Bernie and hoped he was in the same predicament as me.

'Have you ever been with a girl?' I said. 'I mean, really been with a girl?'

'Once. I've been all the way once.' Bernie smiled at the memory. 'It was with one of my sister's friends a couple of months ago. I went home on a first Sunday and my sister had her friend Janice around for the day. My sister has a boyfriend and she asked me to look after Janice while she met up with him before dinner. We were playing records in my room and messing about and somehow we ended up snogging. I was having a good feel of her tits when all of a sudden she undid my trousers and pulled out my dick. She pulled aside her knickers and pushed my dick inside her. She was only thirteen years old but she was a great fuck and we're meeting up the next time I go home.'

'Why didn't you tell me about it before now?' I asked. 'I thought we told each other everything.'

'We do, but this was private. I told her that I wouldn't tell anyone about what we had done.'

'Then why did you tell me now?' I said. 'You could have kept the secret.'

'Fuck off, John.' Bernie was getting annoyed. 'You asked me a question and I answered it. I only told you about it as you are my best friend. I wish I hadn't now you're making a big deal about it.'

'Sorry, I didn't mean to make a big deal about it.' I was embarrassed. 'It's just that I've never been anywhere near a girl. I don't even know what to do and I'm not so sure that I want to.'

Bernie laughed. 'Nor did I a couple of months ago. It is the most natural thing in the world. Take my word for it.

When you get to touch your first pair of tits or mess around with a girl's tush, you'll know what to do and you'll want to do it again.'

Bernie had given me no comfort. It was obvious that he would be after anything he could get from the girls and he expected me to do the same. I had been quite shocked at his revelation about his sister's friend and in awe at his casual indifference to what had occurred. How could he say 'She was a great fuck?' Mum had told me that when a man and a woman went together it should be a wonderful experience and treasured by both of them. 'She was a great fuck' didn't sound like a treasured moment to me. I decided that once again I would have to go it alone and try to do what was right.

'Why the long face?' Bernie asked. 'You should be smiling at the thought of getting your first bit of tush.'

'You smile, Bernie. I don't feel like it.' I scowled at the dilemma I was in. 'It's all new to me and I'll decide what I want to do on the day.'

'I never doubted it. Now can we stop talking about something that won't even happen and go for a smoke instead?' He took a crumpled roll-up out of his sock and rolled it between his fingers until it was smokeable. 'Let's go. You've got nothing to worry about.'

He was wrong. Thirteen days later we knew that there would be girls at Erith. Bernie was jumping for joy. I was quivering in my boots.

Erith Sports Stadium was a modern stadium that had been built as part of a government plan to help England attract some of the big European sporting events. As our coach pulled into the stadium we were amazed at its size. It was huge. The eight-lane running track was freshly marked out into lanes and the huge central plot of land was split into sections for the field events. The only field events that were taking place at this meeting were the long jump and the high jump. A large covered grandstand ran along the entire length of the finishing straight and the remainder of the track was circled by concrete stands that offered good viewing but scant protection from the weather.

There must have been at least fifty to sixty other coaches parked up when we arrived. Bernie was craning his neck to see who was in them. His face lit up as our coach pulled in next to a coach filled with girls. The girls all waved frantically and I could see a few women in grey suits running up and down the aisle trying to restore some sort of order and decorum. They were failing miserably as the girls were totally ignoring them and intent on shouting out of the small ventilation windows.

Brother Michael shouted loudly from the front of our coach, 'Stay sitting down. I don't want any shouting or yelling. Totally ignore those girls.'

His voice fell on deaf ears as boys were scrabbling to open their windows and strike up conversations. I couldn't believe my eyes when one of the girls sitting next to a window pulled up her blouse and exposed a pair of snowy white breasts with beautiful pinky-red nipples. A great cheer went up from all of the boys and Brother Michael quickly got out of our coach and went to speak to a woman on the girls' coach. The woman quickly charged down to where the girl was sitting and pulled her unceremoniously from her seat. The girl's ample bosom wobbled delightfully as the woman tried to pull down her blouse and cover her up.

Bernie sighed, 'This is going to be a great day.' He pointed at a petite girl of about fourteen years old who was staring at us with unbridled interest. 'Me and her are definitely going to fuck today.' He jumped on our seat and shouted out for the girl to stand up by her window.

She obliged and soon they were both shouting suggestions as to how they might get together before the day was over. She signalled to someone behind her and another girl came to stand next to her. She was a pretty girl with brown hair and a nice smile and Bernie told me to join him on the seat.

'That one is for you,' he said. 'I've arranged with my one to bring her along when we meet up. You can come with me and we'll all find somewhere to be alone.'

I smiled sheepishly at my intended partner and she gave me a brilliant smile in return. She undid the top three buttons of her blouse and nodded at me suggestively. I couldn't see anything of her breasts but I knew that she was telling me that I would definitely be seeing them later. I nodded my head like a demented person and my mother's instructions flew out the window and were gone for good.

'Let's go.' Brother Michael was standing on the top step and looking down the coach. 'Bring your running gear and towels as we're not coming back here until after the races have finished.' He looked at Tom Banks and Brother Ambrose and added quietly, but loud enough for us to hear: 'If any of them misbehave, book them and they will be dealt with when we arrive back at school.'

We filed slowly off the coach and towards the main grandstand. Our seats were located halfway up the stand and gave a great view of the whole stadium. The finishing line on the track was directly in front of us and Brother

Ambrose selected his seat so that he could see clearly who won every race. Tom Banks sat on the end of our row and Brother Michael sat with a large group of teachers from the other schools in the VIP section of the stand.

The whole of the stand below where we were sitting was full of boys and girls, seated in alternate rows. Tom Banks told us that they did this to stop two boys' schools sitting together as this generally led to fighting.

Bernie grinned at the news. He said, 'That suits us down to the ground.' He pointed at a group of girls who were making their way up the stand to sit in the seats behind us. He sounded excited. 'It's them, John. It's the girls from the coach next to us.'

I looked eagerly along the line of approaching girls and soon spotted the two girls we were hoping to meet up with. There were about twenty-five girls in the group. The four grey-clad women who were chaperoning them were chivvying them along to their seats. Bernie attracted the girls' attention and pointed to the two seats directly behind us. They nodded and pushed their way along the line and claimed the two seats by slumping down on them.

One of the women shouted, 'Barbara and Jean, you're blocking our way. Move along further.' The two girls ignored her and the remainder of their group had to squeeze past their legs to get to their seats.

My heart was racing fifteen to the dozen. The girl sitting behind me had awakened all my sexual feelings and all I could think about was how I could get her alone. Nothing else in my life had any meaning; there was only this girl.

'Your one is called Barbara,' Bernie whispered in my ear. He chuckled quietly. 'Look around you. Everyone has the same idea as us.'

Boys and girls all over the stand were whispering to each other. Girls were giggling and boys were talking loudly, trying to impress them. The teachers were shouting instructions and getting nowhere. The sexual tension in the air was palpable and it was only relieved when the tannoy system crackled into life and a quivery male voice welcomed us all to Erith Stadium. Everyone was asked to rise and join in the National Anthem. 'God Save the Queen' was sung with exceptional gusto and on its conclusion a great cheer went up.

The tannoy system once again crackled into life and this time a much more assured and stern voice told us the plan for the day's activities. There were going to be three classes of races. The 12–14, the 14–16, and the over 16. Bernie and I were both in the second category and had to wait an hour or so while the younger boys and girls competed for their school's honour. We used our time well chatting non-stop to Barbara and Jean.

Barbara was fourteen years old and came from Battersea in South London. Her mother and father had been killed in November 1944 when an undetected, unexploded bomb had detonated and caused masonry from the house next door to fall on them. She had only been a baby at the time and had been put in an orphanage. She decided to run away when she was thirteen and tried to locate her uncle and aunt who lived in Southend. She couldn't find them and ended up living on the streets and begging for food. She was picked up by the police in London and prosecuted for running away from the orphanage and not attending school. She was given three years in an approved school in late December 1957.

Bernie's girl, Jean, came from Deptford in South-east London. She had run away from home when she was twelve because she was being used for sex by her mother's boyfriend. She had adapted well to living on the streets and had made quite a good living as a child prostitute. When she was picked up by the police in Hyde Park she was being looked after by a fifty-three-year-old Maltese pimp. She went to court on her fourteenth birthday, which was on 6 February 1958. She too was given three years' approved school.

Both girls spoke openly about sex. Jean was definitely more experienced but Barbara was more than willing to learn. They told us of the frustrations they had to endure being locked away in a girls-only environment. We laughed at their raunchy stories of escapades that went on in their school with various tradesmen. Two girls had actually become pregnant by a young bricklayer who had been working on a craft shop extension. He was married with two children and denied the offence but it had definitely been him. He was sacked from his job but he still sneaked back to the school of a night and carried on his affairs. He was eventually caught by the headmistress when she found him hiding in a shower room. He was stark naked at the time of his capture and was led away by the police wrapped in a blanket. The girls didn't know what happened to him as the case was still going on.

Jean told Bernie to try and meet her in the girls' toilets. She left her seat and shouted along the line to one of the women that she was off to the toilet. The woman nodded and said, 'Be back here in five minutes or I will come looking for you.' Jean hurried out of the stand and towards the toilets situated just inside the main entrance. Bernie winked at me and said, 'I'm off. Cover for me.'

'Where do you think you're going, Connors?' Brother Ambrose shouted.

Bernie held the front of his trousers and hopped from one leg to the other. 'To the toilet, Bro. I'm desperate. I think it might be nerves about running in front of all these people.' Everyone in the vicinity who heard Bernie's excuse laughed mockingly.

'Well, be quick about it,' Brother Ambrose said and stood up to look along the line at the rest of us. 'Nobody else goes until Connors is back. I'm only allowing you to go one at a time.'

Bernie hurried away and disappeared from sight. Barbara said to me quietly, 'I don't fancy the toilets. Shall we try and sneak back to the coaches?'

My voice suddenly deserted me. I wanted to say that I'd go anywhere in the world with her. I nodded my head and managed to say huskily, 'I can't go anywhere until Bernie's back.'

'I know,' she replied. 'I heard what that bloke said. We'll have to wait a few minutes after they get back so as it doesn't look too obvious.' She looked into my eyes enquiringly. 'Have you done it before? I've only done it a few times and I'm not that experienced.'

'I'm the same as you,' I lied. 'Just a few times.'

I looked up at the stadium clock and saw that Bernie had been gone nearly ten minutes. The woman who had given Jean only five minutes was engrossed in deep conversation with Brother Ambrose. She nodded her head and then tittered behind her hand. Brother Ambrose didn't know it but he was doing us all a big favour. The time moved on another seven minutes before Jean appeared at the bottom of the stairs and began her ascent. She sat down and smiled at Barbara. I looked anxiously for Bernie and was relieved when he came jogging up the stand with a Cheshire cat grin on his face.

The tannoy system crackled into life and the stern voice announced the start of the 14–16 races. Tom Banks and Brother Ambrose stood up and directed us all towards the changing rooms. I was gutted. I looked at Barbara and she mouthed the word 'later' to me. I felt better and smiled. I nodded my head and jogged down the stand in the direction of the changing areas.

Bernie seemed to be in a state of euphoria. He kept smiling inanely at me and chuckling to himself. I was longing to ask him how he had got on but it was impossible to do so with Brother Michael standing so close. Tom Banks was circulating amongst us and giving us all a large tablespoonful of glucose. We had been told by Brother Francis that glucose would give us extra energy and it would be our secret weapon to make us fitter than the rest of the competitors. Personally I would have preferred something to eat.

A young master from another school called out for the 100-yard runners. Peter Tingle looked nervous but pushed his way towards the entrance to the running track. He was a tall boy with an unruly mop of black hair and protruding ears. He had recently gone in front of the school governors and was due out on licence in a few days' time. Tom Banks and Brother Ambrose left the changing room and went into the stadium to get a good view of the proceedings. They were both standing at the trackside as the 100 yard runners dashed past them.

Brother Ambrose returned to where we were waiting for news of the race. He shook his head and said, 'He came second. The lad from Redhill won it.' There was a loud cheer from the Redhill boys and mumblings of discontent from the rest of us.

David Tate fared no better in the 220 yard race. Redhill won the race and Cobham came second. David Tate came in fifth and returned to the dressing room with a dejected look on his face.

Tom Banks told him that he'd lost because he had been too slow out of his starting blocks. He told Bernie: 'Learn from Tate's mistake. When the gun goes off, I want to see you come flying off the blocks.'

Bernie nodded.

The Redhill boys were shouting and cheering and boasting about their team's ability. One of the Guildford runners took out his dick and pissed in the big sports bag that contained Redhill's towels and washing kit. Everybody in the changing room, apart from the Redhill squad, burst into laughter and only the quick intervention of a group of masters stopped a mass brawl breaking out. The offending boy was given a swift clip around his ear by one of his minders and led away. He left the changing room to the sound of loud cheering.

I was still laughing about the bag incident when Tom Banks returned to the dressing room and gave us the thumbs up sign. Bernie had won his race. The whole of our team jumped up and down and shouted abuse at the Redhill team. We really enjoyed taking the piss out of them and Brother Ambrose had to shout loudly to restore some form of order. It was decided that the teams had to be separated as the rivalry and hostility could easily overflow and turn into outright violence. We were taken out of the changing room and relocated in separate areas in the centre plot of the stadium.

The area we were in gave us a good view of the running track and the main stand. It was easy to pick out the remainder of our school party. We had brought along twenty boys from the school to give us vocal support. They spotted us in the centre and were all on their feet, shouting out words of encouragement. We waved back at them with equal enthusiasm and cheered extra loudly when Andrew Devine lined up for the start of the 880-yard race.

The sound of the gun reverberated around the stadium and the runners sprinted off the line. I watched Devine as he jostled for a good position on the inside of the track when they came off the stagger. After the first lap he was in fourth place. They went past the main stand in a long strung-out line and a thunderous cheer went up from their supporters. The boy who was in second place pulled off the track clutching his side and it was obvious that he had a stitch. The rest of the runners went past him without a glance. Pain was etched on their faces and all of them were willing themselves onwards.

Devine was gaining on the two runners in front of him and as they came off the back straight he was level with them. The three of them came down the final 100-yard straight together with only half a yard between them. When they ran over the finishing line and broke the tape, we saw that Devine had won the race. We were all standing and cheering a Vincent's winner. Tom Banks applauded by clapping his hands together over his head. Brother Ambrose was smiling and nodding his head approvingly. Andrew Devine was lying face downwards on the grass by the side of the track trying to get his breath back.

Tom Banks walked Liam Donovan and me over to the starting line for the mile race. He said, 'Remember not to go off too fast. Run exactly how we practised back at school. Keep a steady pace and you'll win through in the end.' He patted us both on the back. 'Make sure you're not bullied into a bad position on the track. And good luck!'

We lined up on the starting line with fourteen other boys and waited for the starter. He lifted the gun and fired. We were off. Six of the boys went off at a suicidal pace and I am sure that any one of them could have won the 100-yard race. I was in last place directly behind Donovan. By the time we had finished the first lap there were only thirteen of us left in the race. Three of the early sprinters were lying on the grass in the centre of the track gasping for breath.

The second lap I always found was the hardest for me. I enjoyed running the mile race but for some reason I hated the second lap. The second time around the 440 yard track always seemed to me an endurance test and a battle for survival. I started counting the strides I was taking – 1, 2, 3, 4 ... 82, 83 .... The lap seemed endless and the numbers became larger. I had just reached 630 when a boy tripped over some way in front of me and I had to veer to avoid treading on him. We were running down the home straight for the second time and Donovan and I were still bringing up the rear.

We ran past Tom Banks who was standing by the side of the track and he smiled at us. 'Well done, lads,' he said. 'Keep it up.'

I had my second wind by the time we started running down the back straight of the third lap and I began to enjoy the race. The pace of the leaders was visibly dropping and Donovan and I were starting to catch up and overtake several of the other runners. By the time we had completed the third lap we were leading the race and a considerable gap had appeared between us and the rest of the field. We had not altered our pace since the race had begun.

It was now a private race between me and Donovan. I had never been further back than a stride's length behind him and as we approached the final 100 yards I pulled out and overtook him with very little effort. The move took him completely by surprise and by the time he started to respond I was 10 yards in front of him. I sprinted towards the tape and let out a scream of exaltation as my midriff pulled the tape and snapped it.

Donovan ran up behind me and slapped me on the shoulder. He said, 'That was a fucking great race. We killed the fucking lot of them.' I put my arm around his shoulder and squeezed him tightly, our grudge against each other after the fight over Cuddy momentarily forgotten. I didn't have time to say anything because Tom Banks and the entire team came bounding up to us shouting their congratulations. The Vincent's team had won the 14–16 cup and I knew that we would get our photograph on the recreation room wall. For some reason, that was really important to me.

'You've got your wish,' Bernie whispered. 'You're on the wall.'

We returned to our seats in the stand like conquering heroes. Our supporters were standing on their seats shouting out in unison, 'Vincent's are champions. Vincent's are champions.' Tom Banks signalled for them to be quiet and the chanting stopped. I looked in dismay at the empty seats behind us. Barbara, Jean and the rest of the girls had disappeared and my eyes frantically searched around for a glimpse of them.

Bernie pointed to a group of girls who were being ushered onto the grass in the centre of the track. He said, 'I think that's them.'

He was right, it was them and I could see Barbara waving up at me. I jumped on my seat and waved back.

Bernie and I cheered enthusiastically when Barbara and Jean ran their respective races. They tried hard but neither of them finished in the first three. Barbara came fifth in the 440-yard race and Jean came last in the 880-yard. They returned to the stand to Bernie's and my rapturous applause. They laughed loudly when Bernie managed to get all of our boys chanting their names.

Barbara touched me lightly on my shoulder and said, 'Shall we try to sneak away?'

My voice deserted me again so I just grinned and nodded my head.

She whispered: 'Meet me at the back door of my coach.' She stood up and signalled to her chaperone, who was once again chatting to Brother Ambrose. The woman nodded her head at Barbara and immediately returned to her conversation. Barbara smiled at me and hurried down the steps and out of my sight.

I stood up and squeezed my way along the row until I was standing next to Brother Ambrose. 'Is it OK if I go to the toilet, Bro? I think I've got a bit of an upset stomach.'

Brother Ambrose nodded. 'You may have strained yourself when you sprinted for the line. Try the toilet. It might work, but if it doesn't do a few gentle sit-ups to see if you've hurt your stomach.'

'I'll do that, Bro. Thank you.'

I hurried out of the stadium and into the parking area. I ran amongst the coaches until I suddenly came upon

Barbara standing behind one, smoking a cigarette. She smiled and offered me the cigarette. I took it from her and our fingers touched.

'Have a quick puff and put it out,' she said quietly. 'We haven't got much time.' I took one long hard pull on the cigarette and dropped it onto the floor. Barbara took my hand and pulled me gently towards her. I bent my head and very gently kissed her on the mouth. It was the first time I had ever kissed a girl and when her tongue probed an entry into my mouth I wasn't quite sure what I should do.

Before I could make up my mind she stopped kissing my mouth and started sucking on my neck. I tentatively moved my hand so it was resting on her breast and she took my hand and pushed it up under her blouse. By now I was so hard it was bursting out of my trousers and I reached my other hand down to lift up her skirt.

Suddenly we heard the sound of running footsteps. Bernie appeared at the back of the coach. 'They're all coming back,' he said. 'You haven't got time to do anything. They're right behind me.'

Barbara looked sadly into my eyes and suddenly kissed me passionately on my mouth. Her mouth opened wide and her tongue darted in and out of my mouth. Her breath was coming in short laboured gasps and she pressed her pelvis hard against me. Bernie yanked me away and pulled me around the side of the coach and out of sight.

'Where is your coach?' I heard Brother Michael ask.

There was a muffled reply and then the sound of a woman's voice. 'We were looking for you, Barbara. Where the hell have you been?'

Bernie half dragged me back to our coach and only stopped when we were standing by the front steps. He grinned at me. 'That was fucking close. I really thought they'd caught you.'

'I was just about to get a bit of tush, Bernie. Barbara has to be the sexiest and most beautiful girl in the world and I didn't even get to touch her tush.'

Other boys and girls were coming back to the coaches and there was lots of shouting from the staff as they tried to keep the different factions apart. A Redhill boy and a cute little girl of about thirteen started kissing by the back door of our coach. He had his hand underneath her skirt and was definitely playing with her tush. A female minder screamed out an order and dashed past us. The young girl paid no attention and had to be dragged away from the boy, who still had his hand down her knickers. Bernie was cheering wildly at the boy's antics and the female teacher took a swipe at him as she dragged the girl past us and back to her own coach.

'Let's go and see if it's safe to say goodbye to the girls,' Bernie suggested.

We hurried to the back of our coach and ran quickly across to the back of the girls' one. Bernie took a sneaky look along the side of the coach and when he saw it was all clear, signalled for me to follow. We crept along the side of the coach until we were under Jean and Barbara's window. He tapped gently and both girls looked out.

'Let John stand on your shoulders so he can kiss Barbara goodbye,' said Jean.

Bernie nodded and I climbed up and balanced precariously on his shoulders. Barbara smiled impishly, pulled her blouse open and pushed her chest against the open ventilation window so that one of her breasts was directly in reach of my mouth. I kissed it like a ravenous baby would suck on its mother's tit. I didn't have time to do anything else as

Bernie insisted that I return the compliment and let him climb on my shoulders so that he could get at Jean's breasts.

We both managed to do it twice before one of the grey-clad women spotted what was going on and slammed the window shut. We ran back to our coach and watched sadly as the girls' coach pulled out of the parking area.

Tom Banks walked down the aisle of the coach checking numbers. Satisfied that everyone was present, he nodded his head at the driver and our coach engine revved into life. The Home Office Championship was now officially over and we were on our way back to Vincent's. I leant my head against the window and closed my eyes. I could clearly see in my mind Barbara's smiling face and feel the magic of her breast in my hand. I knew that these images would reappear in my mind every night when I climbed into bed and that I would curse my ill fortune at not getting to touch the magical kingdom called tush. I fell into a beautiful sleep where everything happened and all hidden places were revealed. I opened my eyes again just as the coach pulled through the gates at Vincent's.

Barbara was my very first sexual encounter and from that point onwards when I masturbated I often fantasised about having sex with her. Bernie and I would speak about the girls, yet we both knew that we would never see them again. Because Bernie had a girlfriend at home he offered to try and fix me up with his twin sister.

'She's definitely not a virgin, John,' he said. 'I know for a fact she's had sex with quite a few boys. I reckon you'd have a good chance of getting in there.'

So I fantasised about her as well and would sometimes tease Bernie that the stains on my sheet were from the night I had just spent stuck up his sister.

Chapter 16

In August 1959 it had been nearly eight months since I had seen my mother and family. I had lost five days of my summer holiday but I was looking forward to the nine days I was going to spend with them. Mum had written to me every week and somehow managed to send me a five shilling postal order with every letter. I was thrilled to receive the money but couldn't help worrying that she had beggared herself to get it. I spent very little of it and had over eight pounds in my school account to bring home with me. The money felt good in my pocket as I walked towards my house.

I was excited as I rang the front door bell and heard rushing footsteps. The door was flung open and I was enveloped in my mother's arms. She squeezed me so hard that if I had been younger the breath would have left my body.

'He's home. He's home,' she was shrieking for everyone to hear. I hugged her back and lifted her off her feet and swung her round like a spinning top. She squealed with laughter and disengaged herself from my grip, then stepped backwards, her eyes appraising me from head to toe. Happiness shone out of her eyes and I couldn't help hugging her again. I was suddenly surrounded by two of my sisters and my grandmother. They were all laughing and my grandmother was trying to reach me to give me a welcoming kiss. I kissed her and let them all lead me into Gran's living room.

'Why are your trousers so short?' asked Jennifer, my youngest sister.

Everyone looked at my trousers and I was embarrassed. I hadn't had any new clothes for over a year and in that time I had sprouted another three inches and filled out considerably. When I put my clothes on to come home I had struggled with the buttons on my shirt and my trousers definitely looked as though they'd had a row with my shoes as they were at least an inch above my ankles. I kept my jacket undone as I had lost a button trying to do it up and the bottoms of the sleeves were well above my wrists. Bernie had lent me a pair of his shoes as I couldn't squeeze my feet into my own.

Mum saw that I was embarrassed. 'He hasn't been home for ages and in that time he has grown into a young man.' She pushed me into a chair and perched on my knee, hiding my appearance from the rest of the family. 'As soon as he's had something to eat I'm taking him out to get him some new clothes that fit him.'

'I've got some money, Mum. I saved a lot of the money you sent me.'

She smiled and kissed me on my forehead. 'That money was sent for you to use,' she said very quietly. 'To help you have a better time. You can spend it when you go out over the next week or so. I saved up all the keep money your sisters have given me since they started work. There's more than enough to buy you something to wear.'

The door to Gran's room suddenly opened and my father stood framed in the doorway.

'I'm trying to get some sleep and all I can hear is screaming and laughter coming from in here,' he said angrily. He was halfway into the room before he saw me with my mother on my knee. 'What the hell is he doing home?' he snarled.

I eased her off my knee and stood up, making sure that I was positioned between them. 'I'm home for nine days on holiday. I won't come near your fucking stupid television or you. I'll stay out of your way. You make sure you stay out of mine.' I put my arm around Mum's shoulder. 'And, if I were you, I'd keep my hands to myself while I'm at home.'

For several seconds he stood staring at me. 'I suppose you think you're a tough guy now,' he sneered. 'Take a look in the mirror. You look like a clown.'

I took a step forward and laughed contemptuously as he backed away. 'You look in the fucking mirror,' I retorted. 'You look like chicken shit to me.'

He turned around and stomped out of the room, slamming the door so hard it made Gran's ornaments wobble precariously on the mantelpiece. I listened as his footsteps went back up the stairs.

Mum's relief that nothing violent had happened was evident. She took me by the arm and sat me down at Gran's table.

'I'll go and get you something to eat while you tell the others about all the things you've done since the last time you saw them,' she said and, kissing me again on my forehead, hurried off into the kitchen. As I watched her leave I noticed how much older she looked than the last time I had seen her. Her hair was greyer and the lines in her face had become more pronounced. I closed my eyes to shut out the image and prayed quietly that the evil bastard lying in bed upstairs would drop dead.

I checked my appearance in the mirror and was definitely pleased with what I saw. My mother had bought all my clothes but had let me choose them. I was wearing a pair of light-blue jeans, a white T-shirt, a short black leather jacket and a pair of black suede chukka-boots. I had modelled myself on the clothes that Bernie wore as I had always envied the way he looked when he went home. I strutted into the living room and smiled at my mother.

She laughed. 'I can't believe how you've grown up. You've chosen to dress really modern and it suits you.'

She was wearing a flowered print dress and a new pair of sandals she had bought at the same time as my clothes. While she went to the kitchen to make tea, I relaxed comfortably on our living room sofa, puffing contentedly on a cigarette. Suddenly I heard a great crash of falling crockery and a distinctive sob. I rushed into the kitchen and found Dad pushing Mum's face down into the sink. Without thinking, I grabbed a dirty saucepan from the draining board and smashed it into the centre of his face. He let go of my mother and slipped over backwards onto the floor. I kicked him viciously in his ribs and watched him double up in pain.

Before I could do anything else Mum grabbed me by my arm and pulled me out of the room. Her nose was bleeding and the blood was dripping down her chin onto her lovely new print dress. I broke free from her grip and rushed back into the kitchen. My father was struggling to get back up off the floor and I noticed that the hit in the face with the saucepan had broken his glasses and had given him a large swelling over his left eye. I stood over him menacingly and said, 'The next time you hit Mum I'll really do a job on you. I'm not the same boy I was when you put me inside and I'm more than your match now.'

I watched him warily as he struggled to his feet. We stood facing each other for several seconds until he staggered over to the sink and inspected the damage done to his face in the small mirror hanging above the taps. He tentatively touched the swelling over his eye and then turned to face me. His eyes betrayed his hatred. He looked over my shoulder to where Mum was standing behind me and said, 'Are you proud of your precious son now? He's turned into a vicious thug. Look what he's done to my glasses.' He held out his broken glasses for Mum to take but she totally ignored his outstretched hand.

I couldn't believe my ears. 'At least I hit a man and not a woman. You're a gutless piece of shit and deserved everything you got. You're no better than those cunts in Vincent's.'

'At least I don't use disgusting language in front of them like you do.'

I shook my head. 'No, you'd rather punch them in the face and make out you're some sort of hard case. Well, you're not. You're a nasty, wicked old man and I hope you die so my mum can have some happiness in her life.'

He stepped past me and out of the room. As he put on his work coat he said loudly, 'I'll be writing to your school and telling them how you call them disgusting names. They'll know how to deal with you. You won't be so brave then.'

I laughed loudly. 'They frighten me as much as you do. All the Irish are wankers and De Montfort and his bunch of arseholes are the biggest wankers of all. So do what you fucking like.'

I heard the front door slam and knew that he was gone. I put my arm around Mum's shoulder and led her into the living room. The great day we had had was now a fading memory and we were back into our normal way of life. She was softly weeping into her handkerchief and Jennifer was standing by the door looking petrified. I'd wanted to get back at Dad and be able to protect Mum since I was a young boy, but once I'd done it the satisfaction was somehow hollow.

Fuck him, I thought.

The next few days I stayed close to home as Mum wouldn't go out sporting the bruises of her latest altercation with my father. The atmosphere in the house was tense and I waited listening by the living room door every time she went into the kitchen.

I heard him moving around the house but he never came into the room where I was and that was OK by me. I worried about her all the time. She had to be in his company when she was preparing meals and my ears strained to catch every noise. I hated this way of life. It was worse than Vincent's.

Jennifer stayed close to me and Mum and looked nervous whenever one of us left the room. She was only nine years old but I realised that she was suffering as much mental torture as my mother. How many times she must have seen or heard violence in our house didn't bear thinking about. I tried to reassure her that nothing was going to happen while I was at home but she still looked a nervous wreck. I decided that I would take her out to the pictures and give her some respite from her miserable life.

The trip to the pictures was a success and Jennifer talked excitedly about the film all the way home. Because she had enjoyed herself so much I promised to take her again in a few days' time. When we arrived home I was relieved to find Mum busily preparing tea and looking untroubled. Today was turning into the best day of my holiday.

I had started reading *David Copperfield* and every night Dickens would draw me into his imaginative world. I loved Dickens novels and although it took him twenty words to say something that could have been said just as easily in five, I was an avid reader. All his characters lived in my mind: 'umble' Uriah Heep made my flesh crawl and irresponsible Mr Macawber became one of my favourites. While I was lost in reading Dickens, all my troubles vanished and it was as if my father didn't exist. I briefly thought about how wonderful it would be if I could just read and read and never need to be aware what was going on around me.

When I finally put my book down, I couldn't sleep. I was aware of every small sound in the house and could even discern Mum's gentle snoring coming from her bedroom. I must have dozed off for a while as I suddenly woke with a start. In my confused state I thought I was back at Vincent's and Jimmy Wilkinson was assaulting me again. I screamed and began thrashing my legs around and it was only when my mother rushed into the room to see if I was OK that I fully regained my senses. Sweat was pouring down my face and body and the bottom sheet was cold and wet.

'What's the matter, son? Are you all right?' She wrapped me in a comforting hug and my fears dissipated like mist on a sunny day. 'You've just had a bad dream. You're safe now.'

Safe. I will never feel safe again. Wilkinson had made sure of that. I clung to her and said, 'I'm fine, Mum. It was just a stupid dream.'

She pushed me gently back down into my bed and kissed me. 'Do you want me to stay with you until you drop off to sleep?'

I shook my head. 'Go back to bed, Mum. I'm not a baby.'

I listened as the house settled back down and once again I could hear gentle snoring coming from Mum's room. I knew that I would get very little sleep as I had suffered this dream so many times. It always left me wide awake as I battled in my mind with my shame and humiliation. Tonight was no different and I was still awake when Mum got out of bed in the morning.

Two days later Jennifer was pestering me to take her to the pictures again. As we left the house, a group of lads aged between twelve and fifteen were playing football in the road. They stopped playing as Jennifer and I walked past. I had known two or three of the older boys when I had been in St Gregory's and noticed how they smirked to each other as we walked past. Paul Hurley, my biggest tormenter in those days, who had left St Gregory's and was now at St Benedict's High School, said loudly, 'I bet you he's still wearing girl's knickers under his trousers.'

I went cold. It was like the pages of time had been turned back and I was in the classroom again. I stopped walking and turned to look at him.

'Be careful!' Jennifer warned me in a whisper. 'They'll beat you up.'

I laughed and told her that a St Benedict's boy couldn't hurt even the youngest of Vincent's boys.

Hurley was grinning and enjoying heaping further misery onto my shoulders. I strolled casually over to where he was standing and looked into his eyes. I said very quietly, 'I'm not the same silly little boy I was in Gregory's. I think you want to give me an apology.'

His grin got bigger and he looked at the other lads and laughed. He reminded me of all the other bullies I had encountered over the last year or so. I smiled back at him and like a serpent's strike my left hand shot out and grabbed him by his windpipe. His face contorted into a grimace as I pushed and shoved him by his throat towards a holly bush alongside one of the houses. With all my strength I shoved his face deep into the depths of that prickly mass of leaves and branches.

When I released him my hand was covered in scratches from the barbs I had shoved his head through. He screamed in agony as he tried to disentangle his head from the bush that held him prisoner. I looked at the other lads and noticed they had all backed away and were looking at me with fear in their eyes. I smiled. I knew that it would be a long time before any of them ever passed another derisory comment in my direction. I took hold of Jennifer's hand and carried on down the road.

When we returned from the pictures I was greeted by the sight of Paul Hurley and his mother sitting in our living room. His face had several deep scratch marks on it and he looked a sorry sight. Mrs Hurley stood up as I entered the room and just for a moment I thought she was going to hit me. She pointed at her son's face and shouted loudly, 'Look what you've done to Paul's face. I've a good mind to call the police.'

Mum was visibly upset. 'Why did you do it, John?' she asked. 'Why did you hurt him so nastily?'

'You tell them, Jennifer,' I said. 'Tell them who started it.'

Jennifer related the earlier little fracas and left out no details. While she was speaking I kept my eyes on Mrs Hurley and noticed that her expression changed when she heard how her precious little boy had taunted me as I walked past. I saw her glance in her son's direction. At the end of Jennifer's account she looked apologetically at Mum.

'I don't condone bullying,' she said, 'But I'm sure Paul is sorry about what he said. He must have meant it as a joke.'

I shook my head. 'It was no joke. He meant every word. When I was at Gregory's I had to wear my sister's old knickers as my mum couldn't afford underpants for me. He and his friends made my life a misery when they discovered what I was wearing and he tried to do the same again today. The only difference today was that I've grown up since then and made him pay for trying to make me look stupid.'

Mrs Hurley gestured for her son to stand up. 'Before we go,' she said, 'you're going to say sorry to John.'

He shook his head angrily and ran out of the room. I heard the front door open and close.

'I'm sorry about that,' she said. 'I'll get his father to deal with him when I get home.' She gave me a thin smile and hurried after her boy.

I looked at Mum to gauge her reaction to it all. 'Just like you told me to, Mum. I don't get bullied. I fight back.'

She came across the room and hugged me. 'I'm sorry about making you wear knickers when you were younger.'

I laughed. 'That's a long time ago. It really doesn't matter.'

I reached for Dickens. It was time to shut out the day and go back in time and read about other people's misfortunes. I slumped into my armchair and opened my book.

The next three days passed without incident and much to my delight I didn't see any more of my father. Mum was trying to be cheerful but I knew that she was dreading the moment when I had to go back to Vincent's. At every opportunity she would kiss me on my forehead or stroke my arm. I could see the sadness behind her eyes and wished desperately that I could have stayed with her. As I was preparing to leave she could keep her feelings in no longer and started to cry. I hugged her tightly and found that I too had tears streaming down my cheeks.

I walked slowly away from home and kept turning around to see Mum standing forlorn by our back gate blowing me kisses. I knew she was still crying. I blew her a kiss and ran round the corner so that I wouldn't be tempted to go running back to her. I looked up to the heavens and said a silent prayer to Jesus to keep her safe.

The bus journey to Ealing Broadway Station took very little time and before long I was getting onto the Dartford train at Charing Cross. I settled myself comfortably into a corner seat in my carriage and opened my bag to take out my book. Sitting on top of my belongings was a brown paper package. I wondered when Mum had slipped it in without me seeing it. I pulled it out and carefully opened it.

There in all its glory was a beautiful leather-bound copy of Dickens's *Great Expectations*. I opened the first page and read my mother's inscription. It said simply *'Thank you for a wonderful holiday. Lots of love, Mum.'* Tears sprang to my eyes as I thought of how much it must have cost her and how little she had. Also in the package were four one-ounce packets of Golden Virginia tobacco and three packets of cigarette papers. Nobody has ever had a better mother than me.

I was still feeling slightly morose as I walked up Temple Hill and back into the grounds of St Vincent's. I wondered when I would see my family again. I would have liked to see them on the next first Sunday but I knew that would never happen. I sneaked into the chapel and hid my tobacco before reporting back to the duty brother.

It was Brother Arnold and as soon as I saw him it was as though my holiday had never happened. I let him search my bag then wandered out into the yard and across to the recreation room.

Chapter 17

Bernie and I were partners at Vincent's and being partners was like being married without the sex. What it
amounted to was a solemn agreement that no matter what
happened you would share everything and defend your
partner if he was involved in a confrontation with more
than one person. Most of the boys in the school had this sort
of relationship with their best friend and it was treated as a
solemn oath. Bernie and I very seldom had a serious argument about anything. I would get pissed off with him when
I saw him take a smack and not hit back, but I think in all
honesty that the thought of being caned frightened him. I
never insulted him by asking but I am quite certain that was
the case. As well as that, he disagreed with my tactic of
taking on the bullies; he thought life was easiest if you kept
your head down and avoided confrontation whenever
possible, but that just wasn't in my nature.

One day Bernie was taking a roll-up out of his sock and
rolling it expertly between his fingers until it was in perfect
shape. He lit it and sucked in a lungful of smoke, blowing
the smoke downwards in a thin blue stream. He looked
furtively around the yard to see if he had been spotted, but
Brother Michael was looking in the opposite direction. He
was about to take another long drag when suddenly he was

punched in the face and the roll-up taken out of his hand. Standing in front of him were Jimmy Fuller and Trevor Hicks. Hicks was smirking.

I had seen the whole thing as I walked towards Bernie to meet him for our midday smoke before dinner. Both Fuller and Hicks were arseholes who loved to throw their weight around with the younger boys. I didn't much fancy fighting either of them as they could definitely look after themselves and were more than a year older than me but I gritted my teeth and kicked Hicks just above his ankle. He let out a yell and spun to face me. He grinned when he saw it was me.

'Fenton,' he said, 'you're such a wanker.' His left hand flashed out and punched me straight in the centre of my face. I tried to kick him again but he easily avoided it. However, he didn't avoid my right fist that was thrown at him in the same motion of the kick. It landed right in the middle of his lips and I knew that he would have cuts on the inside of his mouth. He was now annoyed to the degree of being reckless and ran at me with both arms flailing. I retreated under the barrage and was relieved when Brother Michael grabbed Hicks and pushed him against the wall. He held Hicks tightly by his neck and signalled for me to come closer. I cautiously walked forward and received a hard slap around my left ear.

'You'll both see Brother De Montfort later.' Brother Michael sounded slightly out of breath. He pushed Hicks away. 'Get over to the other side of the yard. Don't you dare come over this side.' He switched his attention to me. 'And you stay over here.'

I watched as Hicks sauntered away and Brother Michael took up his position again in the centre of the yard. I didn't keep an eye on Fuller, though, and he walked up on my blind side and smacked a perfect punch into the side of my head. It really hurt me and I staggered sideways. Fuller jumped on me and luckily we both fell on the floor. This movement gave me the time I needed to clear my head and I managed to get one of my arms around his neck and pull his head underneath my arm. He was much stronger than me and was pulling his head loose from my grip when Brother Michael separated us. Again, we got the customary slap around the ear and were sent to different locations in the yard.

'Why the fuck did you kick Hicks?' Bernie asked. 'It was only a roll-up and now you're going to get caned and more than likely a kicking from those arseholes.' He took another rollup out of his sock and lit it. He handed it to me after taking two quick puffs. 'You're going to have to be careful when we go for lunch. Either of those bastards may have you.'

I touched the swelling on my cheek from Fuller's punch. It was very tender and I knew that it would turn into a nasty bruise. Bernie was eyeing me in bewilderment. I said, 'I can't choose who I fight. I promised myself that I will fight anyone who tries to bully us.' I spat on the floor. 'I know I stand no chance against Fuller and Hicks but I also know that the cane will hurt them as much as it hurts me.'

Bernie shook his head. 'It seems stupid to me. Why get yourself the cane just so they get the cane as well?'

'Because it hurts them. Because they'll know that every time they bully us they will get hurt.'

'But you're getting hurt twice. Once by them and once by De Montfort.'

'Who gives a fuck, Bernie?' I couldn't understand Bernie's reluctance to look after himself, just as he couldn't understand my attitude. 'I won't be bullied by arseholes any more.'

The whistle blew for lunch. I cautiously made my way to the washroom to clean myself up. I didn't see Hicks lurking in one of the cubicles as I was too busy watching Fuller walking towards me. Suddenly I was grabbed by Hicks from behind and thrown face downwards towards the cubicle floor. The side of my face crashed into the top of the porcelain bowl and I felt a blinding pain in my mouth. I knew that I was kicked several times in the body but because of the pain in my mouth I felt nothing.

A short time later I found myself alone and kneeling on the floor. I stood up carefully and made my way over to one of the sinks. Looking in the mirror, I saw that the side of my jaw had a huge purple swelling on it. I pushed my tongue around the inside of my mouth and flinched as it encountered a very sharp broken tooth. All the nerves were exposed and it was excruciating when cold air reached them.

I staggered back into the yard and approached Brother Ambrose, who had just come out of the recreation room.

'I've had an accident, Bro,' I said awkwardly, my speech slurred from the swelling in my mouth. 'I've broken a tooth.'

The pain must have shown on my face as without another word he took me to matron and she immediately arranged for me to be taken to the dentist in Dartford. An hour later I returned to the school with a completely numb jaw and an empty cavity where the tooth used to be. That dentist never did fillings or repair work; any problems with a tooth and he yanked it out. My face was swollen and out of shape and I had several bruises on my body from where Hicks and Fuller had kicked me. I looked around the recreation room and saw the two arseholes sitting on a bench, laughing at the state I was in. There wasn't a visible mark on them and I was bruised and hurting all over.

Bernie came over and shook his head. 'I told you that it wasn't worth it. You stood no chance against them and look how you've ended up. You're fucking stupid.'

I walked away. I couldn't listen to Bernie's chicken-shit talk. I headed over to the far wall and sat down on an empty bench. Hicks and Fuller immediately came over to where I was sitting and stood arrogantly in front of me.

'How much baccy have you got, Fenton? We want it.'

I stood up and fumbled in my pocket as though I was searching for something. The stupid arseholes thought that they'd beaten me and were grinning all over their faces. They were caught completely unawares when I suddenly crashed my forehead into the centre of Hicks's smiling face. There was a crunching noise and blood streamed out of both nostrils. Fuller immediately jumped on me but as we grappled I managed to get two fingers inside his mouth and rip his cheek outwards. He screamed in pain and pulled away from me. Tom Banks and Brother Arnold rushed over to break it up and the three of us were marched to De Montfort's office.

Forty-five minutes later I returned to the recreation room with the pain of the cane still fresh in my mind. I waited patiently for Hicks and Fuller to return from De Montfort's and smiled in satisfaction as I saw the pain on their faces from their ordeal. I also grinned at Hicks's swollen nose and Fuller's scratched and swollen cheek.

Bernie was wrong. As far as I was concerned at that point in time, it was definitely worth it and, even though you could say I came off worst, I was happy with the result.

'We will have no Jack Spots in this school,' De Montfort's voice whined.

Jack Spot was a notorious East London gangster infamous for his brutal reign over the London underworld.

'I will not tolerate violence of any description and especially the use of razors.'

We all stood listening impassively as he ranted on about a bit of fun that had somehow got out of control. Two boys, Jack Gardner and Dave Stocker, who were good friends, had been joking about who would have the last square of Palm Toffee left in the bar they had been sharing. Gardner had said light-heartedly that they should fight for it. Stocker readily agreed as long as they fought with razors.

Both boys had leapt to their feet and produced the little curved razors we used for sharpening pencils, which they brandished jokingly at each other. They both jumped around pretending to slash each other. By accident, both boys slashed down at the same time and Stocker's razor cut Gardner's hand. Gardner let out a yelp and dropped his razor. Both boys looked at the two-inch cut on Gardener's hand that was bleeding quite profusely. Stocker held up his arm in a triumphant salute, took the last square of Palm Toffee and popped it in his mouth.

Everybody laughed except Gardner. He picked up the razor he had dropped and slashed down hard across Stocker's arm. Stocker jumped backwards like a scalded cat and stared at his bleeding arm. The laughing stopped as the two boys eyed each other warily and we knew that this was no longer a play fight. They circled each other like a pair of gladiators in the Coliseum, both seeking a weakness in the other's defence. Stocker took a wild kick at Gardner's leg and got cut on his knee when Gardner parried with a downward slash of his razor. This cut seemed to send Stocker into a wild frenzy and he ran at Gardner, slashing wildly at anywhere his razor could reach. Gardner fell over under the onslaught and rolled sideways to get away from Stocker's flailing arm. He managed to get to his feet but not before he had sustained several superficial cuts to his arms and chest.

Brother Arnold and Mr Lawson crashed into the midst of the fight and brought it to an abrupt end. I watched in horror as Brother Arnold systematically beat Gardner until he lay in a mangled heap at his feet. He looked down at the prostrate body and kicked him viciously in his ribs. He then went across to where Stocker was being held by Lawson and punched him hard in the face. Stocker sank to his knees and Arnold kneed him in the face.

Now both boys were lying in a dazed and bloody state on the floor and Arnold stood over them, swaying from side to side and panting slightly from his exertions. I couldn't stand it any longer so I went over to the door that led to the infirmary and banged on it hard until Matron appeared. I pointed to where the two boys were lying and she hurried out to attend to them.

Brother Arnold looked far from happy at my actions – he'd obviously wanted to do a bit more damage. I turned my head away and went to sit with Bernie, who was watching Matron trying to organise a group of boys to carry Gardner and Stocker to her surgery. They all disappeared through the infirmary door and slowly the room returned to normal.

Brother De Montfort arrived in the recreation room ten minutes later and lined us all up for his lecture.

It must have gone on for about twenty minutes and Jack Spot was mentioned at least ten times. De Montfort kept on about how it was his job to make sure that we understood what was right and what was wrong. I couldn't help wondering if he was going to give the same lecture to Brother Arnold. I had developed a hatred for Arnold that I knew I would carry for the rest of my life. The man was pure evil. I fervently believed in God and the final Day of Judgement. I knew that one day Arnold would face his final judgement and be given an express ride to Hell. My God would make sure that justice was done.

The next morning, when I went to chapel, I prayed hard that Brother Arnold would meet with a serious accident or illness and die a painful death. I watched him come to the front of the chapel and kneel to receive Holy Communion, his ugly face pious-looking, his hands clasped together in prayer and I wanted to kick him in the head. Then I looked at Gardner and Stocker and flinched at the sight of their bruised and battered faces. They were due to see De Montfort this morning and take a visit to the small dormitory. I wondered if Arnold would stand by the door enjoying watching each boy's misery as they were caned.

Father Delaney leaned forward and whispered in my ear. 'Concentrate, John, I'm returning to the altar for the Ablutions. You've missed two responses.'

'Sorry, Father,' I replied quietly. It took a great deal of concentration to finish the responses as my mind was still full of the horrid images of the day before. I was glad when at last I said, *'Deo Gratias'* and the Mass ended.

I sat quietly in the vestry staring sightlessly out of the window that looked over the small graveyard. Arnold's beating of the two boys had left me with an unsettled mind. I needed to speak to Father Delaney and get some advice.

I think that he had guessed I wanted to speak to him, as he returned to the vestry with two cups of tea in his hands. He handed me one and sat down in the seat next to me. His eyes scanned the graveyard as he spoke to me. 'Well, John, what is troubling you?'

His eyes met mine and his expression softened. 'You can tell me anything. It will go no further than this room.' He pointed towards the door that led into the chapel and added: 'Or, we can go into the confessional box.'

'That won't be necessary, Father,' I said. I felt a little awkward and looked down at the floor. 'I don't think I want to serve Mass any more.'

Father Delaney was surprised. 'Why's that, John? You must have a good reason to suddenly decide that you no longer want to serve God.'

'I would never refuse to serve God, Father. You should know that.' I must have sounded sincere as Father Delaney put his arm affectionately around my shoulder. 'It's just that it seems blasphemous to me to help you serve communion when I think evil of some of the people who are receiving it.'

Father Delaney sat back in his chair and stared up at the ceiling. He shook his head slowly, trying to work out the problem. 'Are you willing to tell me the people you're thinking evil about?'

I nodded. 'It's mainly just one person, Father. It's Brother Arnold. I hate the man.'

Father Delaney nodded. He didn't seem surprised by my revelation. 'How long have you felt like this?'

'Since the first time I saw him, Father.' I closed my eyes remembering how he had beaten a boy for fighting on my first day in the school. 'He enjoys hurting us, Father, and I'm sure Jesus will send him straight to Hell when he dies.'

'You don't know that, John. You may be right, you may be wrong. It's not up to you to decide.' He took a set of rosary beads from his pocket and rolled them between his fingers. 'Maybe Brother Arnold does not see things in the same light as you do. Maybe he thinks that the punishment he dishes out is justified and that he is helping the boys to become better people. I find it hard to believe that he enjoys hurting the boys. I think you're misreading the situation.'

I shook my head vehemently. 'I've watched him punch and kick boys since the first day I arrived eighteen months ago. It doesn't matter what you've done wrong; he hits with the same nastiness. I've watched his eyes and he definitely enjoys what he does. You must have seen it as well, Father. Haven't you?'

'No, John, I haven't.' Father Delaney lit a cigarette and watched the smoke drifting towards the half-open window. 'I haven't witnessed any of Brother Arnold's punishment beatings but I'm certain that they can't be as bad as you say and,' he paused to take a puff on his cigarette, 'I'm sure he wouldn't take any pleasure in them.'

I couldn't believe what I was hearing. I trusted Father Delaney more than anyone else and he was taking Brother Arnold's side. 'You're just protecting him because he's a Brother.'

Father Delaney shook his head. 'I wouldn't do that, John. If I believed that Brother Arnold was taking delight out of hurting you boys I would personally report him to the school principals. You must believe that.'

I did believe him. He had been a good friend to me and I trusted him implicitly. 'Can't you at least stop him from taking Holy Communion?' I said. 'He really annoys me with his saintly looks. I know in my heart he will burn in Hell.'

Father Delaney laughed quietly. 'Of course I can't stop him taking the Blessed Sacrament. What would I say to him? I'm sorry, Brother, but my altar boy doesn't think you worthy?' He took another long puff on his cigarette. 'I promise you that I'll keep my eyes open and if what you say is true, I will deal with it.'

Father Delaney patted me gently on my shoulder and stood up. 'Don't fill your heart with hatred. If you think Brother Arnold is doing wrong, pray for him.'

I smiled weakly. 'I'll try, Father, but I don't think I'm that forgiving.'

Father Delaney opened his cigarette packet and dropped a cigarette clumsily on the floor. 'I love your honesty, John. There is always something refreshing in our conversations.' He pointed at the cigarette on the floor. 'Dispose of that before you leave the chapel.'

I watched him walk away, still fingering the beads on his rosary, and I could just discern the words he was muttering: 'Hail Mary, full of grace.' I picked up the cigarette and lit it. All I could do now was hope that Father Delaney would see Arnold committing one of his frequent acts of brutality. I suddenly remembered that he hadn't mentioned anything about me giving up serving mass. He had skipped over it and ended up ignoring it.

I smiled. He had no intention of letting me stop being his altar boy. I stubbed out the cigarette, put the butt in the thurible and walked quickly out of the chapel, closing the door quietly behind me before I entered the school-yard.

It was mid-October 1959 and the autumn evenings were bringing in a taste of winter with cold winds and colder rain. Bernie had brought back a crib board from his last home visit and we had picked up the rudimentary skills of cribbage. We spent most evenings engrossed in our game and paid scant attention to anything else. Our game was interrupted one evening by Brother Michael. He came over to the bench at which we were sitting and said, 'We are starting ballroom dancing classes on Monday and Friday nights. Are you interested in joining?'

Bernie looked up from our board and said, 'Who's taking the classes, Bro?'

'A lady dance instructor from the local college. She'll only come if we have at least twenty boys attending.'

Bernie winked at me. 'How many have you got so far, Bro?'

Brother Michael looked embarrassed. 'None yet, but once somebody volunteers I am sure I will get more.'

Bernie nodded his head. He said loudly for the boys on the next bench to hear, 'OK Bro, count me and John in. We could do with a bit of female teaching.'

Brother Michael was relieved. He strode purposely away writing our names into his notepad.

I looked at Bernie with disbelief. 'Why the fuck did you volunteer us for that?'

Bernie grinned cheekily. 'We're bound to practise dancing with girls from the college. We might be in for a bit of tush. Tell Pete Boyle and Taffy Jenkins to put their names down. It'll be a good laugh.'

Pete and Taffy looked at me as if I'd lost all my marbles. 'Why the fuck would I want to prance round the classroom like a poof?'

'Bernie reckons that we're bound to dance with girls from the college. He thinks we stand a great chance of getting a bit of tush.' I smiled. 'Or have you two turned queer?'

They laughed. 'You'd better be right,' Taffy said. 'If I volunteer for a load of crap, I'll hold you responsible.'

'No, we'll all hold Bernie responsible. It's his idea.'

Friday evening arrived and Brother Michael led us in an orderly line across the yard and into the brightly lit classroom. He'd got the twenty boys he'd wanted. Bernie pushed his way to the front so that he would be first through the door. We followed him like lambs to the slaughter. I felt very self-conscious as I stepped through the door into the classroom. All the desks had been removed and the chairs were spaced out along the walls. In the centre of the floor stood a slim, elegant woman in her mid-thirties, who was appraising us with lovely hazel eyes. She gestured for us to sit in the chairs. Brother Michael took a seat just inside the door so that he could watch all of us from where he sat.

'Good evening, boys,' she said confidently.

Without any prompting we said in unison, 'Good evening, Miss.'

She smiled, showing gleaming white teeth. 'My name is Mrs Lloyd and I am going to be your dance instructor. I was pleased when I was approached by your headmaster to teach you boys the art of being able to dance properly. You are nearly all young men and it won't be long until you all have girlfriends. Every girl enjoys dancing and wants a boyfriend who knows how to dance. I hope that at the end of my lessons you will all have the confidence and ability to stand up and dance at any venue, whether it's an official ball or a local hop.'

Pete Boyle let out a snort of laughter. 'I can't imagine you, Miss, at any local hop.'

'Thank you, but let me assure you that I've been to plenty.' She chuckled. 'In fact I met my husband at a local hop.' She walked over to a record player that had been placed on the front table and switched it on. She smiled at us again. 'I'd like to start by teaching you the waltz. I've chosen a modern song that has recently been in the charts and which you may have all heard. It's by Jim Reeves and it's called "He'll Have To Go".'

'Where's all the girls?' Taffy whispered to me. 'Dancing with her will be like dancing with my old lady.'

I shrugged my shoulders and looked across at Bernie. He was silently laughing at us and swayed his shoulders in time with the music. I mouthed the word 'wanker' at him and he laughed aloud, which got him a disapproving look from Brother Michael.

Mrs Lloyd stopped the music and said, 'I'd like a volunteer to stand up and be my dance partner.' She looked around hopefully, and Pete, Taffy and I pointed over to where Bernie was grinning.

'He knows how to dance, Miss,' Pete said. 'He told us before we came in.'

Bernie's face was a treat. He looked horrified as Mrs Lloyd reached for his hand and led him into the centre of the room. All the boys were enjoying his obvious discomfort and laughed openly at the redness in his cheeks.

Pete said laughing, 'That'll teach the wanker.'

'The first thing I'll show you is how to hold your partner.' She looked at Bernie and said, 'Put your right arm around my waist and rest your right hand gently against the small of my back. Take my right hand and hold it firmly in your left hand. My right arm should be slightly away from my body and our hands should be at shoulder height.' She guided Bernie's hands and arms into position and told us to memorise the way they were standing.

We all nodded our heads as if we were past masters of the delicacies of dance.

She smiled and said, 'Now split into twos and take up this position in the centre of the room. I'll come to each couple in turn and make sure that you're standing properly.'

None of us moved. I looked at Pete Boyle, sheer horror written on my face.

'Did she say we've got to select one of us for a partner?' I said. 'She must be having a laugh. There's no way I'm dancing with any of this lot. I'm not a poof.'

Pete and Taffy nodded their heads in agreement. 'That's enough of this shit,' said Pete. 'I'm out of here.' He stood up and started walking towards the door. Taffy looked at me and I nodded my head in agreement before we stood up and followed him.

Mrs Lloyd intercepted us before we reached Brother Michael.

'What's wrong, boys?' she asked. 'Where are you going?'

'As far away from here as possible,' said Pete as he stepped round her. 'Do you think we're a bunch of queers?'

'Of course I don't,' she replied. 'Just because you practise dancing with another boy doesn't signify that you are homosexual.'

Pete grimaced. 'It does in this school. You won't find any of these lads prancing around holding onto each other. We don't do things like that. We only came here because we thought we'd be learning with girls.'

Mrs Lloyd appealed to Brother Michael. 'Can you assure them that after they have mastered the waltz and ballroom jive they will get the chance to show off their prowess to the college girls at a social dance.'

Brother Michael came over to where we were standing and said, 'I have no intention of making any of you boys do something you don't want to do, but I believe you should give Mrs Lloyd a chance. She is giving up her own time to come here and teach you. She has said that when you've mastered two dances she will bring girls from the college to dance with you. I think she is being very fair. If anybody in the school questions your sexuality, I will deal with them. Think how envious they will be when they see you all having a social evening over here with Mrs Lloyd's girls.'

'I'm staying, Bro,' Bernie called. 'How about you, John?'

I felt trapped. I hated the thought of looking like a queer, but I had an overwhelming urge to stick it out until we had our social evening. I looked at Pete Boyle and said, 'Shall we give it a go? It'll be a laugh.'

Mrs Lloyd spotted the wavering in our ranks and stepped forward to speak directly to Pete. 'I promise you that no one will think you're homosexual. I can see that you are as straight as a die.'

Pete pointed his finger at Taffy Jenkins. 'If I stay, I'm only going to dance with him. At least I know he's straight.'

Instead of answering, Mrs Lloyd said authoritatively. 'Right, boys. Pair up in the centre of the room.'

Jimmy Johnson, a fourteen-year-old with an unruly mop of jet-black hair and a face covered in acne, came hurrying up to me. 'Can I partner you, John, as then I know that no one will take the piss out of us?'

I nodded. 'I'll partner you, but I'll never practise as the woman. I'll always be the man.'

'That's OK by me.'

Self-consciously we made our way to the centre of the room and stood in pairs. Mrs Lloyd worked her way around the group, putting us in the proper stance and laughing at our clumsiness when she made us hold hands. I held Jimmy's hand in a vicelike grip; he had to know that I was a man and not some stupid fairy. Satisfied that she had the whole group standing properly, she went over to the record player and turned Jim Reeves back on.

'I want all the boys playing the man's role to take a step forward with their right leg. The boys playing the girl's role will move their left leg backwards with the movement of their partner's right leg. Right men, move your right leg forward.'

I stepped forward with my right leg and Jimmy moved his left leg backwards. We took great care to make sure our legs didn't touch. We stood in that position until Mrs Lloyd was satisfied that everybody had made the right movement. She smiled, pleased with us.

'Now, men, move your left leg forward so that your legs are slightly apart. Boys playing women will move their right legs backwards so that they are in the same position as their partner. Men move your left leg.'

I moved my left leg forward and Jimmy moved his simultaneously. I grinned at him. This was a piece of cake. Mrs Lloyd smiled. All the boys had done exactly as she had asked.

'The next movement is easy. I want the men to move their right leg sideways so that their feet are together. The boys playing the women will move their left legs sideways so that their feet are together. Move your legs.'

Again we moved our legs in unison and were back into our starting positions. Mrs Lloyd gave us a round of applause.

'Well done, boys. Let's try the three movements together without stopping. Are you ready? On my command start the movements. Start.'

We all moved forward as we had before and not one of us made a mistake. Mrs Lloyd was in high spirits and clapped enthusiastically. 'You all made that look so easy. It looked like you've been doing it for months.'

For the next two hours Mrs Lloyd guided us through several different movements. She was delighted as we mastered the simple steps. At the end of the evening she sat down next to Brother Michael and watched with pride as we all danced around the classroom to the strains of Jim Reeves. We had lost all our self-consciousness and, like everything in Vincent's, it had become a competition as to who was the best pair. Occasionally one of the boys would make a mistake and would be loudly berated by his partner. Jimmy Johnson was a quick learner and could keep perfect rhythm in his movements, and though he was playing the woman's role he would often pull me through my steps. I was pleased I had him for a partner and decided that he would definitely be the only one I practised with.

Flushed with success we left the classroom at the end of the lesson and planned how we could practise some more before our next lesson. Brother Michael had agreed that we could use the classroom of an evening. It was decided that every evening between six and eight we would assemble in the classroom for practice. There would be no excuses for not turning up.

Brother Michael astonished us all by showing us some fancy manoeuvres on the floor. It was obvious that he was an accomplished dancer. We all managed to learn these moves before our next lesson and Mrs Lloyd shook her head in disbelief as we glided around the floor. She burst out laughing when John Page and Michael Smith did a perfect double turn in a figure of eight movement. She clapped her hands in delight as the dance ended and we turned to face her.

There was a minor dispute between us about the music for the jive. Every boy had his favourite rock 'n' roll singer and wanted to dance to their music. Mrs Lloyd solved the dispute by telling us that she only had two records for practising with and they were Cliff Richard's 'Move It' and The Big Bopper's 'Chantilly Lace'. There were groans of disappointment, as most of the lads wanted Elvis Presley or Bill Haley.

The jive was easier to learn than the waltz as most of us loved beat music. There were so many variations of twisting and turning that Mrs Lloyd allowed each pair to choose two or three moves they liked the best and inaugurate them into their dance. Jimmy Johnson was already good at the jive, as he had been taught by his sister before he had ever come to Vincent's. He showed me the moves and we soon became very adept and quite flashy dancers. By the end of three weeks, all of the class were ready to perform for real and were anxious for Mrs Lloyd to fulfil her promise of a social. She told us that it would take place the following Monday.

Inside the school our little dance class was ridiculed and we were soon referred to as 'The Queers'. Pete Boyle and Taffy Jenkins were caned for kicking seven bells of shit out of one of the stupid lads who said it within their earshot. Jimmy Johnson suffered a lot of verbal and physical abuse so he spent most of his time hanging around me and Bernie. Nothing was said in my hearing as everyone knew what the outcome would be – a fight and a trip to the small dorm. All the aggravation was bringing the dance class into a tight niche and we ended up sitting in a group. This stopped the piss-taking and bullying.

Excitement was intense on the day of the social. All the boys felt sure that a great sexual encounter was just around the corner. Brother Michael had arranged for each of us to be issued with a pair of black trousers and a white shirt. We either owned or borrowed modern slim ties and, wearing our own shoes, we looked relatively smart. Taffy Jenkins had bought a bottle of Old Spice aftershave and assured us that just a small amount on our necks and chins would have the girls eating out of our hands. They would stand no chance and their knicker elastic would immediately loosen with lust. We all bought a little sprinkle off him and Taffy made a huge profit. He then produced a jar of Brylcreem from his locker and sold us all a small dab, making an even bigger profit. When at last it was time to make our way over to the classroom, the smell of Old Spice permeated the air and, with our slicked-back hair, we arrogantly sauntered over to get our hard-earned reward.

The classroom had been spruced up. The wooden floor shone with newly applied polish and two large tables proudly displayed a mixture of sandwiches and cakes and large jugs of different squashes. Mrs Lloyd was waiting at the door as we entered and nodded her head with approval at our appearance. Sitting in the chairs were at least thirty beautiful girls, all dressed in the most wonderful ballgowns. Chiffon, lace and shimmering silk bedazzled our eyes and the glitter of sparkling costume jewellery shone out from all parts of the room. I couldn't help my mouth dropping open. I stood staring with amazement at so many gorgeous girls.

'They're too fucking old,' Bernie said quietly. 'The youngest must be at least twenty.'

I think I must have been the only one who hadn't spotted the age of the girls as the rest of the boys' faces all betrayed their disappointment. Pete Boyle took Mrs Lloyd to one side and said, 'I thought the girls would be the same age as us.'

Mrs Lloyd smiled sympathetically. 'There are no girls in our college as young as you boys. The youngest we have is eighteen.' She put her arm comfortingly around his shoulder. 'Don't worry. All of my girls are nice and are looking forward to seeing how well you boys can dance. Relax and have a good time.'

Pete came over to where we were standing and said, 'There are no girls our age. We stand no chance of getting any tush. The best we can hope for is seeing their tits as they dance.'

Taffy laughed and said, 'None of the lads in the school will know what went on over here so we can tell them we all scored. As long as we agree to keep it a secret, we can make them as jealous as hell.'

Elvis Presley singing 'Love Me Tender' started up on the record player and Mrs Lloyd stood in the middle of us.

'Now go and ask a girl to dance,' she told us. 'Don't be shy. Just walk over as we have practised and say "May I have this dance, please?" Don't worry, you'll be fine.'

I had never imagined that a small walk across a classroom could be so difficult. Gone was the arrogance. The Old Spice and Brylcreem meant nothing any more and my legs were having great difficulty walking in a straight line. I self-consciously headed in the direction of a pretty girl who was dressed in layers of light-blue chiffon. She watched my approach with interest and smiled up at me when I reached where she was sitting. I held out my hand and said nervously, 'May I have this dance, please?'

Her straight white teeth gleamed as she smiled and stood up from her seat. 'Thank you,' she said. 'I would love to.'

She walked with me to the centre of the room and then turned to face me. I had an inward struggle to stop my hand shaking as I slid my arm around her waist and put my hand gently in the small of her back. She held onto my other hand and all of a sudden we were waltzing around the room. She was a very accomplished dancer and guided me through the more difficult turns. I knew that I was blushing and felt sure she could feel the heat from my face.

'You're doing very well,' she whispered to me. 'I find you very easy to dance with.'

I stammered a 'thank you' and promptly missed a step and stood on her foot. I would have felt better if the floor had swallowed me up. I looked at her apologetically and was amazed to find her giggling.

'That was my fault for speaking to you,' she said.

We carried on dancing for three songs and by the end of the third, we were gliding around the floor chatting and laughing as though we had been partners for years. Her name was Daphne and she came from Canterbury. She was twenty years old and in her second year with Mrs Lloyd. I would have been happy dancing the waltz all night with her, but all too soon the music ended and she thanked me and returned to her seat.

When I got back to where the lads had congregated at the far end of the room, I was on a high.

'How did you get on?' asked Bernie.

'Great,' I said. 'She is a great dancer and a real looker.'

'Do you think you stand a chance?'

I found myself getting annoyed. Why the fuck couldn't Bernie see beyond tush?

'Shut the fuck up, Bernie. You know darn well that none of us stand any chance with these girls, but there's nothing to stop us having a good time. Don't tell me that you got anywhere with yours. I'm not an idiot and I wouldn't believe you.'

Bernie grinned. 'You soft fucker. You've fallen in love with her.'

Now I was annoyed. 'Don't be silly. One more word out of you and I'll forget we're best mates. Leave me alone and let me enjoy myself without any of your stupid yack.' Bernie shook his head and wandered away.

Mrs Lloyd announced: 'Take your partners for a ball-room jive.'

I watched with dismay as a young lad called Graham Dodd led Daphne into the centre of the floor. I made a mental note to deal with him later. I hurried over to where another girl, dressed in a bright yellow silk gown, was scanning the room hopefully for a partner. I held out my hand and she stood up and nearly dragged me into the dance area. There was a loud cheer from a few of the lads as Bill Haley and the Comets' 'Rock Around the Clock' blared out from the speakers.

It soon became apparent that we were far better suited to this way of dancing than the girls. They knew how to jive but were not at all adventurous in their movements and looked bemused at some of the twists and turns we led them through. On several occasions, we had to stop dancing and show the girls how we wanted them to move. They loved it. It was obvious that at last they were going to get something positive out of the night.

For the next two hours it was all jive and nothing else. The girls begged Mrs Lloyd to let them learn these new movements with their partners and she was only too happy to oblige. She watched with interest as her girls enthusiastically took on jiving with the boys of Vincent's.

The night was over too soon and we all groaned, both boys and girls, when Mrs Lloyd announced the last waltz. Jean, my jive partner, asked me if I would do the last waltz with her. How could I refuse? This was a first for me and my head swelled with pride at having been asked. Whether for a joke or for sentimental reasons, Mrs Lloyd put on Jim Reeves' 'He'll Have to Go'. Instead of waltzing we all just swayed and chatted to our partners until the music faded and died. We boys made our way along the line of girls and politely thanked them for a lovely evening and were rewarded by each one with a kiss on the cheek. We left the room having had a wonderful evening of just dance and more dance. I can truthfully say I didn't hear one of the lads mention the lack of tush. They had all experienced the same wonderful high that I had, including Bernie.

I walked up to the dormitory with Pete Boyle and he said he needed to have a shower before he went to bed. The other lads in the dorm all assumed that we had conquered the wonderful and mysterious world of tush. We never told them otherwise. That night, I had the most beautiful sleep and when I awoke the next morning, I was still smiling.

Chapter 18

It was late November 1959 and my second winter in Vincent's. I had been away from home now for twenty-one months and I knew I had changed considerably both in size – I was 5 ft 8 in tall and weighed 9 st 7 lb – and temperament. Occasionally boys still tried to bully me but I always fought back. I must have taken the long walk up to the small dormitory a dozen times. Brother De Montfort had increased the number of strokes of the cane I received to eight. It was the maximum he could give, as any more would do too much damage and I would possibly need hospital treatment. I was becoming hardened to the beatings and my hatred was like a bubbling vent of volcanic lava, hidden from view but bursting to get out. Bernie and I were still best friends but we were drifting apart because of my obsessive determination to look after myself, no matter what the cost. I no longer offered him any sympathy when he got hit or bullied. I believed he should do the same as me and look after himself. It was his choice.

I was becoming a student of life. I would often sit alone in the schoolyard and watch the rest of the boys as they went about their business. New boys to the school would generally huddle in corners and whisper quietly to each other. Occasionally I would see an older boy walk past one of them and hit or kick them for no apparent reason. The new boys' eyes always betrayed their fear and they cowered like frightened rabbits in their corners. The older boy would walk away with a swagger and join his friends who were usually leaning against one of the school walls having a crafty smoke.

I grinned when I saw Liam Donovan returning to the yard after visiting the small dormitory for fighting. He was one of the worst bullies in the school. He walked slowly towards his friends with a sullen look on his face. He certainly wasn't swaggering now. David Todd was sitting by the classroom wall as Donovan went past. I shook my head in disbelief as he flinched and cowered when Donovan pretended he was going to kick him. I heard the ripple of laughter from the boys sitting close to Todd and wondered why he let everybody have the satisfaction of seeing his weakness. His problem was fear. He was afraid of everything and everyone.

Todd was a month younger than me and had been in the school three weeks longer than me. He was a good-looking lad with jet-black hair that was always neatly groomed. Over the last few months he had started to develop a nervous twitch that made his head move sideways like a twitching muscle. It only happened occasionally but just recently it seemed to be getting worse. He had become a target for ridicule and also for frequent bullying.

I watched him follow Donovan with his eyes and saw his head shake in an uncontrolled spasm. I idly wondered what he thought about. His life was one of abject misery and humiliation. Why didn't he learn to fight? He was big enough to look after himself, so why didn't he? I watched him stand up and walk to one of the porches and disappear inside. I knew if I went over to the porch I would find him huddled in the corner, alone and friendless. It just confirmed for me that my decision to fight back against all the bullies had been the right one. At least I had my self-respect.

The shrill blast of a whistle summoned us into the recreation room to queue up in houses for lunch. I walked to my place in line and stood patiently waiting for my house to file into the dining hall. Brother Arnold was standing on a bench seat looking angrily all around. He stepped from bench to bench until he had traversed the whole room. Boys were eyeing him warily as this sort of behaviour usually meant trouble. He occasionally stopped walking and stood looking down from his lofty position, swaying from side to side, fists clenched firmly and eyes seeking out anybody who might be stupid enough to attract his attention.

He sniffed loudly through his nose and shouted in his strong Irish brogue: 'You're all bastards. You've been smoking in one of the porches because I smelt it as soon as I walked through the door.' He stepped onto another bench. 'You all deserve to be punished, not rewarded. If I had my way none of you would be going home on Sunday.'

Sunday would be 6 December and the first Sunday of the month.

He stepped onto another bench. 'None of you would be going home if your mothers and sisters hadn't sold their bodies to get you your fares. They're all prostitutes and whores. They're scum, just like you.'

I couldn't believe what I had just heard. That piece of shit was standing on a bench calling my mother a whore. I turned to look at him. He was standing on a bench directly

opposite me and scanning the room. He spotted me looking at him and fixed me with a triumphant stare.

'Face the front,' he shouted. 'Who the hell do you think
you're looking at?'

I couldn't stop myself, I had to say something. I spoke
slowly and deliberately: 'My mother is not a whore and nor
are my sisters.'

Arnold screamed, 'I said face the front.'

I repeated myself: 'My mother and sisters are not
whores.' I watched him as he began stepping from bench to
bench. He was working his way around the room in my
direction. My heart was racing but my resolve was firm. I
couldn't let him insult my mother without defending her.
All of a sudden I sensed his presence and turned my head.
He was standing on the bench next to me. I looked up at
him and said, 'My mother is not a whore.'

The kick would have been hard enough to knock out a
few of my teeth but I managed to turn my head before it
landed. It hit me on my left cheek and the force of it sent me
tumbling across the floor. I pulled myself onto my knees
and stood up. He was still standing on the bench but he was
now swaying from side to side in his usual challenging
stance.

'My mother is not a whore,' I said loudly. 'So what are
you going to do now? You don't frighten me. You're just a
cunt who enjoys hurting boys. One day I'll be a man and
then we'll see who will hurt who.'

His face went white and pinched with anger. He
jumped down from the bench and grabbed me by my
jumper. I stared defiantly into his eyes. He pushed me
towards the end of the room and in the direction of De
Montfort's office, saying, 'This time you've gone too far.'

Brother De Montfort listened to Brother Arnold's account of what I had said to him and his eyes never left me. When Arnold told him that I had insulted him by calling him a cunt, just for a moment his eyes flickered. He couldn't control his anger when he heard about how I had threatened to hurt Arnold when I was older. He held up his hands in a gesture of resignation. He stood and faced the picture of the Blessed Virgin. He must have stood staring at the portrait for at least five minutes and the silence in the room was deafening. I knew that this was just a lull before the storm.

He started to speak before he turned around to face me. His voice was low and threatening. 'Just tell me what gives you the right to speak to Brother Arnold in that manner. Do you think that I won't punish you worse than I've ever done before?'

He spun around. His face was so close to mine I could feel tiny droplets of his spittle bouncing off my cheeks. 'You were put in this school for being out of control and it is my job to put you firmly in control. So far I have failed miserably but that is going to change. You don't respond to caning alone so I will give you another punishment on top of it. You have lost your Christmas holiday. You will not be going home but will be working in the chapel for the whole Christmas period. I hope that when you see all the other boys going home for Christmas you will start learning what is good behaviour and what is bad.'

He turned back to face the portrait and blessed himself. 'Have you got anything to say to Brother Arnold before I take you up to the small dormitory for the first bit of your punishment?'

Brother Arnold was looking at me with a smug expression plastered all over his ugly Irish face. I said slowly and deliberately: 'My mother isn't a whore.'

De Montfort looked at me in open-mouthed amazement. For several seconds he was completely lost for words. After an apparent struggle within himself he said, 'I suppose you think that's a clever thing to say. Well, that remark has cost you your summer holiday as well.'

I shrugged my shoulders. 'No one calls my mum a whore.' I looked at Arnold and I was glad to see that he knew he hadn't achieved anything in getting me punished. I smiled at him and confirmed, 'I meant everything I said.'

Brother De Montfort pushed me towards the office door. He said to Brother Arnold, 'Tell Brother Ambrose I require his services.'

I headed for the small dormitory with a feeling of pride engulfing my whole body. Nothing could hurt me today. I was defending my mum.

Chapter 19

Bernie looked embarrassed as he came towards me. He was dressed in his own clothes: sky-blue jeans, a black shirt with black mother-of-pearl buttons, black suede chukka boots and a short leather jacket. He was ready to leave to catch the early morning train to London. It was Christmas and most of the boys were anxious to be on their way. Brother Cassius stood by the main door that led into the school and was issuing travel warrants to boys who did not have any money in their accounts.

Bernie slipped an ounce packet of Golden Virginia into my hand and a packet of Rizla cigarette papers. 'I wish you were coming too, John,' he said.

I grinned at him. 'I dare say I'll have a better time here than if I'd gone home. My mum has sent me two books and a load of fruit. I'll have a great time.' I put my arm affectionately around his shoulder. 'You have a good time and if you get a chance give that girl Janice a seeing-to.'

'That's for certain,' he said with a wicked grin. 'She's promised to be round my manor when I get there.'

'OK, lads, it's time for you to go.' Brother Cassius had opened the main door and boys were pushing their way through. Bernie hugged me and said, 'Happy Christmas, John. I'll see you when I get back.'

I watched until every boy that was due to go had gone and then trudged over to the chapel. Just inside the door was a lovely nativity scene which had been made in the woodwork department. Father Delaney had supplied the small models of the baby Jesus, Mary and Joseph, the shepherds, the three wise men and the different animals. I always lingered by the entrance as the nativity scene made me feel good. I stood and admired it and when at last I'd had my fill I walked into the centre of the empty chapel and looked up at the large wooden crucifix.

'Well, Jesus, we're alone again,' I said quietly. 'I know I've been a bad lad but I just had to do it. Anyway, it allows me to serve Mass for you on Christmas Day, so it's not that bad a thing is it?'

I heard the catch on the door click so I stopped talking and pretended to be putting the prayer books back in their places on the pews.

Brother De Montfort and Brother Francis came into the chapel and knelt in silent prayer in front of the altar. I watched them quietly. To any outsider they would have appeared to be devout members of the Brotherhood. To me they were the epitome of blasphemy and corruption. I walked quietly into the vestry so I did not have to witness any more of their hypocrisy. I rolled myself a cigarette and stashed it away. I would light it up when they had gone.

The vestry door opened and Father Delaney walked in and gave me a benign smile. He was carrying a profusion of flowers he had acquired from the gardening department. He laid them on the vestry table and said, 'We have to make sure that the chapel is at its best for Jesus's birthday.'

I smiled. To me Father Delaney was the best man I had ever met and I idolised everything he said and did. 'Do you want me to help you decorate the manger, Father?'

'No, John.' He winked at me. 'You work in the vestry for a few hours today. I'm sure you can find plenty of things that need doing. Maybe you could clean out the thurible and put some fresh incense in it. Don't forget to light it and burn the new incense down a fraction.'

I nodded and tried not to smile. 'I can manage that, Father. Is there anything else you'd like me to do?'

Father Delaney sat down at the table and signalled for me to sit next to him. 'I'd like to have a little chat with you, John. It's Christmas and a time most people spend with their families. I know the reason why you're not being allowed home and I don't want you spending the whole of Christmas thinking evil thoughts about Brother Arnold. Christmas is a time of peace and goodwill.'

'I don't think about him at all, Father,' I said. 'He is what he is and my God will punish him. I just hope that one day I have the pleasure of seeing him in his coffin in front of the altar and then I'll know he is burning in Hell.'

Father Delaney shook his head slowly. His face looked sad. 'I wish I could soften your heart. You're just a young boy in the wrong place and you're too young to get eaten up with hatred.' He put his hand gently on my arm. 'I'd like to think we are friends, John.' I nodded. 'And as a friend I would like to ask you to do me a favour.'

'Anything, Father. You know that.' I looked at him with sincerity. 'You've done more for me than anybody in my life has done before. I wish you had been my father and then I wouldn't have been in here.'

He squeezed my arm tightly. 'Thank you, John. That is

a wonderful compliment. So you should have no problem in doing what I ask?'

I said, 'No problem at all, Father.'

Father Delaney stood up and took a packet of cigarettes out of his pocket and placed them on the table next to me. 'Enjoy your Christmas and have no wicked thoughts.' He picked up the flowers from the table and walked quietly into the chapel. For no apparent reason tears sprang to my eyes.

For the first two days of the Christmas holiday there were several other boys with me in the school. They had lost odd days off their holiday entitlement for not achieving the required amount of points every week. On Christmas Eve these boys all left the school and I was totally alone.

Brother De Montfort came into the vestry after Mass to speak to me. 'For the next few days you are going to be alone in the school. I am not going to make any of the Brothers miss the Christmas celebrations by having to look after you. You will be called in the morning by one of the Brothers and then you'll be left to fend for yourself. Matron is preparing all the meals over Christmas and she will provide meals for you also. Breakfast will be at the usual time of eight o'clock. Lunch will be at one o'clock and tea at six o'clock. When you are not required to work in the chapel you may use the television room or the recreation room. You will be in bed with the lights off by nine o'clock. Do you understand what you have to do?'

'Yes, Bro.' I felt like jumping for joy. No supervision meant I could do what I wanted whenever I wanted to do it. Father Delaney had told me already that he only wanted me to sweep the chapel floor daily and that task would take me about fifteen minutes.

Brother De Montfort must have sensed my glee. He said, 'Occasionally one of the Brothers may check on you. So don't be misbehaving.'

I swept the chapel floor with lightness in my step. This could be the start of an absolutely fabulous holiday. I looked up at the crucifix and smiled. 'Thank you, Jesus.'

I hadn't seen Father Delaney standing by the font and I was taken by surprise when he spoke. 'That was music to my ears, John. If only other boys in the school had the same relationship with Jesus that you have.'

I smiled at him and hurried on with my sweeping. I wanted to get back to the school and start reading the books my mother had sent me. They were by an author called John Wyndham and were called *The Day of the Triffids* and *The Chrysalids*. I didn't have a clue what the stories were about but I trusted my mother's judgement. I was sure she would choose the sort of book that I would enjoy reading.

I settled myself comfortably in the television room with my feet up and opened the first of my novels. I lit one of the cigarettes that Father Delaney had left on the table and coughed as the smoke assaulted the back of my throat. Then I started to read.

In no time at all I was lost in a world that had spectacular green comets flashing overhead and the populace all going blind. I could clearly picture William Masen (Bill), the hero of the book, who had not seen the comets because his eyes had been bandaged. I felt his horror at finding himself one of the only sighted people left in the country and having to fight off the large, genetically modified, carnivorous and intelligent plants called Triffids who were uprooting themselves and attacking humans. I reluctantly closed the book and went to lunch. I was five minutes late and found my meal waiting for me on the dining room counter. I gulped it down and quickly washed up after myself. My book was waiting. I was anxious to find out what was going to happen to Bill.

The whole of the afternoon flew past. By teatime Bill had rescued Rosetta from her horrible blind captor and was fleeing out of town with her. I sat quietly eating my tea. My mind was not quiet though; it was filled with images of huge plants walking around the countryside and blind people stumbling into their paths and dying. I had become an enthusiastic science fiction reader.

Brother Michael woke me at six o'clock on Christmas morning. I climbed out of my bed and slowly made my way to the washroom. The corridors and other dormitories were all in darkness and the absolute silence was a little unnerving. I switched on the washroom lights and hurried through my ablutions. I could hear rain beating against the window by the wash basin and I immediately thought about the Triffids. I knew I was being stupid but I imagined there was a Triffid outside and it was trying to get in.

I scampered back to my dormitory and hurriedly dragged on my clothes. Every noise was playing on my nerves and I ran scared along the corridor and down the stairs into the recreation room. I put on all the lights and the large room was suddenly filled with welcoming light. My hands were shaking as I rolled myself a cigarette and lit it. I sat down on one of the benches and puffed nervously. It must have taken five or six minutes before I had composed myself enough to make my way over to the chapel.

I entered the chapel. Father Delaney was lighting the altar candles and called out, 'Happy Christmas, John.'

I hurried down the centre aisle and said, 'Happy Christmas, Father.'

I went to the vestry and pulled on my server's vestments. Father Delaney was singing *'Adeste Fideles'* and his melodic voice soothed my fractured nerves. I found myself humming along with his singing. His voice seemed to grow louder and then he appeared at the vestry door. He handed me a festively wrapped parcel, saying, 'Happy Christmas, John.'

I felt embarrassed as I hadn't anything to give in return. He said, 'Open it. I want to see if you like it.'

I carefully pulled off the wrapping paper and looked down at a leather-bound English Dictionary. I self-consciously opened the first page and read the inscription he had written. It read:

> *To John. A little gift to ensure that you are never lost for words. Fondest regards. Michael Delaney.*

I smiled up at him. 'It's beautiful, Father. Thank you.'

Christmas morning to me was a feast of reading with no interruptions. I lounged in the television room, smoking, reading, completely lost in a world of make-believe.

When it was lunchtime I was amused at the sight of matron serving dinner in a ridiculous-looking paper hat. She smiled a warm welcome and placed a huge turkey dinner on the counter. I hadn't realise how hungry I was and managed to eat every mouthful. I had brought my book with me to the dining room and ate and read at the same time. I was still reading my book at the table when matron returned and gave me a steaming bowl of Christmas pudding and custard. I went back to the television room feeling absolutely sated and relaxed. So far this Christmas was the best I had ever known.

Teatime consisted of two hot mince pies, a large piece of fruit cake and two turkey sandwiches. I decided to take it all up to bed with me. I had my own little picnic laid out in front of me as I rested my head against the headboard and read my book. When I had finished eating I lit myself a roll-up and puffed on it contentedly. It was as though I was in a different world. At nine o'clock I turned off the light and slept the most beautiful sleep I had ever experienced. Life was certainly being good to me.

Boxing Day was as good as Christmas Day. I finished *The Day of the Triffids* and started reading *The Chrysalids*. It took me some time to work out what era the book was set in. I came to the conclusion that it must be a long time in the future, possibly two or three hundred years hence. Something bad had happened in the world because the Canadian government was wiping out people who had mutated. David, the hero of the story, has a hidden mutation; he is telepathic and can send thought messages to his friends, who are also telepathic.

I had to keep stopping and trying to work out what was happening. The book was totally absorbing and I used Father Delaney's gift quite often. After much thought I decided that there must have been a huge war and most of the world had been destroyed. David's sister makes contact with a land called Zealand, which is across the sea and filled with people just like them. To get there they have to escape from their own country and go through the fringes. The fringes are an area filled with dangerous mutations of humans, animals and plants. When I put the book down to go to sleep I found that my mind was still trying to absorb all I had read. I must have been awake for an hour or so before sleep at last came.

'What sort of Christmas did you have here?' Bernie asked.

I could tell by his face that he'd had a special one. Janice must have been a regular visitor.

I told him of all the things I had done and how I had even lain in bed smoking.

He was amazed that I had been left with no supervision. 'Surely they came round to check on you some time during the day?'

I told him that I had seen no one apart from Matron at mealtimes. I don't think he believed me as he said, 'They wouldn't do that. They know you would have smoked if you had been on your own.'

I grinned at him. 'Take my word for it, Bernie. I was left alone.'

I took Bernie over to the locker room and showed him where I had hidden the packet of cigarettes Father Delaney had given me. He opened it and saw that there were only three left in the packet. I then showed him the ounce pouch of tobacco he had given me and there was only enough left in the packet for maybe six or seven thin roll-ups.

'Jesus, John, you must have smoked a lot.'

I smiled. 'I had a great Christmas. I did what I wanted and nobody bothered me.' I followed Bernie over to a bench and slumped down lazily.

'I have to tell you about my Christmas. When I got home Janice was already there. I must have fucked her at least a dozen times during my holiday. She's great. One day we did it three times.' He reached in his pocket and produced a photograph. He handed it to me. 'That's her.'

A pretty blonde girl stared back at me. She looked young but well developed and she posed in the photograph so that her breasts seemed to be trying to bust out of her blouse. It looked very provocative.

'Who took the picture, Bernie?'

'I did,' he said proudly. 'I've got a load more at home. One of them, she's in the nude.'

'Bollocks. You'd never get them developed. They'd hand them over to the police.'

'I know that,' Bernie said smugly. 'My dad has a dark-room and develops all his own pictures. It's his hobby. He developed my film.'

'You lucky fucker,' I said. I took another long look at the photograph and handed it back to him. 'You should have brought the nude one back with you.'

Bernie laughed loudly. He said, 'Yer, that would be great. I'd really be happy seeing you staring at Janice's tush.'

We both laughed at that remark.

David Jones was a new boy who had only been in Vincent's a couple of months but had somehow acquired a reputation as a bit of a hard case, despite the fact that he had never had a fight in the school. He was sixteen years old and quite tall, with white-blond curly hair and a pronounced nose. He had been given the nickname White Wog because of his curls.

'What can we do for you, David?' I asked as he approached Bernie and me in the locker room one day.

He put one of his feet on the seat of the bench and leaned forward so that his arms rested on his knee. I stood up and stepped a few feet away from the bench. He took his foot off the bench and turned to face me.

'Me and my friend Hodges are taking over the baccy trade in this school. I've come to collect all the fags and baccy you two have got.' He clenched his fist threateningly. 'Don't say you haven't got any as I wouldn't believe you. Connors has just returned from holiday so he'll have brought back plenty.'

'He brought back stacks,' I said. 'We've got enough to last us for ages.' I stepped back out of punch range. 'But you're getting fuck all out of us.'

Bernie jumped out of his seat and came to stand next to me. Jones spat on the floor and signalled to Hodges to come and join him. Peter Hodges had been a thorn in my flesh for over a year. He was sixteen years old and fat. He must have weighed at least 15 stone and used all of this weight to push people around. He sauntered over to stand next to Jones and looked at me and Bernie with contempt.

'Fenton's said we're getting fuck all off them,' said Jones.

'Are you sure about that, Fenton?' Hodges moved a little closer to me. 'You know you're fuck all and I can take what I want off you.'

'I know you're a fat cunt,' I said. 'Do you think that just because you've palled up with the White Wog,' I pointed at Jones, 'we're going to hand over our baccy? Kick it off, fatty, and let's all go up to the small dormitory.'

Jones nodded at Hodges and started to walk towards us. I had never seen Jones fight before so I didn't know what to expect. I feinted with my left hand and saw that he jerked his head hard to the right. I stepped back out of range and watched him warily as he came towards me. Bernie was standing close to Hodges but neither of them was making any threatening moves. They were watching Jones coming at me. I feinted again with my left hand and again Jones jerked his head to the right but this time as he jerked his head I kicked him hard on his left shinbone. I knew that I had hurt him because I heard the kick collide with his shin in a sickening thud. He grimaced and sat down heavily on the floor holding his leg. That was all I needed. I ran in quickly and kicked him as hard as I could in his face, then I stepped back, unable to believe it had been that easy. I thought this arsehole was supposed to be a hard case.

Bernie hurried over and pushed me in the direction of the locker room. 'The fight wasn't seen. Let's get out of sight before Jones has to get treatment.'

'Did you see that wanker, Bernie?' I asked. 'He didn't have a clue.'

Bernie nodded. 'I saw it, John, and so did the rest of the boys. You did yourself no harm in finishing him as quick as you did.'

He took one of the last three cigarettes out of the packet and lit it. We smoked in silence, each of us wrapped up in our own personal reverie. I was thinking of Hodges. Would he want to continue the argument? I hoped he wouldn't as he was definitely a strong and heavy lad and not a mug like Jones. We heard the sound of a commotion coming from outside the locker room and opened the door to see what was happening. Several of the boys were attacking Hodges and Brother Ambrose was having difficulty in stopping them.

Bernie grinned at me. 'It looks like we weren't the first ones threatened by those two. Now that they know Jones is just a prick, they're having payback.'

We squeezed our way past the mêlée and went to sit on a bench that gave us a good view of what was going on. Eddie Lawson and Tom Banks ran past us and in a very short time seven boys were on the way to see De Montfort. Jones was sitting against the wall with a dazed look on his face. He had a huge swelling on the side of his head and a bruised and bleeding shin.

'Did you know that you're becoming a hard case?' said Bernie. 'A lot of the younger lads think you're their hero.'

I scowled at Bernie. 'I'm no fucking hero. I'm just trying to look after myself. It's been my plan ever since I decided to learn how to fight. I remember telling you that I would never get bullied again without fighting back. Well, I've done just that and I think I'm reaching the position where people won't even attempt to bully me. It certainly doesn't make me a hero. It means that I'm my own person and nobody can force their will on me. It means that for once in my life I can be proud of what I am and not ashamed.'

Bernie said, 'You've never had anything to be ashamed about. You've always been a good friend and the whole school knows that you're loyal to your family. You were the only one who told Arnold that you weren't going to accept him calling your mother a whore. You lost your holiday and even that didn't affect you. No, John, you've never had anything to be ashamed about.'

But I was still ashamed. I would always feel ashamed about the Wilkinson incident. I stood up and went to the toilet. I needed to be alone. Every time I thought about what happened that awful night I felt like crying and I would creep into a shaded corner to hide my shame and guilt. Today was no different and I sat silently in a toilet cubicle, remembering, shivering and wishing I could turn back the clock. I didn't know that all my wishes would soon be answered.

Chapter 20

January 1960

The 4th of January 1960 was a date I would remember for the rest of my life. It started just like every other day in Vincent's and at midday Bernie and I met up to have our usual smoke before lunch. Bernie lit the roll-up and handed it to me to have the first couple of puffs. He waited for me to hand it back before he spoke.

'I suppose you've heard about Wilkinson?'

'What about him?' I asked. 'Have you got some good news like he's dead or something?'

Bernie laughed. 'No. He's not dead. He's had his licence revoked and is seeing De Montfort now.'

Just for a second it felt as though my heart had stopped beating. I couldn't believe what I was hearing. All my prayers were being answered. 'Are you sure he's back?'

'I'm sure. I saw him walk across the yard earlier with Brother Francis.' He grinned and said, 'He looked really pissed off.'

I needed to be alone. I had to think. Bernie was staring at me. 'You've just made my year,' I told him. 'It's the best news ever.' I started to walk away. My mind was racing.

Bernie called after me. 'John, where the fuck are you going? What's wrong with you? You went as white as snow when I told you about Wilkinson.'

I looked back and smiled. 'I'm fine, Bernie. I just need to go to the toilet before we eat.'

I was alone in my cubicle again. My heart was racing and a nervous twitch in my leg made my foot tap. Wilkinson was back. I was being given a second chance to get even, a chance to cleanse my mind and eradicate the memory. Was I ready? Could I get justice for myself? What would I do if I lost? My mind was in turmoil with all the unanswerable questions. I put my head in my hands and closed my eyes. I had to calm down. A voice in my mind kept telling me to stay focused. I had to keep the memory of Wilkinson's penis between my legs. If I could manage to do that then my hatred would see me through. I stood up and headbutted the cubicle door so hard that a long crack appeared in its entire length. I stared at the damage I had just caused and wondered why I had done it. I didn't mean to; it just happened.

Bernie was waiting for me at the top of the steps as I walked out of the toilet and back into the yard. He took me by the arm and pulled me over to a quiet place by the carpenter's workshop, staring at me intently. 'Are you going to tell me what's going on? I know something's up, John, so why don't you tell me about it?'

Bernie was a good friend. He'd helped me through many difficult times in Vincent's and he never flinched from giving me honest criticism when I deserved it. I owed him more than anyone could ever repay. You can't put a price on friendship. But as much as I honoured and loved him as a friend I couldn't bring myself to tell him the truth about Wilkinson. I was too ashamed. I looked at him staring at me, waiting for me to explain myself, and I felt guilty at having to deceive him.

'This might seem stupid,' I said, 'but I know I'm going to fight Wilkinson. I hate the bastard. I've never hated a person more than I hate him.'

Bernie was incredulous. 'Why, John? Why the fuck do you hate him so badly? What the fuck has he done to you that he hasn't done to everybody?'

'Don't ask me. It's personal. It's between him and me.' I could see that Bernie was upset I didn't trust him. 'I can't tell you anything, apart from the fact that there will be a fight.'

Bernie shook his head. 'You're being stupid. You know he's a hard bastard and will more than likely kick seven bells of shit out of you. So why do it? Just ignore the prick and he'll be gone again before you know it.'

'I can't ignore him. I hate him and I want to fight him.'

Bernie shook his head again. 'Well, if you're intent on going through with it there's nothing I can do to stop you.' He took a roll-up out of his sock and lit it. 'When's it going to happen?'

I shrugged my shoulders. 'I haven't a clue. It could be tomorrow, next week or next month. I just know it's going to happen.'

Bernie handed me the roll-up and I inhaled a mouthful of smoke. It attacked the back of my throat and made me cough. 'What the fuck are we smoking?'

Bernie laughed. 'Boar's Head. It's ten times stronger than Golden Virginia. I brought an ounce of it back from home for us to try.'

I handed the roll-up back to him. 'You smoke that shit; I'll stick to the usual.'

I walked into the recreation room to line up for tea. I still hadn't seen Wilkinson and I scanned the four lines of boys trying to catch a glimpse of him. I didn't have far to look. He was standing in the line next to mine. He saw me looking at him and sneered contemptuously. I turned my head away; I'd seen enough, he was back. A long stream of saliva hit the side of my face. I looked at Wilkinson and wiped the spittle off my cheek with the sleeve of my jumper.

'Fenton, you're a bastard,' he sneered.

Bastard was the worst swear word you could use in Vincent's. It implied that your mother was a slut and you were born the wrong side of the blanket. Wilkinson knew what he was saying.

I looked at his sneering face and smiled. I said, loud enough for the whole school to hear, 'The difference between you and me, Wilkinson, is that I might be called a bastard, but you were born a bastard.'

I spat a large globule of phlegm at his face and was disappointed to see it land on the shoulder of his jumper.

Wilkinson couldn't believe what he had just heard. He pointed his finger menacingly at me. 'After tea,' he said. 'I'll shut your mouth after tea.'

I smiled at him and puckered my mouth as if blowing him a kiss. 'I'll be here, you queer bastard,' I said.

I couldn't believe I had handled the situation so well. I wasn't frightened at all and I had been icy cool with my responses. I think it may have been because I had pictured this moment a thousand times in my mind. I closed my eyes and remembered my shame and humiliation and how I had promised myself that one day I would have my revenge. Well, that day had come, and now it was all up to me.

Bernie was waiting for me when I came out of the dining room, and we went and sat on the backrest of the nearest bench with our feet on the seat.

'Well you've made certain there's going to be a fight,' he said. 'I couldn't believe it when I heard what you said to him. What brought it on?'

'The wanker spat at me and called me a bastard. He likes me as much as I like him.' I looked down at my feet and noticed that one of my work boot's laces was coming loose. I leaned forward and tightened it. I couldn't afford to have my boot flapping about when Wilkinson and I fought. I suddenly had a disturbing thought. 'Do you think he might use a weapon?'

'I haven't a clue. That arsehole is capable of anything. You must be careful, John. You could get seriously hurt.'

I smiled at the stupidity of the warning. Did Bernie think I hadn't thought about the consequences of fighting Wilkinson? I'd gone over all the possible outcomes a thousand times in my imagination. 'I know that, but I'll just have to take my chances.'

I was so wrapped up in my conversation that I didn't check on Wilkinson's whereabouts. He had sneaked along the side wall, clambering over benches out of my line of vision, until he was virtually standing next to me. Suddenly my hair was grabbed and my head pulled downwards onto a fist coming in the opposite direction.

It was as if an explosion had gone off in my skull. For a few seconds I couldn't hear or see a thing but I managed to fling myself off the bench and onto Wilkinson. We both crashed to the floor and my frantic movement cleared my head. As I knelt on the floor I could see a stream of blood gushing from my nose and making a small puddle in front of me. I scrambled to my feet and saw Wilkinson doing the same. He looked at the blood running off my chin and smiled triumphantly. He ran towards me and let fly with a vicious kick aimed at my head. As I had done a hundred times before in the locker room with Bernie, I jumped backwards and grabbed hold of Wilkinson's foot before it landed.

Wilkinson's face showed his shock as he was suddenly balancing on one leg. I moved slightly backwards and watched with delight as he hopped precariously forward. His right leg was now held at a right angle and left the bulge of his crotch a perfect target for my boot. Twenty-two months of torment and suffering went into my kick. I am sure no England fly-half has ever kicked a ball harder than I kicked Wilkinson's crotch. The kick landed with precision and the scream it forced from Wilkinson was music to my ears. He fell over backwards and everything he had eaten for tea spewed out of his mouth. I ran forward and lifted my right boot over his screaming mouth and stamped downwards. I must have stamped on his face at least five or six times before Brother Arnold and Brother Ambrose rugby tackled me to the ground.

I tried in vain to fight my way off the ground. I needed to finish what I had started and ensure that Wilkinson would never be in a position to come sneaking into my dormitory again. Brother Ambrose held me in a vicelike grip and I was trapped and unable to move. Brother Arnold had run in the direction of the school and I guessed that he had gone straight to De Montfort.

I could see Bernie from where I was lying and he was staring at Wilkinson and shaking his head. He looked down at me and mouthed the words, 'You're fucked.'

I didn't understand what he meant. Was Wilkinson getting up off the floor to attack me?

'Let me up,' I screamed at Ambrose. 'I have to get up.'

I heard the sound of running footsteps and tried to turn my head to see who was coming. I could just make out four figures running towards us. The figures stopped in front of Wilkinson and then I saw Brother De Montfort kneeling beside him. He said, 'Brother Francis, go and get Matron, and be quick about it. I think Wilkinson is badly hurt.'

De Montfort stood up and walked over to where I lay trapped on the floor. He shook his head slowly from side to side and said, 'I don't think you'll be with us for very much longer, Fenton.' He turned to Brother Ambrose. 'Let him up but keep hold of him. Take him up to the infirmary and lock him in isolation. Stay there and I'll send for him when we're ready.'

Matron came scurrying along just as I was being pulled to my feet. She took the briefest of glimpses at Wilkinson and said to Brother Francis, 'Phone for an ambulance. This boy needs hospital treatment.'

I had a flicker of alarm. What if I had killed him? I turned my head to look at Wilkinson but found myself staring straight into the face of Brother Arnold. His hand slapped me hard across my face.

What are you doing?' he asked. 'Trying to admire your handiwork?' He slapped me again.

Brother Ambrose pulled me out of the reach of Arnold. 'That's enough, Brother,' he said. 'I think we should allow Brother De Montfort to deal with him.'

I could feel the blood from my nose still running down my chin. With my free hand I wiped the blood sideways across my face.

Brother Ambrose pulled a clean white handkerchief out of his cassock and handed it to me. 'Hold that over your nose.'

I nodded my thanks and placed it carefully over my nose and mouth. I was led away by Brother Ambrose and Brother Arnold. Bernie had taken up a position by the door that led to the infirmary and winked at me as I was pushed past and up the stairs. I was placed in the isolation room and listened as the door was locked from the outside.

I sat down heavily on the infirmary bed. It was hard to say how I felt as it had been a hectic fifteen minutes. I wondered what damage I had done to Wilkinson that warranted hospital treatment? I knew I had kicked him in the nuts and had also done my very best to stamp out his teeth, but surely neither of these things would need him to be carried off in an ambulance? If he died, that would make me a murderer, which was a very scary prospect. I'd go to jail for the rest of my life. Had I been older, I could even have been hanged. I took Brother Ambrose's handkerchief away from my face and stared at the blood that soaked it. I dabbed my nose a few times and threw the bloody rag on the bed then I rummaged in the top of my sock and found a misshapen roll-up and a couple of red matches. I twiddled the roll-up back into shape and lit it. I didn't care if Arnold smelled the smoke. I couldn't be in more trouble than I already was.

Three hours went by before they sent for me. Brother Ambrose led me into De Montfort's office and it didn't surprise me when I saw that he wasn't alone. Standing against the far wall were Brother Arnold, Brother Michael, Brother Francis and Father Delaney. Sitting next to De Montfort was a pasty-faced man I had never seen before. He was definitely someone of importance as De Montfort was fawning up to him. Father Delaney looked stressed. I wondered whether he had been arguing as I'd seen him looking the same way a few months ago when the painting and decorating of the chapel hadn't been finished in time for Sunday Mass. My stomach clenched with nerves. What were they going to tell me?

De Montfort looked at me with disgust written all over his face. 'This gentleman sitting on my right is Mr Davies,' he said, 'the Head of our Governors, and he will help in any decision we take as to the punishment you will receive. I can tell you now that it could well be that you will be handed over to the police and taken to court for further sentencing.' He handed Mr Davies some official-looking forms and a sheaf of blank paper. I surmised that Mr Davies was going to take notes of the proceedings. The seriousness of the situation was obvious. The words 'court' and 'sentencing' rang in my ears.

De Montfort sat forward and leaned on his desk looking at me. 'Wilkinson is in hospital and is being operated on as we speak. There is no doubt in my mind that you knew that you would cause him serious damage when you kicked him. You may well have prevented him from ever being able to have a family of his own.' De Montfort stood up and turned to look at the portrait of the Blessed Virgin. I felt relieved. Wilkinson was alive. At least I wasn't going to have the tag of murderer hanging over me.

He blessed himself and sat back down. 'Explain yourself and your actions. I want to hear what you've got to say about the incident. There's no use in you saying sorry, it's too late for that; just tell us what made you do such a dreadful thing.'

I gave a nervous laugh. 'Saying sorry never crossed my mind. I'm not sorry for what I've done and if I get another chance, I'll do it all over again.'

'What did I tell you?' Brother Francis said. 'He's no good. He doesn't know right from wrong.'

Mr Davies was staring at me, looking puzzled. 'Is that what you're going to say in court? "I'd do it all over again?" From what I've heard about you, you're not stupid. So why would you say such a stupid thing?'

'I wouldn't say that in court.' Suddenly all the emotion of the past two years of nightmares flooded me, all the pent-up shame and sleepless nights and self-disgust. I started to cry and the words burst out in a rush: 'I'd tell them how Wilkinson stuck his prick between my legs when I was thirteen years old and how I caught him interfering with me when I was asleep. I'd tell them how I've had sleepless nights worrying about him coming back to do it again. That's what I'll tell them. So fuck you and your threats about me getting another sentence. I really don't give a flying fuck what you do. I'm glad I did it and I hope the bastard dies in hospital.'

I wiped my eyes angrily with my hand and stared at them defiantly.

There was a deathly silence in the room. All the occupants were staring at me, not believing what they had just heard and undecided how they should react.

Father Delaney broke the silence. 'I told you all there would be a reason why he acted in the way he did. Now you know the reason.' He walked across the room and rested his hand on my shoulder. 'Why didn't you confide in me, John? I would have helped you.'

'I couldn't, Father. I was ashamed.' I started to cry again. I was now sobbing uncontrollably and Father Delaney put his arm around my shoulder. I looked at him through my tears and said, 'I only had any peace when I was in the chapel.'

Brother De Montfort stood up and once again looked at the portrait and blessed himself. He turned to Mr Davies and said quietly, 'I think we should take advice about all we have heard tonight and meet up again in a day or so. What do you think?'

Mr Davies was staring at me and slowly nodding his head. 'I think that John should be kept in isolation until the matter is resolved,' he said. 'It is a very tricky problem and must be handled with some delicacy.'

Brother De Montfort said, 'I agree,' and turned to Father Delaney. 'I think it would be a good idea if you took Fenton up to the infirmary and spoke to him in private. He may have other things to tell you that he's too embarrassed to talk about in front of us.'

Father Delaney led me towards the door. Brother Ambrose reached out his hand and patted me on the shoulder. I was surprised to see that he had tears in his eyes. Father Delaney patted him affectionately on the arm and led me out of the room, shutting the door quietly behind him.

'Well, John, we're all alone.' Father Delaney was sitting opposite me. He opened his cigarette packet and took out two cigarettes and handed one to me. 'I think we can forget about school rules for the moment.'

We sat in silence, smoking our cigarettes, not knowing quite what to say. I had stopped crying and was feeling a little embarrassed at my uncontrolled outburst. There was a soft knock on the door and Matron appeared with a tray with two cups of tea on it. She placed it on a side locker and quietly left the room again.

Father Delaney sipped from his cup. 'I want you to tell me everything about Wilkinson's assault on you when you were thirteen. Don't leave anything out. I want to know it all.' He put down his cup and looked at me expectantly.

I started to speak. At first I was embarrassed and spoke quietly into my tea cup but after a short while I was looking Father Delaney in the eye and speaking with some feeling. I told him in detail about what Wilkinson had done to me in the washroom and how it had made me feel. When I related to him the account about Wilkinson masturbating me in my sleep and Tony Birch doing the same to another boy, Father Delaney muttered the word 'bastards' to himself. I told him about how I had been bullied by older boys and how much it hurt me when I was caned. I told him about my home life and how much I hated my father and feared for my mother. It seemed that once I had started to speak about my problems, I couldn't stop. The floodgates of untold misery had been opened and everything poured out and gushed onto Father Delaney's lap.

When at last I had finished, I felt drained of emotion and just sat staring at him. He was looking at me with an intensity I had never seen in him before.

He noisily cleared his throat and handed me another cigarette. 'John, you are what is commonly known as one of life's unfortunates. Everything you have told me touches my heart and makes me want to thank our Saviour that I never had to suffer like you. How you ever got through it and kept any spark of decency in yourself is a miracle. Jesus must have been holding you in his arms and protecting you.'

He took out a handkerchief and blew his nose. 'Why didn't you speak to me in confession about it? I would never have told anyone where it came from but I could have tried to put an end to it. Why didn't you tell me?'

I shook my head and said, 'I couldn't, Father. It would have been grassing.'

Father Delaney looked annoyed. He said loudly, 'Grassing! You boys and this stupid code of ethics that you all seem to live by.' He stood up and paced angrily around the room. 'If any of you boys had broken the code of silence, the problems of sexual abuse and bullying could have been dealt with. I would have made absolutely certain it was stamped out.'

'How about the physical abuse we get from the Brothers. Would you have got that stamped out?' I stood up and pulled down my trousers and showed him the fading bruises on my backside from the last time I had been caned. 'Don't try and tell me you didn't know about the canings that go on in this school. They've been going on for years and nobody has done one solitary thing to bring them to an end. You told me ages ago that you didn't agree with them but you've done nothing to get them stopped. All you said is that it's school policy.' I pulled my trousers back up and sat down again.

Father Delaney looked taken aback at my little tirade. He said, 'You're right in your rebuke. I agree that nothing has been done about the canings but you must believe me when I tell you that I have spoken to Brother De Montfort about them.'

'I do believe you, Father, but I know that it will have done nothing to stop it. Whether you like to believe it or not,' I went on, 'the Brothers take a sadistic pleasure out of beating us.'

Father Delaney spoke forcefully. 'I don't believe that, John, and you should stop thinking like that. Their punishments may seem cruel to you but I feel certain that they believe they are teaching you boys right from wrong.' His voice mellowed, 'One thing for certain is that there will be no more molesting of boys of a night. I will make sure that there will be a lot more dormitory checks and I'll be insisting there is a permanent night watch. You need never worry again when you go to sleep; you'll be safe.'

I knew that Father Delaney would do what he said and I felt relieved. It had been a long time since I had gone to sleep with an easy mind. 'Thank you, Father.'

He nodded his head and his eyes searched mine. 'Is there anything else you want to tell me? Forget about being a grass, forget about adhering to stupid ethics; if something needs our attention, tell me about it now.'

'There's nothing else, Father.' I looked at him appealingly. 'What do you think will happen to me? Will I be going back to court for re-sentencing? Will I be sent to Borstal?'

For a few seconds Father Delaney looked thoughtfully at the floor. I knew that if it had been up to him I wouldn't have to go to court. He lifted his head slowly and said, 'I don't know, John. I really don't know.' He rubbed his forehead as if he had a headache. 'I'd be surprised if they decide to take you to court as they don't want that sort of publicity. What you did to Wilkinson was wrong but you had strong provocation. You have put them in a bit of a fix. They are more than likely still discussing it now and waiting for me to return with further information to help them in their deliberations'

He rubbed his forehead again and raised his eyebrows, giving me a weak smile. 'I'd like to say you've got nothing to worry about, but this is a difficult one and I don't know how it's going to end up. Whatever the outcome is, John, you can rely on me to speak up for you. I promise you that.'

'Thank you,' I said softly but gratefully.

My question brought our discussion to an end. Father Delaney was clearly embarrassed that he couldn't offer me any succour and I suddenly felt very tired. It had been a long, worrying day for me that had culminated in the fight; I was physically and emotionally drained and needed to shut out the worries that were starting to invade my mind. Father Delaney must have seen the tiredness in my eyes, as he went to the door and opened it. He looked at me and smiled and said, 'Have a good night's rest. Don't worry about tomorrow as I am sure that Jesus will look after you.' He closed the door gently behind him and I heard the click as he turned the key. I lay back on the bed and fell into a deep sleep. I never even took off my boots.

I was left in isolation for three days. Father Delaney brought me a book to read, *The Adventures of Tom Sawyer* by Mark Twain, and he also conveniently forgot to pick up his packet of cigarettes when he left. I asked him if he had any news about what was going to happen to me and he just said, 'Nothing yet, John.'

I tried desperately hard to get involved with the new book but my mind was uneasy and I found that my concentration was at an all-time low. I had no regrets about what had happened to Wilkinson now that I knew I hadn't actually killed him, but I had a real fear of starting a fresh sentence in another school or Borstal. I lay for hours on my bed just staring at the ceiling and imagining what I would do if the news was bad. At night I kept waking up and my mind would immediately go back to worrying. I decided that night worries were ten times worse than day ones. It seemed to me at night that the whole world was dropping onto my shoulders and I was being crushed under a mountain of worry and self-pity.

On the morning of the fourth day I was relieved when Father Delaney came to fetch me and take me down to find out my fate. He looked at me and the relief on his face was evident.

'You're not going to be charged with any offence,' he said. 'I think you're going to get some sort of punishment but it's going to be kept in the confines of the school. I think,' he looked up towards the heavens, 'that your Friend is still looking after you.'

Mr Davies stared at me impassively before switching his attention to fiddling nervously with his tie. Brother De Montfort kept staring for another few seconds and then carried on perusing the document he had been reading as I was led into the room. After what seemed an interminably long time he put the document down and peered at me. His whining voice that day resembled the mewling of a dying cat.

'What you did to Wilkinson was reprehensible. It is only through the grace of God that you didn't do even more damage to him than you actually did. The hospital reports are good and with the help of God he will make a full recovery.' He stood up and as usual faced the portrait and blessed himself. I wondered idly why he did this. Was he trying to look sanctimonious? He walked around his desk and came to stand in front of me. His eyes narrowed and his lips were a thin blue line under his nose.

'If the reports had been different you'd be on your way out of here and I wouldn't be sorry to see the back of you.' He paused and took a long blow of his nose into a greyish handkerchief. I watched with fascination as he inspected the contents of the handkerchief before putting it into some hidden pocket in his cassock. He wrinkled his nose. 'We have taken into account all the underlying reasons behind your savage attack and have decided that we can keep this incident within the school's punishment system.' He looked at Mr Davies. 'Mr Davies and I have agreed that eight strokes of the cane will suffice as your punishment.'

Father Delaney stepped forward from where he had been standing. 'I think that after the caning he should be made to spend several days in the chapel reflecting on the evil thing that he did and how his behaviour should be in future.'

Brother De Montfort nodded his agreement. He was staring at me again with a look of distaste on his face. He whined in his hateful voice: 'He should also reflect on how he can show respect to the Brothers in this school and not use his facial expressions to indicate his contempt for us. We have had enough of his dumb insolence.'

Father Delaney promised, 'I will deal with all these issues in chapel.'

Brother De Montfort said to Mr Davies, 'Would you like to be present at his caning or shall I handle it?'

Mr Davies's face got even pastier. He shook his head. 'I think that it would be better if you handled it.' He stood up from his seat and held out his bony hand. Both Father Delaney and Brother De Montfort shook it and watched him as he quietly slipped out of the room. He didn't once glance in my direction.

Father Delaney looked at Brother De Montfort and said, 'Send him to the chapel when you have finished with him.' He turned to leave the room and patted me on the shoulder as he left. 'I'll see you later, John. You should be thankful that you are getting off so lightly.'

Brother De Montfort pointed to the door. 'You know the way, Fenton.'

I led the way up the internal staircase to the small dormitory. I knew what was in front of me and the pain I was about to endure, but I was calm. Fifteen minutes of misery was a cheap price to pay for having my revenge on Wilkinson. I pulled on the shorts with a smile on my face.

Afterwards, I stepped slowly and painfully into the chapel and found Father Delaney standing by the altar cleaning the chalices. On hearing my footsteps he looked up. 'How are you feeling, John?'

I shrugged. 'I'm OK, Father.'

He gestured for me to come and stand with him and handed me a brilliant white cleaning cloth. 'Don't rub the chalice too hard or you'll leave smear marks.'

We polished the chalices side by side for several minutes, then Father Delaney returned them to the tabernacle. I watched as he locked the small door with a beautifully carved silver key. We both genuflected in front of the altar and I looked up at Jesus hanging on the cross above my head. He seemed to be looking back at me.

'What do you think of when you look at our Saviour hanging on the cross?' Father Delaney asked. 'What's going through your mind? You always look so sincere.'

'I'm just checking to make sure He understands what I've done. I'm also thanking Him for giving me the strength to take whatever punishment I have just had.' I looked at Father Delaney. 'I think of Jesus being scourged when I'm being caned. I think of how He suffered and how brave He was and I try to show the same courage. It helps me.'

We walked slowly towards the vestry. Father Delaney had his hand on my shoulder and squeezed it. 'I'm sure Jesus is pleased that you understand the suffering he endured. That is why he keeps you close in his arms. He will never desert you.'

'I felt He deserted me when Wilkinson abused me, Father. I prayed really hard but nobody helped me.'

'Jesus may have been testing you. Who knows what plans He has for you?' He blessed himself. 'God works in mysterious ways.'

'When Brother De Montfort said that the reports from the hospital were good, what did he mean?'

Father Delaney said gravely, 'It was feared that you may have damaged Wilkinson's testicles so badly that he would never be able to have children. That wasn't the case. You kicked one of his testicles up into his lower body cavity and they had to operate to bring it back down. The operation was a complete success and he should recover completely. You also loosened a few of his front teeth but they also think that he won't lose them. So all in all you were very lucky. Things could have been a lot worse.'

'Do you think what I did was wrong, Father?'

Father Delaney said very simply, 'I can't condone violence, John, but the rights and wrongs will be judged at a much later date in mankind's highest court in Heaven. All I will say is that I understand your actions.'

I held out my hand to him and he took it in a firm grip. I said shyly, 'Thank you for standing by me, Father. I don't know how I would have got through it without your help.'

He smiled and pointed back towards the chapel. 'Why don't you go and thank the real person behind your good fortune?'

I knelt down in the front pew and looked up at the face of Jesus. I felt sure that Father Delaney was right. My Friend kept me close because I understood his suffering. I stayed kneeling in silent prayer for the remainder of the morning.

Chapter 21

It was Easter Monday 1960 and the spring sun felt warm and pleasant. It was three and a half months since the Wilkinson incident and two days before my sixteenth birthday. Bernie and I were sitting on the ground in the yard with our backs resting against the recreation room wall. A group of about twenty boys had formed two teams and were kicking a ball around the yard. Other boys were sitting or lounging in small groups watching the match and having the odd crafty smoke.

We both laughed as we saw Jack Clarke tackle Pete Boyle and run away laughing with the ball at his feet.

Jack Clarke became a legend on his first day at Vincent's. He was a small thirteen- year-old with buck teeth and an unruly mop of mousy hair. He had been sentenced to three years' approved school for being completely out of control at school and at home. He crept quietly into the yard that first day and had gone unnoticed by virtually everyone as he sat in a corner. When the school were called into houses to go into lunch he managed to find his spot without too much bother. He filed into the dining room with all the boys and seated himself at a table near the front.

As usual, the duty brother took his position on the podium and commanded silence by booking and slapping any boy who made the mistake of talking. We were ten minutes into our meal when we saw Brother Ambrose signal to someone to come over. Jack Clarke walked slowly to the podium and stared up at Brother Ambrose, who towered above him.

'What's your name, boy?' Brother Ambrose called down.

'Jack Clarke, sir,' he said quietly.

'Well, Clarke, there's a rule of silence during meal times and you were talking.' Brother Ambrose reached down and pulled the young lad up by his hair and slapped him around the ear. 'Now go back to your seat and keep your mouth shut.'

Jack Clarke put his hand up to the ear that had just been slapped and rubbed it. His whole face went beetroot red and he shoved the podium with all his pent-up anger. The podium began to wobble precariously and Brother Ambrose struggled to keep his balance. With a resounding crash it toppled over and Brother Ambrose flew through the air with his arms and legs flailing wildly. He hit the floor with a resounding wallop and his cassock wrapped around his head. The whole of the school burst out laughing and some of the boys started to cheer loudly. The dining room door was flung open and Brother De Montfort and Brother Arnold rushed in.

Brother Ambrose was still floundering on the floor like a beached whale so Brother De Montfort rushed over to help him to his feet. Jack Clarke stood perfectly still watching the mayhem he had caused and grinning all over his face. Brother Arnold hit him hard in the face and then Jack was the one on the floor. De Montfort looked down at him and instructed Brother Arnold: 'Bring him to my office.'

We all watched with sympathy as Jack Clarke was dragged out of the dining room towards his fate. Brother Ambrose tentatively put the podium back into position and took up his sentry stance on it. The school had quietened down and most of the boys were lost in their own private thoughts about the punishment Jack Clarke was about to receive.

An hour after we had come out of lunch Jack Clarke reappeared in the yard. His face was wet with tears and there were blood streaks on the back of his legs. He was welcomed into our midst like a conquering hero and every boy seemed to want to speak to him. His entry into the school would be talked about for ages and he had earned the nickname of 'Shover'. Talk about arriving with a bang!

I was reflecting on how my life had changed since the 4th of January when I had my fight with Wilkinson. After my caning I had returned to the school and found that I had gained enormous respect overnight. The bullying Bernie and I had once faced daily disappeared and we were left alone. Bernie said, 'Nobody would dare bully you now. They're too frightened of losing their bollocks.' Wilkinson had never returned to the school and I was told by Father Delaney that Davies and De Montfort had given him back his licence, thus solving a very difficult problem for them.

A school choir was formed and both Bernie and I became members. We joined because there were special privileges given to choir members. Twice a week after choir practice we were allowed to watch an hour of television and after singing at High Mass once a month, we were allowed to go to the pictures on a Saturday afternoon. These privileges were too good to turn down so we were two of the first volunteers.

I found choir practice a laugh from start to finish. Bernie and the rest of the choir didn't have a clue how to pronounce any of the Latin Mass and listening to them sing words they couldn't pronounce was one of the funniest things I had ever heard. Brother Michael was the choirmaster and if it wasn't for his accomplished and melodic voice drowning out the mumblings of the boys, the whole thing could have been a disaster. Father Delaney even laughed when he attended a rehearsal and heard the boys' attempts at singing the *Nicene Creed*.

There had been a lot of licences granted over the last three months and consequently a big influx of new boys. I watched all the comings and goings with interest. I'd see a new boy being pushed around and remember how, not so long ago, Bernie and I had suffered the same kind of treatment. I found myself studying the different ways some boys handled the bullying. There was still brutality being dished out daily by the staff for the most trivial of offences and some boys seemed to handle it well, while others cringed in corners and were not averse to snivelling when they were given the most basic of slaps. Brother Arnold always seemed able to single out the weaklings and revel in the fear and power he had over them. I'd watch him strut his stuff around the school and let it feed my insatiable hatred of him.

My thoughts were interrupted by the football hitting and breaking one of the large ventilation windows above my head. A few slivers of glass showered down on me and I carefully flicked them off my hair and jumper.

Bernie commented, 'You're lucky most of the glass fell into the rec and not onto your head.'

I noticed how the football players had suddenly dispersed and were hiding themselves among the various groups in the yard. The schoolroom door opened and Brother Arnold came hurrying out. He immediately came over to where Bernie and I were sitting and stared up at the shattered glass above our heads. He looked down at me and pointed at the window.

'Who did that?' he asked menacingly.

I shrugged my shoulders and said, 'I haven't got a clue, Bro.'

Arnold kicked out his right foot and it caught me high on my thigh. 'You must have seen who did it. You're sitting right underneath it.'

I jumped to my feet as I was at his mercy sitting down. 'I saw nothing at all,' I said quietly. 'The first thing I knew about it was when I was showered with glass.'

My hatred for him must have shown on my face as without any warning he backhanded me across my mouth. I knew he had split my lip as I immediately felt the trickle of blood running down my chin. He was swaying from side to side in front of me and I knew that meant he was planning to hit me again so I quickly moved out of his reach.

'Get back here,' he shouted. 'You're going to tell me who did it.'

My temper was roused and I wiped the blood angrily off my chin. 'I don't know fuck all,' I said loudly, 'so piss off and find someone that does.'

He smiled sadistically at me and stepped forward but I stepped backwards and further out of his reach.

'That just cost you a trip to Brother De Montfort's office,' he said. 'The way you're behaving makes me think that it was you who broke the window.'

'Think what you like. I know I didn't do it and that's all that counts.'

He pointed at the door that led towards De Montfort's office. 'Get going. I'm sure Brother De Montfort will be delighted at the way you have just sworn at me.'

I turned to Bernie and raised my eyebrows in disbelief. 'Can you believe this fucking wanker? I've done nothing wrong.'

Arnold ran forward and grabbed my arm and pushed me towards the door. 'You've got a foul mouth,' he said, slightly out of breath, 'and deserve everything that's coming your way.'

I allowed myself to be pushed along to De Montfort's office and nearly stumbled as I was pushed through the door-way. De Montfort listened in silence to Arnold's account and never took his eyes off me. When Arnold had finished De Montfort stood up and walked towards the door.

'Follow me, Fenton,' he said. 'You know where you're going.'

I followed him out of his office and up the stairs to the small dormitory, riled by the injustice of it all. He slung a pair of blue silk boxing shorts onto the nearest bed.

'Put them on.'

'Not a chance.' I spoke without thinking. Somewhere in my subconscious I must have decided not to take the cane. 'I'm not being caned for doing nothing wrong. I've been caned at least a dozen times and I've always accepted my punishment, but this time I've done nothing that deserves a caning so I'm not taking it.'

Brother De Montfort's eyes were cold and unfeeling. He was silent for some considerable time, digesting what he had just heard. He eventually said very quietly, 'Put the shorts on.'

I shook my head and said, 'No.'

We had reached an impasse. He turned around and walked to the open door.

'I'll give you five minutes to think about what you're doing. When I come back you had better have those shorts on.' He closed the door behind him and I was left alone.

I started to pace the dormitory nervously. My heart was racing and my hands were sweating. I knew I was right in refusing the cane but I was terrified at what might happen now. What could they do? I kept my eyes fixed on the door. Eventually it opened and Brother De Montfort walked in. He saw I was still not wearing the shorts and said, 'Are you going to put on the shorts?'

'No. I've done nothing wrong.'

I watched him apprehensively as he turned to the door and signalled with his finger. In walked Brother Arnold, Brother Michael, Brother Francis and Mr Lawson. They were followed by Brother Ambrose carrying his usual bundle of canes. They all walked towards me and I backed away until I was stopped by my back pressing against the far-end wall. This was the signal for them to rush me and suddenly I was struggling violently with four grown men who were considerably stronger than me.

Kicking and screaming abuse, I was lifted bodily off the floor and thrown face downwards across a bed. Brother Michael and Brother Francis each had hold of one of my legs, Brother Arnold and Eddie Lawson each had an arm and I was being stretched and pulled downwards over both sides of the bed. I thrashed my head from side to side in a vain attempt to break loose. Brother Ambrose began lashing a cane down on my body like a demented person and when I strained my head and neck to look at him, his face had a maniacal expression.

Suddenly, what Brother Ambrose was doing didn't matter at all; my right hand was being pushed so hard downwards that my wrist was close to snapping like a twig in winter. My scream of agony reverberated around the room. I looked down and saw Mr Lawson kneeling on the floor pressing hard on my hand and arm.

'You're breaking my fucking wrist,' I screamed. 'Let go. You're breaking my fucking wrist.'

He totally ignored my screams and kept the pressure on.

The pain was excruciating and I screamed again, 'You're breaking my fucking wrist.' There was still no let-up on the pressure so I screamed again, 'OK. I'll take the cane. Let me up. For God's sake let me up.'

My legs and arms were suddenly released. I struggled to get up to kneeling position and Mr Lawson put both his hands under my arms to help lift me. That was the chance I'd been waiting for. I crashed my head into his face and felt my forehead collide with hard bone.

'Fuck you, you ginger-headed cunt,' I screamed.

Hands grabbed me and once again I was stretched across the bed and was being lashed unmercifully with the cane. I think all in all I was probably hit fifty or sixty times but I was so angry I didn't feel the pain. I craned my neck to look at Mr Lawson and grinned through gritted teeth when I saw a massive swelling starting to close his left eye.

Finally I heard De Montfort say, 'That's enough,' and I was free to move again. I pushed myself off the bed so I was kneeling on the floor and stood up slowly. I noticed that they were all keeping well away from me. They were taking no chances because they could see my temper was up.

De Montfort pointed to the door. 'You can go back to the yard now.' He decided to brave it and came to stand directly in front of me. 'You will never beat the system. Let this be a lesson to you.'

Bernie and a few of the older boys came to greet me when I returned to the yard. I felt like a conquering hero and bragged about refusing the cane and sticking a nut on Eddie Lawson. The Eddie incident was initially met with a degree of scepticism but this quickly turned to open-mouthed amazement when he walked out of the school-room door sporting a closed and puffy left eye.

I told them how Brother Ambrose had lashed me over and over with the cane and Bernie said, 'The nutty fucker.' I burst out laughing and said, 'That's a great nickname for him. Nutty Ambrose.'

'How many times did you get hit?' Bernie asked. 'If he was going loopy it might have been hundreds.'

'You tell me. I can't see behind me.'

The boys gingerly lifted my shirt and jumper up and I heard a few gasps and expletives.

'Jesus, John,' Bernie said, 'you're like a fucking zebra you've got so many stripes.' My trousers and underpants were pulled down and there were even more expletives. 'There are even stripes down the back of your legs. The nutty fucker must have been hitting you all over.'

'I know he was but the best part is, I never felt a fucking thing. I was too busy struggling and shouting to feel anything. I've decided that if I ever have to have the cane again, I'll do the same thing. It doesn't hurt a quarter as much as when you're wearing those fucking shorts.'

Bernie nodded. 'You could well be right as you haven't got a single cut.'

I looked at Brother Arnold as he walked across the yard and said, 'The next time, I'll stick a nut on that cunt.'

Bernie lit a roll-up and handed it to me. I sat down carefully with my back against the recreation room wall and resumed my study of the different boys of St Vincent's.

I watched as Brother Arnold beat Pete Boyle for smoking. As usual, I could see he was taking a perverse delight in inflicting pain. For several minutes I imagined what it would be like to have Arnold on the floor and kick the shit out of him just as he had done to so many boys. I hated the man and felt sure that he was a pious hypocrite. He had no right to wear any church attire. I knew that because I'd witnessed him sinning at first hand.

A few weeks earlier I had been told to go to the Brothers' living room and ask for the key to the television room. The room was situated near De Montfort's office and was where all boys reported when they returned from holiday or from their home visits on the first Sunday of the month. I tapped gently on the door and opened it in the same motion.

The room was comfortably furnished and looked very similar to any lounge in any house. Brother Arnold was lying along the couch with his head resting on the cushioned arm rest. I was taken completely by surprise to see that a young Irish nurse who worked in the infirmary was also lying on the couch with her head resting on the opposite arm rest. Brother Arnold had his hand resting on the nurse's knee in what could have been a perfect scene of domestic bliss. He snatched his hand away and quickly swung his legs onto the floor then jumped up and smacked me hard around the face. He said viciously, 'Don't enter a room until you've been asked to enter. What do you want?'

I walked out of the room with the key and with the almost certain knowledge that Brother Arnold and the nurse were more than just common acquaintances. Why else would they recline in such an intimate fashion? He was fucking her. It stood to reason. That was another reason he should burn in hell.

I watched him shove Pete Boyle angrily away and take out his notebook. I spat on the floor and contemptuously stood up and went to retrieve my book from my locker. I had to shut out the sight of that wicked bastard.

Chapter 22

I watched torrential rain falling from the sky and bouncing six inches off the ground before dropping into the rivulets that were streaming towards the drains. The school was deathly quiet and I could clearly hear the raindrops beating against the recreation room windows. I was once again left to my own devices as all the boys had gone home on their summer holidays. I didn't envy them at all. If I had gone home my father would have made my mother's life even more miserable than it already was and I would have had an awful time.

I cursed the rain. It was the middle of August and I had been looking forward to lying on the playing field, sunbathing and reading a book. I chuckled softly to myself as I thought of Bernie. He was going with his family for a week in Blackpool and he had talked about nothing else for the last three weeks, but in all of his plans, he had never predicted rain and the need for galoshes. A sudden crack of thunder made me jump and I looked eagerly at the black clouds in the hope of seeing some lightning. I didn't have long to wait as a bright jagged streak illuminated the sky followed almost immediately by a booming clap of thunder.

Father Delaney suddenly appeared, coming out of the chapel. He peered up at the sky and then unfolded an umbrella before splashing his way across the yard. I wondered what was bringing him over to the recreation room and I hurried to the door and held it open for him. He stamped into the room and shook his umbrella into the porch. He smiled at me and said, 'It's a lovely day for the fishes, John.'

There was another flash of lightning, which was immediately followed by a crackling clap of thunder.

'It must be right overhead,' he said. 'Let's hope it soon passes over.'

He reached into the side pocket of his jacket and pulled out a thin booklet and handed it to me. 'It's a brief history of St Thomas à Becket. Have you ever heard of him before?'

I shook my head and peered down at the front cover of the booklet. It showed a picture of a bishop kneeling and looking up to heaven with four medieval knights surrounding him, one of them plunging a sword down through the back of his neck.

'Why have you given me this, Father?'

Father Delaney looked pleased with himself. 'I've arranged with Brother De Montfort that I can take you on an excursion to Canterbury Cathedral tomorrow. It's not too far away and I'm certain that you'll enjoy it.' He pointed at the booklet I was holding. 'That tells the story of Thomas à Becket, who was an Archbishop of Canterbury and was murdered on the 29th of December 1170. He was a person who stuck by his beliefs, no matter what, and was even prepared to die for them.'

'When was he made a Saint, Father?'

Father Delaney nodded his head, pleased by my interest. 'He was canonised in February 1173. That is quite soon after his death as lots of saints are not canonised until they have been dead for decades or longer.'

'Is he buried in the Cathedral, Father?'

'He was once, but his tomb was destroyed in Henry VIII's reign with the Dissolution of the Monasteries.' He patted me on my shoulder. 'I won't tell you anything else for now. You can read all about it in the book I've just given you. Let's hope the weather is better tomorrow.'

'What time are we leaving, Father?'

He thought for a moment. 'I think we should be on our way by nine o'clock. It would be nice if we can spend a whole day looking at the wonders that Canterbury has to offer.'

The excursion to Canterbury Cathedral was possibly the most educational thing I had done in my life. Father Delaney was better than any official guide and pointed out and explained everything of significance in the Cathedral. I was thrilled to stand next to the small dark-coloured stone square on the floor of the Martyrdom where Thomas à Becket was slain. Father Delaney insisted that we said a decade of the rosary there for the sick and dying in the world. We moved on to St Michael's Chapel (the Warriors' Chapel) and he pointed out the large book of remembrance. He told me how a soldier from the Royal East Kent Regiment (known as the Buffs) marched to the chapel every day and turned the page so a new list of soldiers who had died for their country was on display.

I was excited when at last we arrived in the Crypt. I don't quite know what I had expected to see but this exceeded every stretch of the imagination. The Chapel of

Our Lady Undercroft was the most simple and beautiful place of worship I had ever seen. I asked Father Delaney if we could stay a little longer in the chapel as I wanted to say a few prayers for the well-being of my family. Father Delaney smiled and knelt next to me in front of the altar.

When we returned to the main floor Father Delaney led me over to the tombs of Henry IV and his wife, Joan of Navarre. He explained to me that Henry IV was the only monarch buried in Canterbury. He wasn't the only member of the royal family interred in Canterbury as earlier he had shown me the tomb of Edward the Black Prince, who had been heir to the throne of his father, Edward III. My brain was being swamped with tales of previous Archbishops of Canterbury and Father Delaney spoke with such authority and could deliver such wonderfully descriptive narratives, it brought the majestic building to life. At the end of our day in Canterbury I was a convert to England's history and heritage and couldn't remember ever having had such an interesting time.

Father Delaney was quiet on the journey back to Vincent's and it was only as we approached Dartford that he spoke. 'That was a marvellous day out, John. Did you enjoy it?'

'It was great, Father,' I said with passion. 'I never knew that there were such wonderful things to be seen.'

'The world is full of wonderful things,' he said. 'England is full of ancient castles and churches. When you leave the school you will be free to seek them out and learn about your country's history. History has thrown up some great people who have achieved great things. I watched you today and you showed me that you appreciated the wonders of Canterbury Cathedral. Don't let it be a one-off experience. Every chance you get to go and see some place of historical interest you must grab with both hands.'

'I will, Father. I want to learn; I enjoy learning.'

'I know, John. That is why it's so tragic you're in St Vincent's.' He turned the car on to Temple Hill, which led up to the school. 'How long have you been with us?'

I had to think for a moment. 'Two years and five months, Father.'

He shook his head sadly. 'And with your history I would say you have another seven months to go. I don't think there's any chance of Brother De Montfort putting your name forward for licence; you've been too much of a pain in the backside to him.'

I laughed. 'I've never even thought about getting licence as I know what the Brothers think of me. Seven months is no bother, I've got used to the place.' I turned my head to look at him. 'Who are you going to get to serve Mass when I've gone, Father?'

He shrugged. 'I haven't a clue, John, but I'm sure I'll find someone.'

He turned the car through the school gates, sped along the drive and pulled up outside the front door to the chapel. I reluctantly opened the car door and climbed out and stepped back onto Vincent's ground. 'Thank you, Father. It was a great day.'

'It was my pleasure, John. I'm glad you enjoyed it.'

I walked slowly around the small graveyard and into the schoolyard. I was alone again and the wonderful day was finished. I looked wistfully at the booklet of Thomas à Becket and wished the day was just starting again. For the first time in over two and a half years I became discontented with my life. I was yearning for the unobtainable. I wanted a life with a loving family and all the treats that went with it. I felt tears coming behind my eyes and cursed. 'For fuck's sake, John, get a grip,' I muttered. 'You'll get nowhere feeling sorry for yourself.'

Later that night, alone and lying on my bed, I let the tears flow freely.

Chapter 23

'Shut the fuck up,' Pete Boyle screamed out. He picked up one of his work boots and slung it at the bed next to me, where the sound of someone crying was disturbing the whole dormitory. It just missed me and I picked it up from the floor and lobbed it back at Boyle.

'Sorry about that, John,' he said. 'It was meant for that noisy cunt in the next bed. Get out of bed and give him a slap.'

I looked across at the mound of bedclothes the boy was hiding under. His muffled sobs touched my heart. I had become a student of life and of the boys at Vincent's and prided myself on assessing what sort of character they were within hours of their arrival in the school.

The boy hiding under the mound was John Lacey. He was just thirteen years old and had been in Vincent's for a little over a week. When he came into the yard on his first day I noted how he kept himself to himself and, apart from a little fear in his eyes, looked confident enough to fit into the ways of the school. I was surprised to hear him crying under his pillow as I'd thought he was stronger than that.

I slowly climbed out of my bed and crept over to Lacey and shook the mound of bedclothes.

'John, stop crying,' I whispered. 'You're keeping the whole dorm awake.' I was startled at his muffled scream when I touched him. 'What's up? Why did you scream?'

His pillow moved and tentatively his tearstained face appeared. His broken sobs became louder and he buried his head back under the pillow to muffle them from the other boys. I pulled the pillow off his head and threw it on the floor.

'I'm taking an awful chance being out of my bed,' I said. 'If Brother Arnold comes along on his night patrol and finds me here, I'll be in deep shit. So tell me quickly what's wrong with you?'

Desperately trying to control his sobs he said, 'I sneaked out of school this afternoon to ring my mother and I was caught by one of the Brothers as I climbed over the fence. They said I was trying to run away. I was taken upstairs and they made me put on boxing shorts and then caned me.' He started to sob again. 'They hurt me bad. Really bad.'

'Do you mind if I have a look?'

He kicked back the bedclothes and rolled over onto his front. Very gently I lifted up his nightshirt so his backside was exposed. I couldn't believe what I was looking at. His whole backside was black and blue with no sign of any untouched flesh. There were five large cuts criss-crossing his buttocks and trails of dried blood running down the backs of both legs.

I gently covered him up again. 'How many times were you hit?'

His sobbing had eased. 'I think it was eight times. I don't know for certain as I was hurting too much to count.'

My mind went back to the first time I had been caned by Nutty Ambrose and I could imagine the torment and suffering John Lacey had gone through. I cursed loudly, 'Those fucking arseholes.'

I looked over to where Pete Boyle was sitting up in bed, looking at me. 'Get your arse over here, Pete, and see what those cunts have done to this kid.'

He scampered over to where I was standing and I pulled up Lacey's nightshirt again. 'No wonder the kid was crying,' I said.

Pete had been in the school for two years and was a few months younger than me. He had been caned a few times himself and, like me, hated Nutty Ambrose and De Montfort for the pain they had inflicted on him. He stared down at Lacey's backside. 'Those cunts,' he muttered. He didn't need to say any more. Cunts was an appropriate word for what we were looking at. He leant forward and covered Lacey over. 'When is this ever going to stop?'

I had no answer. What could I say? This treatment was common in Vincent's and had been going on, I should imagine, since the school was first opened in 1878. I said in a whisper for only Lacey and Boyle to hear, 'Try to go to sleep, John. I'll have a chat to you in the morning and me and Pete will do our best to make sure you're OK.'

Lacey wiped his eyes on his nightshirt sleeve and smiled weakly at me. I pulled the bedclothes over him and climbed back into my own bed.

Pete Boyle sat on the end of my bed. 'We've got to do something, John,' he said. 'We can't allow this to keep going on.' He stood up. 'I'd better get back to my bed before the Kraut catches me.' The Kraut was a recent nickname given to Arnold by one of the boys. It was a great name for him as he was just like a Gestapo officer with his general nastiness and inhumanity. I nodded my head and watched Boyle as he tiptoed back to his bed.

I couldn't sleep. What Boyle said had touched a raw nerve. *We've got to do something* kept going through my mind and I searched over and over for a solution. I had thought for a long time that something should be done about the constant assaults we were subjected to. Somehow we had to expose the cruelty to the outside world. But how could we do that?

Suddenly I thought of Bernie and his new hobby. He had returned from his summer holiday, two months ago, with a camera his father had given him. It was a Box Brownie and it was his pride and joy. He had used at least three rolls of film photographing different boys and different locations in Vincent's. His father developed the films for him when he went home on his first Sunday visit and he brought the pictures back for us all to see. I could get him to take pictures of any boy who was caned and show the damage done to them. Then it would only be a matter of getting the pictures out of the school and into the hands of someone who would take up our cause. Who the hell could I get to take up our cause?

I thought back to a recent conversation I had had with Father Delaney. He had been reading an article in the *Daily Mirror* that said 60 per cent of American pensioners live in poverty. He was annoyed that the American government could allow such a thing to happen and he was glad that the *Mirror* was exposing the scandal. I asked him why an English newspaper would be interested in what goes on in America. He told me that there were two sorts of people in the world – doers and dreamers. Dreamers thought about doing something; doers did it. The *Daily Mirror* was a doer.

If they thought a thing was wrong they would publish it so the world could see what was going on. It was only right, he said, that America's bad treatment of its pensioners was exposed to the whole world. Maybe the *Mirror* would take up our cause. But how could I get the photographs to them and who would I address them to?

I turned over restlessly in my bed. The idea was good but I wasn't happy with it. I wanted more than that; I wanted payback as well. Maybe, if we did something big enough, the *Daily Mirror* would come to us. The word riot flashed into my mind. Just the thought of it made my body tingle. All I had to do was get fifteen to twenty boys who could look after themselves. If the boys were committed enough, the Brothers would stand no chance. A picture was shaping in my mind of us barricading the small dorm and fighting off the Brothers. Boyle, who worked in the gardening group, should be able to get hold of some of the petrol that was used in the motor mowers. We could collect some of the small bottles that we got our daily ration of milk in and half fill them with petrol. Put a petrol-soaked rag in the neck of each bottle and we'd have petrol bombs. I kicked off the bedclothes as I was sweating with excitement. Everything was taking shape in my mind and I knew we could succeed if we kept our nerve.

The night seemed interminably long and I tossed and turned and got very little sleep. I kept thinking of the boys I'd want with me in the small dorm when it all kicked off. Bernie and Pete Doyle immediately sprang to mind. Taffy Williams and his mate Jack Harker would be good inclusions as they could both look after themselves and were always in De Montfort's bad book. Jimmy Smith was a bit of a loner but had an air about him that suggested he too could look after himself. I'd link up with him in the morning and try to persuade him to join us. Liam O'Connor would be a definite as he hated the Brothers and had been caned several times for swearing at them. David Brown and Paul Curtis were new to the school but had both been caned recently for fighting and hadn't stopped griping about it ever since. Smudger Smith would jump at the chance to have another go at Nutty Ambrose – after he had been caned he had tried to attack Nutty but had been restrained by De Montfort. I also asked Andrew Devine, the poor boy who was best known for wetting his bed. Pete Boyle didn't agree with me. 'What are you playing at? He's a wanker, John. I wouldn't trust him as far as I can spit.' But I felt sorry for Devine and he seemed to be keen to be involved. The list was taking shape and I smirked to myself. If all those lads took part in the riot then we would definitely win. At last my eyes were growing heavy and I settled myself down to catch a bit of sleep before the Kraut called us at six o' clock.

A week had passed since I had conceived the idea of the riot. I was amazed by the enthusiasm shown by everybody I mentioned it to. Even Jimmy Smith, who I'd thought might refuse, was keen on the idea. 'I've only been caned once by Nutty Ambrose but I owe him big time,' he'd said. 'Count me in.' The hatred the Brothers had inspired with their cruel treatment of the boys made my task easy. I had found sixteen willing conspirators and now all we needed were the photographs.

Bernie was enjoying his task of gathering the evidence we would need to convince the *Daily Mirror* of the cruelty that went on behind closed doors at Vincent's. He always made sure that the light was bright enough to take a good photograph when he got a boy who had just been caned to drop his trousers. Everything had to be done in secrecy and we took elaborate precautions to make sure our plans were not discovered. Eventually, after twelve days, Bernie had taken photographs of six boys who had been caned and we agreed that should be enough. He went home the following first Sunday with the film securely secreted on his body and returned with nine photographs of excellent quality.

I looked critically at the photographs and nodded my head in satisfaction. They all clearly showed the bruising and cuts on the boys' backsides and, much to my delight, in two of them you could clearly see the trails of blood running down their legs.

'They're great, Bernie. It's exactly what we want.'

'My dad wasn't happy about it. He said that what we're doing is stupid and could get us in deep trouble. I'm supposed to give you the photos and then drop out of the riot. I told him I'd do that, but that was just to keep him quiet. I'm still in.'

I smiled. 'Good. It wouldn't have been the same without you.' I tucked the photos down the back of my trousers. I'd decided to hide them somewhere nobody but me would know where they were because without them, there would be no hope of us succeeding. It took me hours to think of a suitable hiding place but in a moment of brilliance I came up with the ideal place. First of all, I needed a small pin hammer and a few pins from the carpenter's shop. I had spoken to Smudger Smith, who worked there, and he agreed to get them for me.

After that, I had to serve evening Mass with a Franciscan priest who was doing an ecclesiastical retreat with the Brothers. When I finished, I was anxious to get away and hide the photographs I had secreted down the back of my trousers. The Brothers would all be tied up in the chapel for at least the next two hours and I could do what I wanted without any fear of getting caught. I hung up my server's vestments and looked hopefully at Father Delaney.

'Is it OK if I go now, Father?' I asked quietly.

He looked at me enquiringly. 'You seem distracted, John. Is anything the matter?'

'Nothing, Father.'

'I know you're rushing off to do something but I don't think I want to know what it is.'

I smiled at him. 'You know me too well, Father. I'll see you in the morning.'

I felt his eyes boring into my back as I hurried away. I virtually ran around the outside wall of the graveyard and along the front of the building until I arrived at the small side door that led into into the Brothers' private quarters. The door was never locked as it was in constant use. Once inside, I crept along the corridor that led to the reception hall and De Montfort's office.

I turned the handle to the office and, with my heart pounding, I slipped inside and closed the door gently behind me. I hurried over to De Montfort's chair and punched out its leather seat base. It popped out easily and I quickly turned it upside down then, with the little pin hammer, I removed a row of pins that was keeping one side of the leather attached to its plywood base. Underneath the leather there was a small amount of padding which helped cushion the seat. I removed the photos from down the back of my trousers and, one at a time, I slipped them between the padding and the plywood. I was careful as I put in the new pins to make sure they went through the same holes in the leather as the old ones had come out of. The seat went back onto the chair and I pushed it firmly into its place. I picked up all the old pins and put them in my pocket with the small pin hammer. My heart was still pounding as I slipped quietly out of the room and back out of the building.

I sat down behind the graveyard wall and lit a roll-up. I was smiling all over my face as I thought about what I had just done. It was a fantastic hiding place for the photos, somewhere they'd never dream of looking. I leaned my head against the stone wall and in a mood of utter contentment I enjoyed every last lungful of smoke. From the chapel came the muffled sounds of a Gregorian chant and I took that as a cue to have another smoke. Fuck them, I thought; they'll have something else to chant about in a few days' time.

When I walked into the recreation room, Pete Boyle came over looking flushed with excitement. He said conspiratorially, 'I've managed to get four of the bottles filled and ready to go. I've put thick paper corks in the tops to keep the fumes in; otherwise they'd stink of petrol. I'll get another four tomorrow.'

'Where have you stashed them?' I asked.

'They're in my locker.'

I nodded my head approvingly. 'Put the next four into mine. I reckon we need about twenty. Will that be OK?'

'No problem at all. There's a ten-gallon drum of petrol in the shed.' He looked around furtively. 'How about the photos? Have you got them safe?'

I smiled. 'They're as safe as houses. They wouldn't be found in a hundred years.'

'So when are we going to do it?'

I thought for a few moments. 'Next Thursday night. The Kraut's on night duty on a Thursday and he's the one I want to take. Make sure you've got all the bottles done by then.'

Boyle gave a nervous laugh. 'I'll make sure my job's done. Jesus, I'm so fucking excited. I can't wait for it to kick off.'

'Don't get so excited that you blab to the wrong person,' I said. 'We've got to keep it close until it actually happens. I'll have a big meet with everybody involved on Wednesday night. We'll go over everything so there's no mistake. We'll only get one chance, so it's got to be right.'

I walked away from Boyle and went over to where Bernie was sitting. 'They're safely tucked away,' I said.

'Where'd you put them?'

'Safe, Bernie. That's all you've got to know. If nobody knows and they get found, then I'll know it's bad luck. If they get found and everybody knows, then I won't know if we've been grassed.'

Bernie grinned. 'Listen to you; anybody would think we're master spies or something.'

'We'll get treated worse than spies if we get caught. Take my word for it – worse than spies.'

Bernie looked thoughtful. 'Are you sure we're doing the right thing?'

I sat down next to him and told him the story about dreamers and doers that Father Delaney had told me. After I finished I said, 'We're doers, Bernie. Not dreamers. How we get treated is wrong and the world should know about it. This riot will bring it to the world's attention.'

Bernie shook his head. 'Where's the frightened kid from St Nick's gone? I'd never have believed a person could change as much as you have over the last two and a half years. Every kid in the school looks up to you for leadership, including me.'

I gave him a weak smile. 'The kid's still here, but he's well hidden.'

The whistle blew and we stood up to go to supper. Bernie said as he walked away, 'Make sure you look after the kid and don't get suckered into something you can't control.'

I laughed and shouted after him, 'I'm relying on you to keep me safe.'

He shouted back, 'If you rely on me, we're both buggered! I think I'd rather rely on you!'

I was chuckling as I went to get my cup of cocoa.

Chapter 24

Istood by the open recreation room door and stared out at the rain. My eyes shifted to the main building and up at the windows of the small dorm. It was all lit up and the lights shining out of the windows illuminated the ever-deepening puddles of water in the yard. Tomorrow, I thought; everything we had planned would start tomorrow. I shivered in nervous anticipation. Had I thought of everything? I was sure I had. Were all the lads I'd enlisted reliable? I'm sure they were. Was everything ready and in place? It was. Pete Boyle came to stand next to me. He didn't say a word and I wondered whether he was having the same thoughts as me.

I pulled the door closed and looked at Boyle. 'I wonder if it'll be raining tomorrow night? Not that it will make any difference. We've come too far to worry about a little rain.'

Boyle was quiet and looking very serious. I guessed he had last-minute nerves, as I'd had all day. What had begun as a harmless remark in the dorm had grown into a well-oiled plan for a riot. Everyone involved was showing signs of nervous tension. We all knew we'd be in deep trouble if it went wrong and that, once it started, there would be no turning back.

'Are you OK, Pete?'

'I'm OK. Just a little nervous.' He held out his hands and I could see that they were shaky. 'I just hope that nothing goes wrong tomorrow.'

'So do I. I don't know what will happen to us if it fails.'

He shrugged. 'Does it matter? Things in this school need changing and someone has to do it. I'm proud of what we're doing. I've been in kiddies' homes since I was eighteen months old and I've never been treated as badly as this before. No, everything we've done has been worthwhile, no matter what the consequences.'

I felt better. Pete Boyle had given me the reassurance I needed. We were trying to change a code of practice that was barbaric and cruel, so it was worth any amount of risk. I smiled at him.

I walked away and sat down on an empty bench, wondering where I would be at Christmas. That night I had a troubled sleep.

Thursday morning started like any other and I hurried over to the chapel for early morning Mass. It was still raining and the wind had freshened to give the late autumn weather a winter chill. I hurried into the vestry and pulled on my vestments. I wondered whether there would be a service tomorrow morning or whether we would still be barricaded inside the small dorm.

Father Delaney came in and got dressed in his vestments. I watched him surreptitiously as he changed and felt a pang of remorse. He had been a good friend to me and I hated the thought of letting him down. I knew he wanted me to do well in life and to put all of this behind me when I left. He would not approve of what we were going to do tonight as he was totally opposed to any sort of violence and there would definitely be violence involved. I closed my eyes and tried to think of something different. I needed a clear head when I served Mass as I had a few favours to ask of Jesus. We would need all the help we could get, including spiritual help.

After Mass, Father Delaney told me that he planned to attend choir practice. He felt that we could do with a little encouragement before the High Mass on Sunday. I thought we needed far more than encouragement to sing the Mass properly; we needed a miracle. I smiled at him and watched him as he hurried off to give communion to one of the older Brothers who was sick and unable to attend Mass. I looked out of the vestry and up to the large hanging crucifix. I knew it was just my imagination but Jesus looked even more brutalised and tortured than he had a few months ago. I blessed myself hurriedly and whispered, 'Please forgive me. I have to do it.'

All twelve choir members filed into the television room for our hour's viewing. It had been a long two hours in the classroom with Brother Michael and he had shown great patience with our attempts to sing the *Kyrie Eleison*. Father Delaney had shown a little less patience and had returned to the chapel after our tuneless third attempt. At the end of the lesson Brother Michael exaggerated when he said we were improving and I'm sure that he would have to confess that lie the next time he went into the confessional.

Groans of displeasure echoed around the room as a police series called *Z Cars* appeared on the screen. None of us were big fans of the police.

Bernie nudged me and said, 'Look behind you. We've got no-one supervising us.'

I turned around and the chair that was usually occupied by Brother Michael was empty. I shrugged. He could have gone to the toilet, he could be speaking to someone outside the door, he could be anywhere; I wasn't really interested.

'Shall I light up a fag?' Bernie asked.

'Wait a while. He could walk back in here at any moment.'

Bernie nodded but decided to roll a cigarette anyway. He waited about fifteen minutes then the harshness of a flaring match illuminated his face as he sucked the roll-up into life. After two puffs he handed it to me.

'There's still no sign of him so we might as well take a chance.' I nodded my head and inhaled. When I blew the smoke out it was clearly visible in the light of the television screen and it hovered over our heads in a wispy haze. 'Fucking hell,' I said, 'we'll definitely get booked if he comes back now.'

Bernie laughed. 'Who gives a fuck? After tonight, being caught having a crafty smoke will be the least of our troubles.'

He was right. 'Give me some baccy. I'll have my own smoke.' I rolled the cigarette and relaxed back in my seat to enjoy it. When *Z Cars* finished I expected the door to open and to be ordered out of the room to line up for our supper. Nothing happened. The door stayed shut and the next television programme started.

'They've fucking forgot us,' Bernie said. 'What a result.' He took out his tobacco and made another roll-up. He chuckled to himself and shook his head. 'What a great result.' A match flared and another wave of blue smoke hovered over our heads.

I looked at the door. It had been two hours now and we were still in the television room. The nine o'clock news was starting and we should be having lights out upstairs, not sitting smoking. I stood up and walked to the door and tried the handle. It was locked.

'We're locked in,' I said. 'Something's wrong.'

Nobody believed me until they all came over to try to open the door. I said, 'It's locked. It's fucking locked.' I kicked the door hard to attract attention from anybody who might be around. There was no sound or response from the outside so I kicked it again. Still there was no response. I gave up on the futile attempt and went back to my seat.

Bernie was nervous. 'Do you think they've found out?'

Before I could answer, the door was flung open with a resounding crash. Brother Francis was standing outside and he shouted, 'Everybody out. Get your arses out here now.'

We filed slowly out into the recreation room. When I got to the door I was shaken to see all the boys in the school kneeling on the floor naked with their clothes piled in front of them. There must have been at least ten policemen standing along each wall and every Brother and master was searching the piles of clothes. As I stepped into the recreation room I was grabbed firmly by my arm. I spun around to see who had such a firm grip and looked straight into the face of a six-foot policeman. His fingers were digging into the muscles of my left arm and then my right arm was grabbed by another policeman.

Brother De Montfort appeared in front of me, his face deathly white and drawn. 'Bring him up to the infirmary. I'll show you the way but keep a firm grip on him as he's the main culprit.'

I was pushed and half-carried all the way to the infirmary and the door was slammed shut and locked behind me. I didn't realise until I was alone that I was shaking and my heart was pounding. Something must have gone drastically wrong with our plans and now we would all pay the price. I wondered what was happening to the rest of the lads.

The key turned and the door opened. Brother Francis stood in the doorway and demanded, 'Where are the photographs? We know it's you who has them, so you may as well give them to us.'

I forced a smile. 'I haven't a clue what you're talking about.'

Brother Francis' face showed his annoyance. 'Tell me where the photographs are,' he said impatiently. 'We will find them and then you'll be in even worse trouble.'

I looked innocent. 'What photographs, Bro? I haven't got any photographs. Honestly I haven't.'

His face was twisted and red with anger. 'Don't you come smart with me,' he growled. 'I know you're lying and I've a good mind to beat the truth out of you.'

'You could try, Bro,' I said quietly, 'but I will be a little bit tougher to beat than I was when I first came here. You might not find it so easy.'

His face got even redder and he seemed to be having trouble standing still. He slammed the door shut and fumbled with the key as he locked it.

I shouted, 'Fuck off, you sick cunt.' I knew he had heard me as I listened to him stamping angrily down the stairs.

I sat down on the bed with an ever-growing feeling of trepidation. Our plans had been found out and someone had told them that I had the photographs. I felt relieved that I alone knew where they were and that they had no chance of finding them. Who had broken the code of silence? Whoever it was had definitely dropped me in the proverbial shit. I sat quietly on the bed growing ever more disillusioned. One of the boys must have grassed.

After about an hour the door was unlocked and Tom Banks and Eddie Lawson came in. Tom looked at me and shook his head sadly. 'OK, John. They're ready for you now.'

I walked apprehensively towards them.

Tom said, 'You've never given me any trouble, John, so please don't give me any now. We've got to hold on to you as there's a lot of police downstairs and we have to be seen to be doing our job.'

They each took hold of one of my arms and led me out of the room. Tom said, 'Before I take you downstairs I want to tell you that I don't agree with what's going on tonight. I think most of what Devine told Brother De Montfort is a pack of lies and it was made up so he could get his licence. I've got his measure and if I can stop him getting it, I will.'

Andrew Devine. It had been Andrew Devine. I thought about the way I'd included the smelly, bed-wetting bastard because I felt sorry for him and cursed myself for being too soft. I should have listened to Boyle's misgivings.

I was led down the stairs and out into the recreation room. Much to my surprise all the boys were still kneeling naked on the floor and most of them turned to look as I was led through their ranks. Bernie held up his thumb in a gesture of solidarity. I shouted loudly, 'It was Devine. Devine grassed us.'

Tom Banks held my arm tightly just in case I tried to kick Devine, who was kneeling just to my left.

'It's sorted, John,' Bernie shouted. I was rushed through the door into De Montfort's office, but not before I heard the loud hissing noise all the boys were making behind me. Devine was fucked. He would have to be put in isolation or face their wrath. I hoped he'd face the boys as I knew then that justice would be done.

I was amazed how many people were in De Montfort's office. De Montfort and pasty-faced governor Davies were sitting behind his desk. Along the back wall was Brother Francis, Brother Arnold, two burly policemen and a police inspector. Standing in the far corner was Father Delaney, who was looking at me sadly. Tom Banks and Eddie Lawson stood on either side of me. De Montfort stood up and leaned over his desk to get as close to me as he could.

'What you planned tonight was wicked and evil,' he said, 'and if we hadn't intervened when we did Brother Arnold could have been seriously injured or even murdered.'

I smiled. What a crock of shit. We had no intention of murdering anyone.

'What are you smiling at?' De Montfort's voice sounded hysterical.

'Devine's a fucking liar,' I said, 'and you're fucking stupid for believing him.'

De Montfort looked taken aback. 'What's Devine got to do with this? Who said anything about Devine?'

I grinned. 'Only a piss-bed like Devine would even speak to you. The rest of the school would be only too happy to piss on your grave.'

De Montfort's eyes narrowed. 'Such great bravado. Did you know that Boyle has already been taken out of school and is at this moment languishing in a cell in Dartford Police Station?'

All of a sudden I was brought face to face with the seriousness of my situation. My heart seemed to jump into my mouth. What the fuck did they intend to do to us? I'm a doer, I thought, not a dreamer. I must be brave and face up to what we started. I must keep believing I was right. I looked round the room at the faces staring at me. I was pleased to see that Arnold wasn't looking smug and I couldn't resist giving him a knowing smile. He broke eye contact and looked at the floor. *Good*, I thought, *you know how fucking lucky you were*.

De Montfort said, 'I want the photographs. I know you are the only one who knows where they are. So, where are they?'

I shrugged. 'I haven't a clue what you're talking about.' I looked at the police inspector. 'Aren't you interested in why he's so worked up about a few photographs? Do you think he's got something to hide?'

The police inspector turned his head to show his lack of interest in what I had just said.

I said, 'That's why the kids don't talk to the filth. You're as bad as he is.'

This remark got a response from the inspector. 'I take it from that remark that you've been reading some tacky crime novel. The only filth in this room is you.'

'Not me, inspector; I've got an IQ of 95. I can't read.' I pointed at De Montfort. 'Ask him. All of us boys have the same IQ. We're as thick as two bowls of shit.' I smiled. 'We're thick enough to join the police force.'

De Montfort interrupted our exchange of pleasantries. 'I want the photographs. Tell me where they are so we can bring this to an end.'

'I told you. I haven't a clue what you're talking about.' I smiled. 'Anyway, where would I get photographs showing the cuts on kiddies' arses from the caning you've given them?'

De Montfort was losing his temper. 'Don't come smart with me. You've just said that you know what's in the photographs, so don't tell me you haven't got a clue what I'm talking about. Where are they?'

I smiled again as I knew I was irritating him. 'I haven't a clue and, if I did, I wouldn't tell you Jack Shit.'

De Montfort shook his head angrily. 'That's enough. I don't want to hear another word out of your mouth.' He turned to the police inspector. 'You can take him away now.'

Father Delaney stepped forward. 'May I have a few words with him in private before he goes, inspector? He's been my altar boy for over two and a half years.'

The inspector shook his head. 'I'm sorry, Father, but I daren't risk it.'

I smiled at Father Delaney. 'Do you remember our conversation about the poor pensioners in America? Well, I'm a doer.'

Father Delaney shook his head and I saw tears well up in his eyes. 'I wish you well, John. I'm sure your Friend will look after you.'

A policeman took my wrists and shackled me in large metal handcuffs.

I hadn't actually been arrested. I was to be held overnight in Dartford nick at the request of Brother De Montfort. If a boy ran away from the school he would be detained by the police and held until he was collected by the staff. An approved school was a place where you were sentenced to go to by the court, and the Brothers at Vincent's could also be called guards: the police and the different juvenile establishments worked hand in hand.

I called to Father Delaney, 'Thanks for everything, Father. I'll never forget you.' I looked at Tom Banks and said, 'You're the only good one in this entire place.'

Tom acknowledged my remark with a wink.

Then I looked at De Montfort sitting in his chair. *I've beaten you*, I thought, *you didn't break me. And wouldn't you be pissed off to know you're sitting on the photos?* Two burly policemen led me to the door. I turned around and shouted, 'I hope all you bastards are dead by Christmas.'

I was led out of the main doors and put in the back of a police van. I looked out at the school, which was silhouetted in the moonlight, and I thought how quiet and peaceful it seemed. It was difficult to believe that it was in fact a sanctuary for cruelty and misery and, even at this moment, young boys were kneeling naked on rough wooden floors as hooded monsters walked amongst them disguised as Brothers of the Catholic church.

Bernie often said to me that he thought I got more out of control during my time in Vincent's than I had ever been at home, but this wasn't the case. I just grew out of the school and their barbaric customs. You can only hurt a person so much and then he doesn't feel the pain any more. A hard man can take a kicking and not whine about it. Vincent's taught me to be hard.

The van pulled away and St Vincent's approved school faded from my sight.

Chapter 25

Dartford town centre was in darkness and the streets deserted as the van pulled through a side gate and into the courtyard of the police station. The back door of the van was opened and a police sergeant ordered me out. A policeman held my arm and led me up three steps and in through the station door and stood me in front of a counter where another sergeant wrote down all my details.

I was ordered to empty my pockets, which took no time at all as I had nothing in them. My laces were removed from my boots and put in a large brown envelope and I was led through another door and into a holding area. The sergeant opened a cell door, removed my handcuffs and pushed me into it. The door banged shut with a resounding crash and the clinking sounds of a key turning in the lock took away my cloak of bravado. As I looked around me, I was very scared.

The cell was about ten feet in length and eight feet across. The walls and ceiling were all bare brick, which had been distempered in a sickly yellow colour. There was a window made of reinforced panes of glass and three bars embedded in the outside wall that prevented any chance of escape. In the left-hand corner of the cell was a white porcelain toilet without any seat. On the floor was a toilet roll. Attached to the right-hand wall was a sturdily built, thick wooden bunk. There was no mattress or pillow but there was a thick blanket folded neatly at the head of the bunk. I sat down and fumbled in my sock to retrieve a crumpled roll-up and a red-tipped match. I scratched the match along the wall and sucked my roll-up into life.

I could put on a front for other people but in the loneliness of the cell there was no audience and my bravery evaporated like a snowflake on a summer's day. My hands were shaking and I had difficulty putting the cigarette in my mouth. I had to rush to the toilet, suddenly bursting to pee. My stream squirted erratically around the porcelain until I realised it was the shaking of my hand that was causing the problem. When I'd finished, I sat down again suddenly awash with self-pity.

Self-pity is the most useless emotion given to us by the creator. It serves no purpose at all and instead of helping us through a problem it makes everything so much worse. I cursed loudly at being such a moron. The only way I was going to get through this ordeal was to stay positively focused on what we had attempted to do. There was no place for tears in my present dilemma. Did the Jacobites cry at Culloden? Did Jesus cry at his trial in front of Pontius Pilate? They certainly did not. So why should I cry at this minor bit of misfortune?

I angrily wiped my eyes and knelt on the floor with my arms resting on the bunk bed. I clasped my hands together and closed my eyes and prayed quietly so that no one could hear but me and Jesus.

'Jesus, please help me. Everything has gone wrong and I've been put in this awful place. You know why we planned the riot

*and what we wanted to achieve. Please protect me and the rest
of the lads as we tried to do a good deed. There was nothing evil
planned except for Brother Arnold having a good slap and you
know how much he deserves that. Let Father Delaney know
that I meant well and that I'm truly sorry if I hurt him.*

 *'Jesus, that's about all I want to say except that I need you to
give me plenty of strength over the next few days to last out
whatever they have in store for me. Thank you, Jesus, and
forgive me all my sins. Amen.'*

I slowly got up and sat on the bed. I felt better. My
Friend was helping me again.

I tried to figure out how I was supposed to sleep and
decided that the best thing was to get undressed and pile my
clothes together to make some sort of pillow for my head. I
wrapped myself tightly in the blanket and lay down on the
bunk with my head on my clothes. The wooden base was
far from comfortable and it took me several attempts to find
a bearable position to lie in but at last I was semi-comfort-
able and I shut my eyes to black out my miserable
surroundings. My mind was racing with thoughts of my
predicament and no matter how hard I tried not to, I was
sinking into an ever-deepening well of despair. Mercifully,
a veil of darkness was drifting over my tired eyes and I fell
into a troubled sleep.

I was awakened in the morning by a policeman opening
the small food hatch in the cell door. I lifted my head and
stared blearily at him.

'You have a visitor,' he said. 'Get up.'

I heard a key turning in the lock of the cell door and
then a loud clank as the handle was pushed down. The door
swung open and the policeman stood to one side to let
Father Delaney in. I couldn't believe my eyes – the one

person in the whole world I wanted to see. I quickly sat up and swang my legs onto the floor.

Father Delaney handed me a brown paper package. 'It's your own clothes, John, I have to take the school clothes back with me. You'll also find all the tobacco you had hidden in the vestry.' He sat down beside me and shook his head sadly.

'Why did you do it, John? You only had a few months to go and you'd have been released. God only knows what's going to happen to you now.'

I started to dress myself in my own clothes. 'If you had seen John Lacey's arse, then you would understand why I did it. The amount of time I had left never entered my head.' I pointed my finger at him. 'You, and you alone, knew my feelings on the canings and you also knew what I thought of Arnold and his beatings. Nobody was willing to do anything about them, including you, so we decided to do it ourselves.'

'But where has it got you, John? I'll tell you.' He stood up and walked over to the toilet and peered disapprovingly at the bare bowl. He shook his head. 'It's got you into deep trouble, and to cap it all, nothing was accomplished.'

He handed me a cigarette. I took it gratefully and relished the smoke I sucked into my lungs.

'The photographs were a good idea. I would have understood it if you had sneaked out of the school and delivered them to the *Daily Mirror*. Why didn't you do that? Why did you have to concoct a plan for a riot? It was plain stupid.'

'I wanted a bit of payback, Father,' I said. 'I wanted to give a bit of hurt to Arnold like he's given to me over the last two and a half years. What's wrong with that?'

He looked deep into my eyes and said very quietly, 'If you don't know what's wrong with that, John, then you're not the boy I think you are.'

I felt saddened that Father Delaney couldn't see why I wanted to hurt Arnold. I could still see the fear in Arnold's eyes when I was in De Montfort's office and it gave me a warm feeling that we had scared the shit out of him. Was that so wrong? 'Isn't it written in the Bible somewhere, an eye for any eye? If that's the case, then God will approve our actions.'

Father Delaney replied, 'It also says turn the other cheek. But I don't think our last few minutes together should be used up in theological debate. Let me tell you about what's happening to you next.' He stubbed his cigarette out on the sole of his shoe. 'The police will be moving you today to Stamford House in London. It's a secure remand home for older boys. I don't know how long you'll be kept there but I should imagine it will be a week or two while they decide what to do with you. You've created a real panic in St Vincent's with those missing photographs. Until they have them in their hands they won't make any decision about your future.'

He gave me a knowing look. 'I'm not even going to ask you where you've hidden the photographs as I know you wouldn't tell me. I will give you a word of advice though; don't give them up to anyone as they are what is commonly known as your "ace in the hole". While you have them, Brother De Montfort's hands are tied.'

The cell door clanked open and a young spotty-faced policeman stood in the doorway. He said, 'Time's up, Father. We've got to get him washed and fed before we move him.'

Father Delaney nodded and put both his arms around me in an affectionate hug. He whispered quietly, 'Good luck with the photos.' As he left the room, he stopped and smiled warmly. 'God bless you, John, and good luck for the future.'

The door was slammed shut and my friend, my confessor and the best man I had ever known in my life was gone. I put my head in my hands and cried bitter tears.

I was taken out of Dartford Police Station just before midday and put in the same van they had brought me in. The journey out of Kent and into London was just a haze of houses flashing past and stopping and pulling away from numerous sets of traffic lights. I stared out of the window but I was seeing nothing.

My mind was back in St Vincent's with the other boys. I smiled at the thought of De Montfort turning the school upside down in search of the photographs while all the time he was sitting on them. I thought fondly of Bernie and remembered all the good and bad times we shared together. I wondered where they had sent Pete Boyle and how he was coping. I thought of John Lacey and recalled how he had looked at me with complete trust in his eyes when I asked if he would drop his trousers and let Bernie take a photograph of his backside. Images of boys' faces I had come to know over the last two and a half years were flashing through my mind along with the barbaric cruelty of the hooded Brothers.

When the van stopped, the driver got out of his seat and opened my door. We had arrived at Stamford House in Shepherd's Bush. I was led into a large Victorian building.

The policeman holding me handed a sheaf of papers to a tall, well-built man in a grey tweed suit. He nodded his head and led us through a door and then down a flight of stairs to a spacious room in the basement.

The room was large and had several long trestle tables laid out symmetrically and approximately twenty wooden chairs behind the tables. Against the side wall was a smaller wooden table that had lots of different packets of cigarettes on it with the owner's name scribbled on a piece of paper next to each of the packets.

The man pointed at the table. 'Put any tobacco or cigarettes you have in a pile on that table.'

I emptied my pockets of two packets of Golden Virginia, and my matches and cigarette papers. The man tore a piece of paper out of a small notebook and handed it to me with a small stub of a pencil.

'Write your name on it and put it with your tobacco.'

I quickly wrote down my name and put it beside my small pile of contraband.

He nodded. 'Right, you can go and join the others in the yard.'

He led me out of a small latched door and up a flight of stone steps into a small, paved yard. The first thing I noticed was that it had metal mesh stretched above it which was firmly attached to the high yard walls and to the back wall of the house. There was no chance of anyone being able to climb the walls and escape.

In the yard there were about twenty young men who looked roughly eighteen to twenty-one years old. I was pretty sure that, at sixteen, I was by far the youngest. None of them took the slightest notice of me and I went and sat on the ground against the far wall. I thought it would be best not to stare at any of the boys so I stared up at the mesh and the billowing clouds in the sky instead.

A short stocky man with a handlebar moustache and an unruly mop of brown hair appeared at the top of the steps that led into the small yard. 'Fenton. John Fenton,' he shouted.

I held up my arm and he signalled for me to come over. I walked apprehensively across to where he stood. He looked me up and down with a critical stare and said in a soft Scottish accent, 'You have a visitor. Come with me.'

I followed him back down the stairs and into the basement room. Sitting at a table and looking very uncomfortable was Mum. I was overwhelmed with emotion. As soon as she saw me she rushed up and held me close. She squeezed me tightly and whispered, 'What have you done, son? Why are you here?'

I sat her down and over the next twenty minutes I told her everything. I told her about the damage done to John Lacey, the photographs taken by Bernie, the petrol bombs Pete Boyle had stored in our lockers, the plans we had to get the *Daily Mirror* to expose the cruelty and how I had hidden the photographs so that they would never be found. When at last I had finished my account she looked at me with an expression that was both understanding and sympathetic.

'Are you certain they will never find the photographs?' she said.

'I'm absolutely certain. If they were going to find them they would have found them by now.'

She offered me a cigarette and I signalled to the man sitting at the far end of the room for permission to take it. He nodded and she lit two cigarettes, handing me one.

'Trust me, Mum; they have turned that school upside down looking for our photographs. They will never find them.'

She nodded her head and puffed thoughtfully on her cigarette. 'I just need to know where we stand when your Brother De Montfort comes to visit me tomorrow. He rang me this morning to tell me where you would be this afternoon and then said that he and another man called Davies would be visiting me tomorrow afternoon. I wondered why they were coming; now I know. They want me to find out where your photographs are.'

I said firmly, 'I'll never give them up, Mum.'

She shook her head, 'I don't want you to give them up. I wouldn't do a thing to help those bastards after what they've put you through over the last couple of years. They're evil and all of them deserve to burn in hell. I'm really looking forward to our little meeting tomorrow when I can let them know what I think of them.'

When, after an hour, my mother stood up to leave, there was something reassuring in her manner that made all my misgivings about my future float away like matchsticks in a river. She took my hands in hers.

'Leave everything to me,' she said. 'I'll be back the day after tomorrow and I'll let you know how things went.' She kissed me warmly on my cheek and walked out of the room. Her self-assurance convinced me that she had some sort of plan and I wondered how De Montfort and Davies would react to the unbridled hatred she had for them.

The next two days seemed to drag by. The age gap between me and the other inmates was an obstacle that I wasn't willing to try to overcome so I spoke to nobody but the occasional member of staff. The only highlight of the day was when, after I had eaten, I was allowed to go to the table and take two cigarettes from my pile. I hadn't slept well for days and I noticed in the mirror, as I shaved the bum-fluff off my chin, that my eyes had lines of fatigue under them. I was having nagging doubts about what I had done and I had to keep convincing myself that it had been worthwhile. My imagination was running wild with different scenarios and none of them was positive.

My mother, good as her word, arrived mid-afternoon on my third day. She was sitting facing the door that led into the yard and smiled with pleasure as she saw me walk in. I kissed her and sat down opposite. 'Don't look so worried, son. I haven't brought you bad news.'

I leaned forward in my chair and took her hand. 'Tell me everything that happened. I've been worried sick for the last two days.'

She smiled sweetly at Jock Wallace, the man supervising visits, held up her cigarettes and pointed at me. He returned her smile and nodded his head. She lit two cigarettes and handed one to me.

'I told you that I'd get it sorted and I have.' She took a long puff on her cigarette and blew a cloud of smoke up in the air.

'They arrived at eleven o'clock yesterday morning. I didn't like De Montfort at all and his attitude annoyed me straight away. He came with a little weasel of a man called Davies and another brother; I think his name was Francis. I took them into the living room and made them a cup of tea. De Montfort looked around the room as if it wasn't good enough for him. I told him straight away that if it wasn't good enough for him to sit in he could talk to me through the window from outside. That took the wind out of his sails and from then on it was outright war.

'He told me all about what you'd been involved in and what a horrible boy you were. I said if he was rude about you one more time I'd throw him out the window. He said that you had some photographs and he wanted them. He wouldn't tell me anything about what was in the photographs except that they were school property and he wanted them back. He told me, the cheeky bastard, that I had to come here today and get you to tell me where they were. He said it would make the difference between you getting nine months to three years Borstal, or three to five years.'

She stubbed her cigarette out in an ashtray. 'The bastard was threatening you with five years if you didn't hand over the photos. That really got my rag up. I told him that you couldn't give him the photos as I had them. The little weasel asked me to give them to him. I told him to keep out of the conversation or I'd throw him out. De Montfort then demanded that I give them to him. I told him that they could lock you away to keep you quiet but they couldn't do sweet Fanny Adams to me. I'd got De Montfort on the run and he knew it.

'I told him what was in the photos and where I would take them if he didn't do right by you. That really annoyed him but I could see it also terrified him. He said that he could see where you got your bad attitude from and I should be ashamed of myself. I told him that the next time he had the cheek to criticise me, my feet wouldn't stop running until I was standing in the Editor's office of the *Daily Mirror*. The weasel whispered something in his ear and they said that they would go away and discuss what should happen next.'

She lit another cigarette and puffed on it hungrily. 'They returned after about an hour and De Montfort's whole attitude had changed. He grovelled around me like the rat that he is and said that they'd had a rethink about what should happen to you. He asked if I'd be happy for you just to be transferred to another school to finish your sentence. I told him I would agree to that as long as it wasn't one run by his bunch of wicked bastards. He didn't like that but he agreed without any argument. He said that you would be transferred to a new school in a few days. He then asked me for the photos and I told him that I was keeping them for security in case he didn't do what he had promised. He didn't like that either but, because I had the upper hand, he had to accept it.' She smiled. 'So now you know everything. Are you happy?'

I sat there stunned; so that was it. I knew Mum was clever – De Montfort wasn't even in the same league as her – but I had never in my wildest dreams expected her to bluff him so cleverly.

I shook my head and exclaimed, 'Wow, Mum!' and we both burst out laughing as if we had nothing in the world to worry about.

Tom Banks arrived at Stamford House three days later along with Eddie Lawson, Brother Francis and Brother Michael. I had been warned of their arrival by Jock Wallace and I had been looking out for them since eight o'clock in the morning. I was looking forward to being on my way, as Stamford House had been an ordeal. I must have spent half of the last three days sitting at a table working out problems from a sheaf of test papers that had been put in front of me.

When, at last, I had solved most of the problems and handed the papers back to a geeky-looking man in a scruffy cardigan, I was told it had been an assessment to decide which school they would send me to. He said I had done well and that I would be going to a school for boys with above-average intelligence. It was called Ardale and was in a place called North Stifford in Essex.

Tom Banks greeted me with a smile. He put his arm around my shoulder and gave me a fatherly squeeze. 'How are you, John? The old school is quiet without you.'

'I'm fine, sir. Who has come with you?' I looked over his shoulder.

'Mr Lawson, Brother Michael and Brother Francis. They're waiting in the car. I don't think they wanted to do this trip. They're frightened you're going to give them trouble. I told them I'd take responsibility for you and that made them a bit happier.'

'I'll give you no trouble, sir. You've always been good to me.'

'I know that, John. You don't have to convince me of anything. Are you looking forward to your new school?'

I shrugged. 'I don't really know. I got used to Vincent's and now I'm going to have to get used to some new place. I wish I could have finished my time in Vincent's.'

Tom Banks laughed. 'I'm sure Brother De Montfort would have loved that.'

Jock Wallace came in with a large brown envelope and handed it to Tom. 'Everything is in there.' He looked at me. 'Take your cigarettes and tobacco off the table as I'm sure you'll be glad to have them when you reach Ardale.'

I wondered if that meant something ominous? Was it going to be even worse than Vincent's there? If so, I thought grimly, I'd just have to look after myself using all the fighting techniques I had learned. I stuffed the tobacco and cigarette papers in one of my side pockets and put the two packets of cigarettes my mother had given me in the other. I was surprised when Jock held out his hand and shook mine firmly. 'Good luck, young man. Look after yourself.'

I had no one else to say goodbye to as in the seven days I had been in Stamford House I hadn't spoken one word to any of the other inmates. I walked to the car without a backward glance.

Tom Banks opened the back door and I climbed in. Eddie Lawson was sitting in the back seat and moved across to sit staring out of the far side window and Tom Banks squeezed in next to me so that I was securely wedged between them. Brother Francis was in the driver's seat and was staring at me via the rear mirror with utter hatred in his eyes. Brother Michael sat in the front passenger seat and never gave me a glance. I brazenly stared back at Brother Francis and smiled when he averted his eyes.

Fuck you, you piece of shit, I thought. *You'll never get the better of me.*

The car weaved its way out of London and after maybe half an hour it pulled off the road and up a small grassy bank. Tom Banks opened his door and signalled for me to follow. I was surprised when all the others got out of their seats and came to join us on the verge.

'We're having a short smoke break so if you feel like lighting up, go ahead.'

Brother Francis stared at Tom in disbelief. He opened his mouth as if he were going to say something and then thought better of it. I pulled a packet of cigarettes from my pocket and offered Tom one. He shook his head so I just took out one cigarette and lit it. The only non-smoker in the group was Brother Michael and he stood a little distance from us as we all smoked. I found it strange standing smoking in front of them all as it had only been a week since I had left Vincent's, where smoking was a bookable offence. Brother Francis kept giving me sideways looks of disgust and every time I caught his eyes I smiled contemptuously at him and blew a cloud of smoke in his direction. He hated it and I'm sure he would have loved to have given me one of his famous beatings but he knew that I was beyond taking any more of that sort of treatment. He would have stood a better than average chance of getting his head stamped on.

When we got back under way I closed my eyes and dozed off. I don't know how long I was asleep but I woke up as we pulled off a quiet road and turned through a gate onto a winding driveway. I could see three large detached houses further down the road as we stopped outside a modern bungalow. Brother Francis got out of the car and disappeared inside the front door. He reappeared and signalled for us to come in.

I walked into what appeared to be a very neat and tidy office. Behind the only desk in the room sat a woman of about forty years of age. She was neatly dressed and my first impression was that she looked like a schoolteacher.

She smiled. 'Mr Shaw is waiting for you.' She gestured to a door behind her desk.

Brother Francis tapped on the door and I heard a muffled voice say, 'Come in.' I was led into the room and saw a friendly-looking man in his early fifties rise from his chair and shake Brother Francis's outstretched hand. Brother Francis handed the man a large brown envelope and he removed the contents and started reading them.

Occasionally he looked up at me and shook his head then carried on reading. I hoped he wasn't judging me on my reports from Vincent's. I was apprehensive about what kind of place this was going to be.

After five minutes he pushed the papers to one side and looked at me. 'My name is Mr Shaw and I'm the headmaster of this school. I've read the reports compiled on you from St Vincent's and Stamford House. The least said about the one from St Vincent's the better. You will find this school completely different to what you have been used to as we put our emphasis on higher education. Most of our pupils are studying for GCE 'O' or 'A' levels. We expect our pupils to behave in a dignified manner and at all times to show respect for each other. All of our masters will treat you with respect and they expect the same from you.'

Brother Francis interrupted to say snidely, 'He's got cigarettes and tobacco in his pockets.' He looked triumphantly at me. 'Put them on the table.'

I removed the cigarettes and tobacco and piled them neatly in front of Mr Shaw. Brother Francis patted my pockets and nodded his head in satisfaction when he felt them empty.

Mr Shaw watched the proceedings with interest but said nothing until we'd finished. 'What is that for?' he asked, pointing at my pile of contraband.

'For smoking, sir.'

He chuckled. 'I know it's for smoking. Why have you put it on my desk?'

I didn't understand what he meant so I shrugged.

'In this school you are responsible for your own belongings. Why would I want to look after your tobacco and cigarettes? Put them back in your pocket; I don't want them.'

I turned my head to Francis and mouthed the words 'Fuck you' as I pushed my cigarettes and tobacco deep into my pockets. Brother Francis couldn't help letting his mouth hang open at what Mr Shaw had just told me and slowly shook his head in obvious disapproval.

Mr Shaw looked at Brother Francis and Brother Michael and then at me. He asked, 'What religion are you?'

'Roman Catholic, sir.'

'Are you a practising Catholic? I am agnostic myself.'

'Yes, sir, I am.'

'There's a Catholic church in the town. I don't know what time any of the services are so you will have to take a walk into town later on today or any time before Sunday and find out. I'm putting you into Gordon House and your Housemaster is Mr Reid. Before you go into town you have to let him know when you are going and what time you'll be back. Is that clear?'

I couldn't believe what I was hearing and must have sounded slightly aghast. 'Yes, sir.'

'You sound surprised. Well, don't be. We trust all of our pupils until they give us a reason not to. You'll be required to visit the dentist in the town and if you need any books for your studies you may have to get them from the library in the town. All we ask of you is that you do nothing to bring our school into disrepute.'

I felt light-headed. Everything I was being told sounded too good to be true. I had never imagined an approved school could be anything but harsh and here I was being told about rules that virtually gave me unlimited freedom.

Tom Banks gave me a thumbs up sign. I smiled back.

Mr Shaw stood up and much to my amazement held out his hand for me to shake. He said, 'Welcome to our school,

John. If you have any problems and need to see me, just make an appointment with Mrs Evans.'

I shook his hand and noticed how firmly he squeezed mine. I had been told by my mother that you could judge a man by his handshake. A weak handshake meant a weak person that couldn't be trusted. A firm handshake signified honesty and reliability. Mr Shaw was definitely in the latter category. 'Gordon House is the second big building on the right. Report to Mr Reid and he will fill you in with all the other things you should know.'

As I walked past Brother Francis I said quietly for him to hear, 'See you, shithead.' His face reddened and I smiled to myself.

Tom Banks walked me out of the office and shook my hand. 'Good luck, John,' he said, 'and keep up the football.' As I walked away towards Gordon House he said loudly, 'You should have been here from the start.' I waved my arm in a final salute.

Mr Reid was a grey-haired, heavily built, softly spoken man who had been Housemaster of Gordon House for over a decade. He and his family occupied a large four-roomed flat that took up half the ground floor. His wife was slim and her face was thin and lined but it was obvious that in her younger years she would have been beautiful. They had a son who was twenty-two years old and his photograph stood proudly in a silver frame in the centre of the large mantelpiece that dominated their living room wall.

Mr Reid sat looking at me, appraising me with his dark-brown eyes. 'You will be the youngest person in my house,' he said. 'Most of the boys who come to me are nearly eighteen years old and have academic potential. I don't know exactly what I should arrange for you as your educational level is so much lower than the rest.' He adjusted a cushion on his chair and sat back. 'I find it hard to believe that you have been out of proper schooling since you were thirteen. It's scandalous. What the hell were they thinking about?'

'I'm not thick, sir. I've read a lot of books and I've always managed to understand what I was reading.'

Mr Reid responded immediately: 'I never said you were thick. You have to be bright to have been sent here but it is going to be difficult to find out exactly where to slot you in.' He thought for a moment. 'Maybe you can be set separate work by the teaching staff and they can give you extra tuition in their night classes. I'll have to speak to G.B. about it.'

'Who's G.B., sir?'

'Mr Shaw, the headmaster, who you met earlier. His parents must have had a love for the works of George Bernard Shaw to have given him the same Christian names. Most of the boys and all of the staff call him G.B. and I think he quite likes it.'

I reached into my pocket and pulled out a packet of cigarettes. 'Is it all right if I smoke, sir?'

Mr Reid nodded, reached into his pocket and pulled out a squashed box of Swan Vesta matches and held them out for me. I took one and lit my cigarette and handed them back, shaking my head in disbelief, 'I can't believe that two schools can be so different. I would have been slapped and booked just for having cigarettes in Vincent's and here I can sit and smoke while I'm talking to you.'

He smiled. 'That is nearly all down to G.B. When he came to this school he changed everything. All of the old ways went out of the window and G.B. rules came in through the door. He said that if boys were shown respect, they would give respect and he was right. As soon as G.B. rules had been implemented the behaviour of the boys improved. It is second nature to all of us now to help our boys, not punish them. Our exam results are as good as any of the local schools and I think that our boys are better behaved than any of them. We occasionally have a hiccup when one boy misbehaves, but that happens in any school.'

'G.B. said that I had to clear it with you to go to town and find out the times that masses are said on a Sunday.'

Mr Reid looked surprised. He sat back in his chair and his eyes reappraised me. 'I'm not often taken unawares but your request did just that. In all my years in this school that is the first time I've been asked by a boy about going to church. Of course you can go. What church are you looking for?'

'Catholic, sir. I'm a Roman Catholic.'

'St Mary's is in the town. I'm sure there is a board outside that gives all the times.'

'When can I go and check, sir?'

'Any time this afternoon. Just give a tap on the door when you're leaving. By the time you get back I will have sorted out some sort of timetable for your lessons.' He looked me up and down. 'I'll also sort you out some overalls and boots as you don't want to ruin your own stuff.' He stood up and walked to the door and opened it. 'Come with me and I'll show you the rest of the house and where you will be sleeping.'

I followed him on his grand tour. There were two large rooms downstairs, a television room and a home study room. There was also a washroom and toilet. On the first floor there was a small dormitory on either side of the staircase. Both dormitories had beds for ten boys. In the middle of the landing and opposite the stairs was a large washroom with showering facilities and toilets. The top floor was identical to the first floor.

Mr Reid opened the right-hand door and pointed to a bed in the far left-hand corner. 'That's yours. If you have anything of value you can leave it with me and I will look after it for you. Don't leave it in your locker as we have thieves in the school and it will go missing. There are a lot of clever boys here, but they were not put here for their honesty.'

I went over to my bed and sat down on it to test the springs and mattress. It was comfortable enough and I stood up and opened the small locker by the side of the bed to check that it was empty.

Mr Reid smiled. 'Is it up to your standard, John?'

'Compared with Vincent's, this is great.'

'Stay here for a little while and adjust yourself to your new surroundings. When you're ready you can take a walk around the school grounds to familiarise yourself with the layout of all the different classrooms and workshops. Don't forget to tap on my door when you decide to go into town.'

He closed the dormitory door quietly and left me alone. I was glad of the time alone as my brain was trying to come to terms with everything I had been told and to accept the enormity of the changes in my circumstances. I slumped back down on my bed and closed my eyes feeling a sense of optimism about the future for the first time in ages.

Chapter 26

January 1961

The low winter sun blazed unrelenting rays through the home-study room window and completely obscured the words on the page I was reading. I turned my chair so that the sun was behind me. I was having trouble reading Dickens' novel *A Tale of Two Cities* and doubted if I would be ready to précis it in two days' time. I loved history but I knew very little about the French Revolution so there was no chance I could skip any of Dickens' dialogue. What the fuck was a French émigré? I reached for my dictionary and thumbed through the pages.

The first three months in Ardale had been a bigger ordeal than I thought they would be. Most of the lads in the school were studious and pleasant but there were also a few arseholes. I had come across the biggest arsehole on my third day. I walked into the television room and took one of the back seats as most of the others were occupied. A lad came and sat next to me and whispered in my ear, 'Have you got a spare cigarette?'

I reached into my pocket and gave him one and asked him if he wanted a light. I never heard anybody tell me to be quiet and after I had given him a light, I asked him his name. Suddenly, a tall lad appeared in front of me and said,

'I told you to shut the fuck up.' Before I had time to react, he slapped me hard with his open hand across my cheek.

As far as I was concerned, there were people who walked around with a bullseye in the centre of their faces saying 'hit here'. This arsehole was one of them. I came flying out of my chair and crunched my head into the centre of his face and pushed and ran him, knocking over chairs, to the far wall, where I smashed another head-butt into his unprotected face. It was possibly the most one-sided fight I had ever had. As he slid down the wall I stepped back and kicked him hard in his midriff. I heard someone running towards me and turned just as his friend was about to jump on me. I leapt backwards and grabbed an overturned chair and hit him with it. By this time the room was in chaos and Mr Reid came running out of his flat. He hurried over and took the chair out of my hands then turned around to a big-built red-headed lad and said, 'What started this?'

Unlike Vincent's, the lad told him exactly what had happened and left out none of the details. Mr Reid listened carefully and when the lad had finished he said, 'Thank you, Paul.'

He pointed to me. 'Come with me. We need to have a few words.' I followed him out of the room, making sure I bumped into the arsehole's friend as I walked past. I grinned at him through clenched teeth and said quietly, 'We'll finish it when I come out.'

Mr Reid ushered me to one of his dining chairs.

'Sit down there, John; we have some serious talking to do.' He walked around to the other side of the table and sat down opposite me. 'If that had been anybody else except Bainbridge and Thomas you would be in serious trouble. I know what Bainbridge is like and I know how quick he is to use physical violence. His friend Thomas is no better. But this still doesn't exonerate you because of the level of violence you used. I know in your eyes it was self-defence but that is no excuse. You can't go through life hitting people. When he slapped you, instead of beating him into a pulp, you should have come to me so I could deal with him. That is what a responsible adult would do. If you had hit him first, I would be accusing you of bullying. These boys have not had the same background training that you have.'

He stood up and walked me back towards the door. 'It all ends here. I don't want any afters. It's finished. When you go back out there I want you to shake hands with both boys. Is that clear?'

I reluctantly nodded my head. The ignominy of being slapped by an arsehole was troubling me and I could still feel the burning sensation on my cheek.

I looked angrily at Mr Reid. 'I'll never let anyone hit me without hitting them back. I was thumped and bullied for years. It will never happen again no matter what the consequences.'

He reconsidered his decision. 'In that case, I think you'd best stay in here for a few minutes, John.' He placed an ashtray in front of me on the table. 'Have yourself a smoke and calm down. If you feel up to it, why don't you tell me about what went on in your last school? It might help me to understand you a little better.'

For the next half an hour I told him all about Vincent's. I even told him about Jimmy Wilkinson. He was a good listener and sat quietly looking at me as I related all the different instances that led up to the foiled riot. I explained in graphic detail about the damage done to the boys' backsides after they had visited the small dorm and the brutality of Brother Arnold.

When I told him about Brother Francis making me stand on the recreation room roof he shook his head sadly. 'I've heard that things like that go on, but I never believed them.'

After I had finished my account, he said, 'That explains a lot to me and now I know why you reacted the way you did when Bainbridge slapped you. I think it would be advisable if I had all three of you in here to make the peace as I don't want any silly remark to start it all off again.' He stood up. 'You wait here and I'll get the others.'

When Bainbridge and Thomas were led into the room I watched them warily from my seat. The fear in Thomas's eyes was evident and I watched contemptuously as he held out his hand for me to shake. Mr Reid nodded at me to accept the apology and I briefly squeezed the offered hand. Bainbridge was completely subdued. His nose and mouth were swollen and there were still traces of blood under his nostrils. When I accepted his hand I had to restrain myself from pulling him towards me and giving him another head-butt. I thought that the whole thing was probably a farce and that Bainbridge was smarting over what had happened to him and Thomas. I stared deeply into his eyes so that he knew without doubt that I was ready for him any time of his choosing. He looked away and it was then I realised I would never have any more trouble from him. Mr Reid seemed satisfied and led all three of us back into the television room.

Life settled down and I slotted into a routine of study-ing and reading novels I borrowed from the library in the town. Most of the lads accepted the fact that I was nowhere near their academic level and quite often would help me try to understand whatever assignment I had been given. The only two subjects I had no trouble with were English and History. Most of the mathematics was gobbledygook to me and I dreaded going into the classroom and making myself look stupid.

One day soon after, I had another fracas with someone who made the mistake of targeting me. When I was asked by Mr Gray, the Maths master, what the letter d stood for in the formula $P = dgh$, I shrugged and said, 'I haven't a clue, sir.' Before he could ask someone else, the class joker, Michael Ball, piped up, 'Poor old Vincent's, he slept through that lesson. He was tired.'

The whole class burst out laughing, even though it wasn't particularly funny, and it reminded me of the way I had been teased and ridiculed at St Gregory's all those years before. I looked at Ball and promised myself that after class I would deal with him – and I did just that. Before we went to our next lesson I followed him into the toilet and head-butted him in the face. He slipped over on the wet floor and I kicked him hard in his ribs.

I said to him, 'Poor old Ardale, did you fall asleep when they taught you how to look after yourself?' I kicked him again. 'Don't ever take the piss out of me again or I'll really give you a kicking.'

I had hardly sat down in my next classroom before I was called out to go and see Mr Reid. He was far from happy when I walked into his room and gestured angrily for me to take a seat.

'Why did you attack Michael Ball?' he demanded. 'Tell me exactly what led up to it.'

I couldn't believe he had found out. What sort of school was this where boys ran around grassing each other up? I stared stubbornly at the floor. I wasn't going to get involved in dropping Ball in the shit for taking the piss out of me. I had more backbone than that.

'Look at me when I'm speaking to you.' Mr Reid's voice commanded respect and I looked up at him towering over me. 'I heard that he made a joke in class. The big word in that sentence is *joke*. Ball is always joking. There's not an ounce of nastiness in the boy and yet you decided to beat him up in the toilet. Explain yourself and your actions.'

'You know why. You just told me that he made a joke out of me in the classroom. I'm nobody's fool and I won't allow someone to take the piss out of me. I've just made sure that he won't do it again.'

Mr Reid banged his hand down hard on the table, 'So you decided to beat Ball up for an inoffensive joke directed at you? How dare you! You acted like a mindless thug. I'm withdrawing all town visits for you for a month. You can go out once a week to church and no more than once a week. You cannot use the television room for a month either as I can't trust you not to attack someone for looking at you the wrong way. I want to give you time to reflect on your thuggish behaviour.'

'I'm not a thug. I just look after myself.' I was puzzled. It seemed that all the rules were different in this school and I was feeling my way, trying to understand them.

'No, you don't just look after yourself.' Now he was shouting, 'You attack people to make them do your wishes. You use extreme violence in response to minor provocation. You're a thug and nothing but a thug. We won't have this sort of behaviour in our school and until I can sort something out, you are suspended from classes. Now get out and go up to your dormitory.'

I had seen a new side to Mr Reid and I left his room feeling chastised and ashamed. I spent the next few hours questioning myself and the way I acted. I knew why I hit Ball and in my mind he deserved it, but in Mr Reid's eyes I acted like a thug. Was I a thug and didn't know it? I decided that after Mr Reid had calmed down, maybe tomorrow, I would go back and ask him to clarify his remarks.

It was ten o'clock the next morning when I was taken by Mr Reid into his inner sanctum. He sat down opposite me and his whole demeanour told me that he was no longer riled about yesterday's incident. He said quietly, 'John, before you even start, I can tell you that the restrictions I set yesterday are staying as they are. Once I've given a punishment, I never change my mind.'

'I understand that, sir. I just want you to tell me why you think I'm a thug, as I don't think I am one. There has to be something about me that makes you think I am. I just want to know what.'

He nodded his head thoughtfully and shifted in his chair. 'Why do I think you're a thug?' He reached into a bookcase next to his chair and brought out a large dictionary and handed it to me. 'Look up the word thug and read out its definition.'

I thumbed quickly through the book until I reached the word I wanted. 'It says *vicious and brutal ruffian*.'

'I think that sums up your behaviour yesterday precisely. You were vicious in your assault on Ball and quite brutal in the way you targeted a boy who was no match for you. Whether you like it or not, you have been socialised into becoming a thug. You see nothing wrong in using violence on people who have done nothing to deserve it and I blame it entirely on the school you came from. Somehow I have to try and correct this awful flaw in your character and make you realise that normal people will not tolerate this way of behaving. If I don't check it while you are in this school, I fear that you are in for a lot of heartache and misery in the outside world.'

'Don't you find anything wrong in Ball's behaviour, sir?' I was still puzzled.

'No I don't. He joked about you possibly falling asleep in a lesson. He didn't for one minute think you had; he said it for humorous effect. There will be numerous people in your life that like joking and messing about, and if you decide to hit them all, then I predict a lonely and troubled future for you.'

I stood up to leave. I respected him but what he was saying was the exact opposite of everything I believed. It had taken me over two and a half years to reach a position where people left me alone and now I was being told by Mr Reid that I was in the wrong. I didn't want to stand by and let someone take the piss out of me without doing something about it. To act any other way would be a contradiction of everything I believed in. I walked to the door none the wiser and went back to my dormitory to continue my book.

My worries about someone taking the piss out of me again were not necessary as the lads in the school were wary of me from then on and kept their distance. They didn't ignore me but it was obvious they would have preferred me not to be there. All the help they had given me before was withdrawn and I was left to struggle alone with my homework and assignments.

I'm lucky that I don't need other people's company. I guard my solitude like a dog guards his bone. If nobody is around to bother me then I can lose myself in the imaginary worlds and meet the wonderful characters that authors have pulled out of their minds. Time is no longer a problem when I am reading. The only problem is having enough time to finish a novel.

After a month had passed I was called back into the presence of Mr Reid. He had just finished rollicking Bainbridge for yet another misdemeanour. Bainbridge stood to one side as I came into the room as the last thing he wanted was to break the fragile truce we had established. I nodded at him and went and sat at the table.

Mr Reid ushered Bainbridge out and returned to sit opposite me. 'Well, John, the month is up. I'm pleased that you stayed out of any further trouble and am more than happy to restore all your privileges but I want to emphasise the point that I won't think twice of taking them back if you misbehave again.'

'Thank you, sir, I'll try not to.'

He nodded. 'I've had progress reports from all of the masters and they have told me that you're trying hard at your studies but you don't seem to want to integrate. Why is that?'

I shrugged. 'I prefer to keep myself to myself. What's wrong with that?'

'Nothing at all if that is what you truly want to do. I just thought that it might be better for you if you developed some sort of friendship with some of the boys.' He looked at me enquiringly, 'Is everything OK with you and the boys?'

I shrugged again. 'It's all right. None of them bother me and I most certainly don't bother them. I speak to Brian Hawkins and he comes to church with me on a Sunday and that's enough for me.'

Mr Reid nodded slowly. 'Brian's a nice boy. You could do far worse than become friends with him.' He reached for some papers and briefly scanned them. 'Mr Pitt is impressed with you. He told me that he is thinking of putting you in for your 'O' level English in the spring. Mr Larkin is also entering you for History. Well done.'

I smiled, pleased at the news. 'I like English and History.'

'That's why I saw G.B. and arranged for you to drop all the other subjects and concentrate on the ones you like. In future you will attend only English and History lessons, and Mr Pitt and Mr Larkin will set you work to do in the home study room at the times you would have been in other lessons. I can help you with any queries you have, as I know a fair amount about both subjects. With any luck, you should leave us with a couple of good results under your belt.'

To me this was the best news ever. I was struggling in Maths and Science and Geography bored the pants off me. Just the thought of not having to sit through those awful lessons again pleased me. I could now concentrate on reading Dickens and learning about the English Civil War. I returned his smile and said, 'That will be great, sir.'

Chapter 27

Brian Hawkins leaned casually against the church wall. He was the same height as me and had recently celebrated his eighteenth birthday. His face was handsome in a boyish sort of way and the self-confidence he oozed could be disarming to people who didn't know him. He had been put in Ardale for breaking into his headmaster's office and stealing a copy of the following day's physics paper then trying to sell copies of it to his classmates. He pointed at two girls walking down the opposite side of the road in Salvation Army uniform and grinned cheekily. 'I think we could score with those two. Look how they're eyeing us up.'

I looked where he was pointing. The girls both appeared to be in their early teens and he was not exaggerating when he said they were eyeing us up. The taller girl had her hair tied back in a ponytail and she had just a little too much makeup on. She wiggled her hips saucily as she stared at us. Her friend was more buxom and her chest pushed her Salvation Army uniform jacket outwards to the point of bursting. Her face was half hidden beneath a Salvation Army bonnet and Brian Hawkins prodded me gently in the ribs.

'You've got the bible puncher,' he said and laughed.

Brian signalled to the girls to cross the road and they sauntered over. He immediately put his arm around the taller girl's shoulder. He smiled at her and I could tell she was keen on him.

'My name is Brian and my mate is John. We thought that maybe you'd like to come for a walk.' He smiled his disarming smile and I saw the girl wilt under his gaze. 'What's your name?'

She giggled at her friend and said coyly, 'My name is Brenda and her name is Gillian. Where do you want to walk to?'

'Where do you suggest? You must know the area better than us.' His arm slipped to her waist and she sidled in closer to him, 'Any place we can be alone and have some fun.' He squeezed her waist and said, 'You know what I mean.'

I couldn't believe this was happening. Brian was arranging for the four of us to go somewhere and I might possibly lose my virgin status. Just the thought of it brought a stirring to my loins and I put my arm tentatively around Gillian's waist. She didn't resist and the two girls started walking us towards the open grassland at the end of the road. Brian and Brenda were going faster than us and had soon disappeared from sight into the heathland beyond some overgrown shrubs.

Gillian guided me in the opposite direction, towards a small dale that ran alongside a large hedgerow obscuring a major trunk road. I let myself be led along like a lapdog and revelled in the feeling of her thigh touching mine as we made our way into an extremely overgrown part of the little valley. When we reached a spot where we could see nothing but the high shrubs around us, Gillian stopped and removed her stupid Salvation Army bonnet. I was pleasantly surprised when her long auburn hair tumbled out and cascaded over her shoulders.

She laughed and said, 'I hate that dreadful bonnet. I have to wear it as my parents wear the full uniform and make me do the same.'

I hardly heard a thing she said as I was trying to pluck up enough courage to sneak my hand onto those lovely mounds that were straining to break free of her jacket. She must have sensed this as she started unpopping her tunic buttons. I couldn't resist any longer and eased my hand over one breast and squeezed it lovingly. She grabbed me and pulled my head down so that her open mouth nearly swallowed me up. Her tongue was so far down my throat that I thought I would surely choke. Her hands were all over my body and I was pushed unceremoniously onto the floor. Everything seemed to be happening at once and before I knew it she was underneath me and I was entering her. She writhed around like a wriggling serpent and suddenly the whole world seemed to explode in a feeling of pure ecstasy. I lay on top of her trying to catch my breath as she sucked hungrily on my neck.

So that was it, I thought. *I've had my first bit of tush*. My thoughts went back to Bernie and I wished I was still in touch with him so I could have told him all about it.

In the distance I heard a girl shouting out the name 'Gillian' and I quickly stood up and pulled up my trousers. Gillian struggled back into her knickers and readjusted her skirt and blouse. By the time she stood up, she had her bonnet back on her head and looked ready for another prayer meeting. I tried to kiss her again but she pushed me away and said, 'We've got to get back to the others.'

Across the heathland I saw Brian and Brenda standing on top of a small knoll, searching out our location, calling our names through cupped hands. I shouted, 'We're over here.'

Brian held up his arm as soon as he spotted me. Gillian rushed ahead of me and I had to jog to catch her up. As soon as we reached the others, Gillian and Brenda linked arms and started walking back in the direction of the church.

I looked at Brian in a state of bewilderment. What had we done wrong? Where were they going in such a rush?

'What the fuck is wrong with them?' I asked Brian.

'Who cares?' he laughed.

I watched them disappear in the distance, feeling embarrassed and uncomfortable. It had been my first real sexual experience and I hadn't even found out Gillian's last name; in fact, I had hardly said two words to her. It didn't seem right. It was too clinical and impersonal. I had always believed it would be meaningful and unforgettable. Mum had told me to respect women, and that sex was a special experience when you are in love. Maybe Gillian felt the same discomfort as I did about the occasion and that's why she walked off so quickly without saying goodbye. Whatever the reason, I never bumped into her again.

I rolled myself a cigarette and switched my thoughts to my approaching mock exams.

Chapter 28

7 April 1961

It started off as just another day. I was sitting in the home study room staring sightlessly out of the window and trying to memorise important dates in the English Civil War. I only had two months to go before I sat my exams and was devoting all my time to revision. I looked around as the study room door burst open.

Mr Reid stood in the doorway, his face flushed. 'G.B. needs you in his office immediately,' he panted, slightly out of breath.

I closed my book on Cromwell and stood up. 'Why does he want to see me?'

'He'll tell you when you see him.' He flapped his hand impatiently. 'Hurry up, it's very important.'

Suddenly I had an awful feeling that something nasty might have happened to my mother so I ran down the driveway to G.B.'s office. Mrs Evans stood up as I rushed in. She knocked on G.B.'s door and, in the same motion, opened it and ushered me in. I nearly stumbled into the office in my haste and said, 'What's up, sir? Is my mother OK?'

G.B. looked worried. His lips were pursed and his eyes were flitting to and fro over a document in front of him. He shook his head. 'There's nothing wrong with your mother; it's you – you shouldn't be here.' He looked at Mrs Evans over my shoulder, 'How did a thing like this happen? I rely on you to check these things. It should never happen. It's a complete and utter shambles.'

He turned his attention back to me. 'Didn't you know that you were due for release on the 24th of January?'

I shook my head. 'Nobody told me, G.B.'

He read from the paper in front of him, 'You went to St Nicholas House Remand Home on 24th January 1958. On 7th February you were sentenced to three years approved school. Your three-year sentence began from your first day on remand. It is now 7th April 1961, which is three years, two months and ten days since your sentence began.' He looked again at Mrs Evans. 'How did it happen?'

'I thought he was a new boy. I forgot he had been transferred here and was near the end of his sentence.' She seemed close to tears. 'I know it's my fault but it was a genuine error.'

'Well, there's nothing we can do about it now. Write him out a travel warrant and while you're doing that he can go and gather his belongings from Gordon House.' He stood up and looked at me. 'Get your belongings and hurry on back. You haven't time to say your goodbyes. You have to be on your way.'

I walked out of the office still trying to comprehend what had just happened. I was going home. I had finished my time. I was free at last. It was happening too quickly for me to appreciate the magnitude of the moment. I hadn't thought about how long I had been away, as I had been wrapped up in adjusting to my new surroundings and engrossed in studying for my 'O' levels.

I walked into Gordon House. Mr Reid had cleared my few belongings from my locker and put them into a brown paper bag. He handed them to me and held out his hand.

'Good luck, John, and try to stay out of trouble.' He walked me to the front door. 'If you get a chance, take your exams.' He patted me on the shoulder and watched as I walked back down the driveway.

G.B. was standing just inside the office doorway. He handed me a neatly folded piece of paper. 'That's a travel warrant that will take you all the way to West Ealing. I've tried ringing your parents to let them know you're coming but they must be out as there's no answer.' He held out his hand and I squeezed it hard. 'Good luck,' he said.

As I walked towards the bus stop just outside the gates it seemed to me that the sky kept getting bluer and the grass got greener. Everything seemed to be brighter and my senses picked up the fragrances of the hedgerows and flowers. I looked up towards the heavens and said a quiet 'thank you' to Jesus. He had helped me survive all the rigours and torments of the last three years and had made me into a stronger person.

I leaned against the wooden bus stop and puffed contentedly on a roll-up. The smoke drifted out of my nose and I closed my eyes. Father Delaney's face came into my mind and I smiled. He smiled back at me. A tear slowly trickled out of my eye and I climbed on the bus.

Epilogue

Not long after I was released from Ardale, I got in touch with Bernie. He had been signed up to play football for Barnet Town FC and had high hopes for his future. He told me that although the riot never took place, St Vincent's was never the same after I had left. All canings were stopped and physical beatings ceased. I never told him that this was probably due to my mother's threat hanging over De Montfort's head like the Sword of Damocles. I congratulated myself that everything had been worthwhile and that our actions had resulted in a better life for future boys who were sent to serve time under De Montfort and his crew of sanctimonious thugs. Bernie now lives in Canada with his family and, regretfully, I have not had any further contact with him.

After the intended riot, Pete Boyle was transferred to St Swithin's on the Isle of Wight, where he was forced to finish the remainder of his sentence under the same conditions he had fought so bravely to get rid of in St Vincent's. I never had the pleasure of seeing him again and I only hope that he had a successful and happy future. I'll always remember him as 'a man's man'.

It took me another four years of struggle before I realised that Mr Reid had been right in his assessment of me: I *had* turned into a violent thug. In the years after I left Ardale I was always getting myself into fights in bars and hanging out with a bad crowd. I had such a poor opinion of myself that I was intimidated by other people and responded with violence at the slightest provocation. My Dad sent me over to Ireland to get me out of the way and I was destitute for a while, sleeping rough on the streets.

One day I met a young prostitute who said I could come and sleep on her couch. Her twelve-year-old brother was a thief and soon I had agreed to help him sell the goods he nicked to pawn shops. It didn't take long before I was arrested and sentenced to two years' in Dublin's Mountjoy Prison.

Two things turned my life around in 1964, the year I came out of prison. Within days of returning to England, I met my wife on a blind date, arranged by my sister, and I was immediately smitten by her. I did not hide my past from her and she sympathised and understood what I had been through. Within ten days of meeting her, we were engaged and I joined the army. Eleven weeks later, after my basic training, we were married. We have now been together for forty-three years, so I believe, once again, my Friend was looking after me.

In 1968 I was interested and pleased to read in the *Daily Telegraph* that the headmaster of St Swithin's Catholic Approved School, Yarmouth, Isle of Wight, had been sacked for caning boys, I quote, 'with excessive severity'. The article goes on to say that he had been reported to the Home Office by an ex-member of staff. Although the Home Office recognised the headmaster's long service and dedication to the boys, he had, contrary to the approved school rules and over a long period of time, made them wear drill shorts whilst being caned. The report went on to say that the procedure was abandoned as soon as its irregularity was pointed out.

I returned recently to Dartford in the hope of seeing the places and maybe meeting some of the people I've written about in this book. I was disappointed when I found that St Vincent's had been bulldozed and where the grounds used to be a modern housing development had been erected. An ultra-modern church now stands on the site of the main school building and it has retained the name St Vincent's. The new parish priest was very helpful and gave me the telephone number of Tom Banks, who still lived locally.

Tom remembered me well and reminded me of the riot and my departure from the school. He emphasised that if he had had the power, I would never have been removed from the school. He disagreed with the way I had been treated over the incident. I asked him what had happened to the Brothers and he told me that Brother De Montfort had died a few years ago. Brother Francis and Brother Ambrose had also died but Brother Michael was alive and in good health. Brother Arnold had left the Brotherhood in 1968 and had got married. He also died a few years ago.

My friend and mentor Father Delaney is now with Jesus. The world is a smaller place without him and I still mention him in my prayers for the comfort and shelter he offered me, and for his support and belief in me, so freely given in the face of so much wilful hostility, ignorance and cruelty. Even after fifty years I vividly recall his face and can often hear his voice correcting me if I stray from his guidelines.

When I climbed back in my car to drive home, I couldn't help but feel sad that so many years had passed. In my head I still feel young and I can clearly see and hear the sounds of yesteryear.

As I drove out of the development I was sure I could hear Bernie's voice saying, 'I hope you're all dead by Christmas' and in my head, I answered, 'Well, Christmas has come at last.'